The Bells of Old Tokyo

The Bells of Old Tokyo

Meditations on Time and a City

ANNA SHERMAN

Picador | New York

picadorusa.com • instagram.com/picador
twitter.com/picadorusa • facebook.com/picadorusa

Picador® is a U.S. registered trademark and is used by Macmillan Publishing Group, LLC, under license from Pan Books Limited.

For book club information, please visit facebook.com/picadorbookclub or email marketing@picadorusa.com.

The Library of Congress Cataloging-in-Publication Data is available upon request.

ISBN 978-1-250-20640-4 (hardcover)
ISBN 978-1-250-20641-1 (ebook)

Our books may be purchased in bulk for promotional, educational, or business use. Please contact your local bookseller or the Macmillan Corporate and Premium Sales Department at 1-800-221-7945, extension 5442, or by email at MacmillanSpecialMarkets@macmillan.com.

Originally published in Great Britain by Picador, an imprint of Pan Macmillan

First U.S. Edition: August 2019

10 9 8 7 6 5 4 3 2 1

for Ian

Tokyo is one vast timepiece. Its little alleys
and great avenues, its forgotten canals and temples,
make up the face of a great watch. Its months and
weeks are beat out in traffic bearing into the
capital from the northern rice paddies. The city's
hours and minutes and seconds are meted out
in buildings torn down and the ones that rise;
in land reclaimed from the sea. Time is counted
out with incense sticks; with LEDs; with atomic
lattice clocks. It is measured by the lives of all
who move within the Yamanote Line that circles
the city's old heart and the Kantō Plain beyond.

Contents

The Bells of Time

The Five O'Clock Chime sounded, its notes drifting across Shiba Park. Every night, all over the city, Tokyo's loudspeakers broadcast what's called the *bōsai wireless* at 5:00 p.m. sharp. It's a xylophone lullaby that tests the city's emergency broadcast system. Across Japan, the tunes vary, but Tokyo stations usually play the song 'Yūyake Koyake'. The words are: *With sunset, the day darkens./ On the mountain, the Bell of Time sounds./ Hand in hand, shall we go home, along with the crows?/ Once the children are back, a great full moon shines./ In the dreams of the birds, a sky of sparkling stars.*

The evening loudspeakers weren't playing 'Yūyake Koyake', but something else. I didn't recognize the song, and was wondering what it was, when twining through the recorded broadcast I heard another sound, the bell from Zōjō-ji, the ancient temple near Tokyo Tower.

The single toll rang out almost like a chord: one high note deepening out into a low one. I followed the sound. Passing through the temple's Triple Gate, I could see the huge bell in an open stone tower and the bell-ringer in his dark indigo robes. He was very young. A thick rope of purple, red and white threads dangled from the horizontal *shumoku*, the wooden bar used to ring the bell. The boy hung on to the cord, rocking the *shumoku* back a little, and then again, before he slammed it like a battering ram into the green bronze bell. Dragging on the rope, the boy threw his entire weight backward, falling and falling until he was almost sitting on the tower's flagstones; then the recoil drew him up, up again. The entire motion looked like a recording run backwards; a fall magically reversing itself.

Japan is a country of bells. When I was little, someone gave me a Japanese wind chime, a flimsy thing shaped like an airy pagoda: the five eaves of the three-tiered roofs each jangled with little bells, and five pendant hollow cylinders that rang when they struck each other. Fishing twine held the toy together. Maybe because the threads were clear, the wind chime always looked as if it were about to fly away from itself.

No one ever hung it up, and eventually the lines tangled until their knots were snarled past straightening: the music would not come at all.

But the chime was my first East: the shine of metal, shimmering notes, night winds.

After the last toll, the ringer unhooked the multicolored cord and threw it over his shoulder and set off up a long flight of stairs until he disappeared into Zōjō-ji's Main Hall.

A small metal plaque on the tower read: 'Shiba Kiridoshi. One of Edo's Bells of Time.'

Before Tokyo was Tokyo, it was called Edo. From the early seventeenth century, Edo was the *de facto* political center of Japan, though Kyoto remained the country's capital until 1868, as it had been since the year 794. At first, only three bells sounded the hours: one in Nihonbashi, inside the prison at the city's heart; another near the northeastern temple to the goddess of mercy; and the third in Ueno, near the city's northern Demon Gate. As Edo grew – by 1720, more than a million people lived in the city – the Tokugawa shoguns licensed more time-telling bells: in Shiba, by Tokyo Bay. East of the Sumida River, in Honjo. In the western district of Yotsuya, at the Heavenly Dragon temple. Southwest of the center, in the hills of Akasaka, where the Tokyo Broadcasting System stands now. To the west, in Ichigaya, near the Defense Ministry. And far to the northwest, in Mejiro, where the city's worst fire broke out in 1657.

The bells tolled the hours, so the shogun's city would know when to wake, when to sleep, when to work, when to eat.

Beside the metal plaque was a map showing the sound range of each bell, a series of circles overlapping each other like raindrops in a still pool. Raindrops frozen at the moment they strike water.

Just before he died in 2003, the composer Yoshimura Hiroshi wrote a book called *Edo's Bells of Time*.

Yoshimura once worked as a sound designer. He could build an entire universe from a scrap of music, a few verses, the name of a hill or a well or a river. In his last book, Yoshimura described Tokyo as the blind must know it: the footsteps of workers going home through Ueno Park; the clattering of coins thrown into offertory boxes at temples and shrines; hecklers yelling at a clumsy bell-ringer for the *joya no kane*, the bells rung on the first midnight of the New Year. 108 times; 108 for the number of corrupting worldly desires.

The shogun's city has almost completely disappeared, Yoshimura wrote. Not just the buildings and gardens, but the city's soundscape, too. In *Bells of Time*, Yoshimura drifted through the vast city, listening for noises unchanged in five hundred years. Some were too subtle for twenty-first-century Tokyo – the sound of lotuses, opening at dawn. *Crowds would gather every summer, listening out for the crack of buds rippling across Shinobazu Pond. Can we imagine how sensitive people were then?* But some sounds of Edo do survive: vendors shouting in the markets; the glass wind chimes carried through the city on carts every July; and the tolling of the time-telling bells.

Yoshimura believed that a temple bell's sound was as much about silence as about its ringing. And that when it tolled, the bell drank up all life around it.

The shogun is gone, but you can hear what he heard, Yoshimura wrote. *The note opens outward. The sound holds within itself the movement through time.*

I decided to follow Yoshimura, and look for what was left of his lost city. I would take not the elevated expressway routes, or the Yamanote Line railway that rings the heart of Tokyo, but trace areas in which the bells could be heard, the pattern that on a map looked like raindrops striking water. Winds could carry the ringing notes far out into Tokyo Bay; or the rain silence them as if they had never existed.

A circle has an infinite number of beginnings. The direction I walked would change, just as the circles on the map could change.

There were boundaries, but they were not fixed.

Daibo Katsuji was famous, though for years I didn't know how famous, for his coffee and especially for the way he poured it. Over fine coffee grounds he would let fall one drop, two drops, then three, until the water trickled down in a glittering chain.

Daibo's black hair was cropped like a monk's. Every day he wore a shining white shirt, black trousers and a black apron: a uniform that never varied and that resembled an ascetic's robes. He had fine dark eyes and a dark blue stain on his lower lip, perhaps a birthmark. He was a slight man, but not when he stood behind his counter.

No one found Daibo's cafe by accident. You had to know it was there, before you climbed the narrow stairs. The room was small – just twenty seats – the kind of narrow rectangle the Japanese call an eel's nest.

Tokyo is a restless city, where everything changes and shifts, but not Daibo Coffee. It was always the same.

It was a small cafe on the first floor, above a ground-floor ramen counter. Then the ramen counter turned into a coin locker for left luggage. Before the ramen counter existed, there had been a boutique. The floor above the cafe was a sword-dealer's. On the top floor, I think, someone sold *netsuke*: tiny people, animals, imaginary creatures carved out of bone or wood. Then the other owners retired or moved and the entire building emptied out, except for Daibo. He never left, except for three days every August when he went north to the Kita-Kami mountains in Iwate, where he was born.

From one end of the room to the other flowed a rough counter made of pine that Daibo had retrieved from a lumber yard where, he said, it had been 'floating'.

Every morning, Daibo roasted coffee beans. He would open the windows and the smoke would drift down Aoyama dōri and even to Omotesandō Crossing. Summer and winter, spring and fall.

The beans rattled with a sound like a child's rainmaker toy, like lottery balls. Drifting over that sound was the jazz Daibo loved. The music would disappear – drowned out by a siren, traffic, rain, shrilling cicadas – and then reappear as if it had never been gone.

Daibo cranked his one-kilogram roaster barrel with one hand and held a book in the other, putting it down to test the beans inside the barrel with a blackened bamboo scoop. Then he picked up his paperback, and read on.

'Hibiya'

Hibiya contains relics of all Tokyo's eras – trees said to be as old as the city, a fragment of the castle escarpment, a bandstand in the original park, a bronze fountain . . .

Edward Seidensticker

Hibiya

Night and the city poured into the room.

The hotel's north wing opened out onto Ōtemachi's office blocks. Opposite my window, an unbroken wall, from the tarmac to the sky, and beyond it wall after glassy wall, every vertical plane broken by square or rectangular panels; in each frame, a human figure, and in some, two or three. Where the windows were blank the glow was watchful and the buildings that crowded up against the hotel might have been television monitors that instead of projecting little dramas watched me looking outward, me with one hand on the blinds.

I moved to another wing. The new room faced Hibiya and the waters of Wadakura bori, one of the canals that ring the Imperial Palace: a labyrinth of waters around the old citadel. Instead of ten thousand windows, the huge dry-walled stones carved for the old citadel.

The city had disappeared.

I was almost at the heart of the spiral of canals around the palace, but I couldn't see it.

*

'So, you're interested in time,' Arthur said. We were sitting at Daibo's long counter, drinking milk coffees from tea bowls. Arthur was an American translator who wrote books in Japanese. 'Well, the original space–time word is *kan*.'

I thumbed through my dictionary, frowning. '... What about *jikū*?'

Arthur smiled. 'That's just the *official* word. I take the official word, dissect it and pull it apart. If you come up with something good and get the word out there first, you win.'

Where English has a single word for 'time', Japanese has a myriad. Some reach backward into the ancient literature of China – *uto*, *seisō*, *kōin*. From Sanskrit, Japanese borrowed a vocabulary for vastness, for the eons that stretch out past imagination toward eternity: *kō*. Sanskrit also lent a word for time's finest fraction, the *setsuna*: 'particle of an instant'. From English, the Japanese took *ta-imu*. *Ta-imu* is used for stop-watches and races.

'In the West,' Arthur said, 'we look at time as a progression, as something abstract marching toward some end that we don't know and can't see. But you should remember that Japanese time is told in animals, in the Zodiac. The Japanese used to see time as a *creature*.'

'I don't know that story.'

'You don't know about the Zodiac? You've never heard about the Great Race? It goes, "Once upon a time, the Buddha summoned all the animals in the world to visit him before he left earth for nirvana. But only twelve animals bothered to show up – the mouse, dragon, monkey, ox, snake, rooster, tiger, horse, dog, rabbit, sheep and pig. To thank them, the Buddha broke time down into a twelve-year cycle. And then he made each animal a guardian of one year." People still feel connected to the Zodiac here. The year you were

THE BELLS OF OLD TOKYO

born defines who you are. I was born in 1967, the Year of the Sheep.'

Arthur said something I didn't understand to Daibo, who was across the counter. Daibo laughed.

'The Zodiac clock answers questions like, why isn't the cat there? (The mouse didn't wake the cat, so the cat missed out on seeing the Buddha. That's why the cat and the mouse are enemies.) Why is the mouse first? (It sneaked onto the ox's hoof and jumped off before the ox could greet the Buddha.) Each animal has its own identity and a reality to go with it. Don't forget that for the people of old Japan, the mouse was in the kitchen, not a picture book. On old Japanese clocks, each number was also associated with its own animal. And everyone knows that ghost stories begin, *It was the hour of the cow . . .*'

'"The hour of the cow". . . !?'

'That means 3 a.m. The depth of night. When the ghosts come out.'

Arthur finished his coffee. Then he walked to the end of the bar, paused by the telephone stand and bowed to Daibo. After the door shut, I could see him through its glass panes, hoisting his backpack on his shoulders and then dashing down the narrow staircase.

He was late.

Daibo began to recognize me. After I had been in Japan a few months, we could at last speak to each other. I recited dialogues straight out of a Berlitz phrasebook. When I didn't know a word, I would mime what I wanted to say.

Always, between sentences, long gaps while I flipped through my phrasebook. Some pauses lasted almost a minute, while Daibo waited across the counter, unhurried, expectant.

Daibo liked slowness. He once wrote that he wanted customers to fall asleep while he made their coffee. He had been born in Iwate, in the far north of Honshu: snow country. But though he wasn't from Tokyo, Daibo said, it was Tokyo that had made him who he was.

The English poet James Kirkup, who was living in Tokyo at the time of the first Olympics in 1964, wrote that the coffee bars were 'a way of life to Tokyo's students, who study there, write letters, keep dates, telephone, and even sleep in them.' Coffee houses were like London's clubs in the days of Dr. Johnson. But you had to watch out for 'phoneys, both Japanese and Western', all very consciously scribbling poems or 'planning "daring" exhibitions.' Which was rich, coming from a poet.

Daibo had come of age in those jazz cafes of the 1960s, when, in their hushed darkness, coffee bars began to resemble temples. But though Daibo Coffee had the stillness and the austerity of a Zen temple, it had a generous atmosphere, a forgiving one; Daibo had nothing of the judgmental strictness of the coffee master at Ginza's iconic Café de l'Ambre. That man was rumored to throw out anyone who dared ask for milk or sugar with the holy liquid without warning him first.

The coffee bars, Kirkup wrote, were one of Japan's few democratic institutions because they were open to everyone. At Daibo Coffee, a famous painter might sit beside a runaway schoolgirl, the conductor Ozawa Seiji beside a flamenco artist; an advertising executive beside a flea-market trader. Daibo treated everyone the same.

Daibo said the customer already had to work hard just finding his cafe; and the great boulevard Aoyama dōri below was chaos enough. Let someone climb the narrow stairs, sit and strip away armor built up over a week, or even over a lifetime.

If you leave them alone and make their coffee right, said Daibo, then slowly, gently, people will return to their true selves.

日本橋

'Nihonbashi'

Throughout the Tokogawa period, Nihonbashi was the zero point from which all distances throughout the realm were measured, and it was across Nihonbashi that all formal processions visiting or departing from the shogun's court passed.

Theodore C. Bestor

Nihonbashi: The Zero Point

For more than two hundred years, the first Bell of Time rang the hours from within the prison of the Tokugawa shoguns. Three strikes, twelve times a day.

The clock and the jail were one.

'The execution ground was over there,' the groundskeeper said. He wore a pink T-shirt under a faded black jumpsuit. He pointed. 'The jail went as far as that primary school.' He sported aviator shades, and his gelled hair whipped into peaks like a J-pop star.

The Kodenmachō prison has been reborn as a children's park, its earth hidden underneath gravel crushed into gunmetal grains and silver grit. The place felt antiseptic, clean, as if it had been singed or cauterized. Everything was monochrome, except for the metal stairs up to the children's slide: those were painted a brilliant red.

The bell itself still hangs in the upper story of a pale yellow brick tower built in the Imperial Crown Style of the 1930s. The bronze bell is remote, unreachable. A dragon coils itself around the bell's crown.

The park smelled of hot tarmac and dust and rain. A few office workers huddled together under construction hoardings near the school fence, smoking. At the bell tower's base, a homeless man slept. As I watched him, he turned over, tucking his knees up to his chin, like a child. Beyond him grew two pine trees and a few yucca plants in flowerbeds shored up with dull rocks. Beyond them were rough stones carved with calligraphy, and an obelisk roped away behind iron chains.

I asked the groundskeeper what the writing on the stones read.

'I wouldn't know,' he answered. 'Got no interest in them.' He turned away from me and went back to raking up cigarette butts, dry leaves, trash. The broom's bristles left round swirls in the pale grit: a circle, a zero, traced backward. The groundskeeper was surrounded by these swirls, like Zen *ensō*, those almost-complete circles that represent the emptiness of all things.

A salaryman in suit and shirtsleeves walked over to the concrete pavilion and said a few words, his voice low, to the sleeper, who woke up, slowly.

Beside the climbing frame stood three worn playground animals mounted on springs: a panda, a koala, a red creature that became invisible if you looked at it head-on.

When I glanced back at the bell, the homeless man had moved away from the tower, and was lashing his possessions onto a wooden dolly which he covered with a light blue tarp. Then he threw his weight against the handle and dragged everything off toward Dai-Anraku-ji, a temple founded in the 1870s 'to comfort the souls' of the tens of thousands who had died at Kodenmachō from the 1610s, when the jail was first built, until 1875, when it closed.

The salaryman threw down a cigarette and stamped it out.

He leaned backward against one of the bell tower's pillars and closed his eyes.

The jail was older than the Tokugawa shogunate and outlasted it too. For more than two hundred years, Kodenmachō housed the city's prison: home to pickpockets and arsonists and murderers, troublemakers and gamblers and dissidents. Judgments were not subject to appeal and death sentences were carried out immediately. One inmate described the prison's atmosphere as 'reminiscent of the Warring States period – with desperate men spurring each other on and learning to laugh in the face of impending doom.'

Edo also had two public execution grounds, which stood at its northern and southern gateways. As the city grew, so over time the execution grounds relocated further outward, following the city limits as they moved: from Shibaguchi to Shinagawa and then Suzugamori in the south; in the north, from Asakusabashi to Kotsukappara on the Sumida River's eastern bank. But the walled city within a city that was Kodenmachō remained where it was. Outside its Great Gate, criminals were flogged; inside the condemned were tattooed, or waited for judgment; or for exile on the penal islands to the south and west; or for death.

Public punishment in Tokugawa Japan, Daniel Botsman has written, was a form of popular drama. 'The creation of a horrifying spectacle was more important than [inflicting] pain on an individual wrongdoer.' The shogunate was careful, though, to hold open-air executions only for the most terrible crimes, lest the crowd sympathize with the condemned, and riot.

In 1876, eight years after the last Tokugawa shogun left

the city, the jail was moved westward to Ichigaya. But even after the prison disappeared, Kodenmachō was still considered unclean. The earth itself was believed to be contaminated by *kegare*, the spiritual pollution brought on by blood and crime.

The writer Hasegawa Shigure grew up near the Kodenmachō district; within the sound of its blacksmiths' forges and the smells of frying sea snails and camellia-oil shops. In her memoirs, she wrote that the prison was believed to be filthy, which she thought unfair, since 'innocent people were locked up there as well as the guilty.' When the jail shut in 1875, the buildings were razed and Hasegawa's father was offered part of the block where they had stood, but he refused: *Absolutely not. Ya da kara, na.* He was not a weak man, Hasegawa wrote: he was a samurai, and carried a long sword and guarded Edo Castle in the months after the shogun left and the emperor's new capital was almost lawless. But for no amount of profit would he overcome his aversion to the site.

Hasegawa's mother pleaded that he reconsider – we could be land-rich! – but her father was adamant: 'I heard the shrieks of people being tortured there, tortured for nothing. And men about to be executed. I saw one dragged by his hair to the execution ground. He kept trying to escape. Even after his head was lopped off, his hands were still bound behind his back. And the body was twitching even though he was dead. – I want no part of that place.'

'Did you come here because you're a Christian?' the priest Nakayama asked. 'I can always tell when a Christian has just visited. They leave white lilies for the Jesuit who was tortured and executed in that jail.'

'I'm looking for the Bells of Time.'

'Oh.' The priest glanced back toward the bell tower. 'That one used to be in Edo Castle, but it was moved to the prison because the noise irritated the shogun. We only ring it on New Year's Eve now. It doesn't have the best tone. Though the more often you strike it, the better it sounds.'

The priest – Nakayama Hiroyuki – was around eighty years old, and had lived at Dai-Anraku-ji since he was fourteen, when his family moved from Kyoto.

Dai-Anraku-ji's courtyard is a tidal pool, filled with objects brought from other temples, other places and other eras.

A polished stone block considered sacred by the Ainu, the indigenous people of Japan. Inside that stone are the calcified remains of a snake. The sick come to run their palms over the snake's diamond-shaped head and its scales, and pray for healing. The fossil curves like a whip, or a letter in some unknown alphabet.

A wooden image of the goddess of literature and music: eight-armed Benzaiten. She has enamel eyes, and a smoke-darkened face; in the late nineteenth century she was brought to Dai-Anraku-ji during the Meiji restoration when all across Japan Buddhist temples were being ransacked and destroyed.

'This Benzaiten is a thousand years old. She was made for the warrior wife of a shogun.' Nakayama smiled. 'Four of the goddess' arms were repaired recently – it cost twelve million yen for each! – and when the craftsmen went to work, the neck wobbled. The woodcarver removed the head and found a tiny copy of the Golden Light Sutra inside. When the sutra was unscrolled, the paper stretched twenty-five meters. There were *nine* more sutras like that one inside the Benzaiten.' Nakayama held up his thumb. 'This was how big it was.'

The Golden Light Sutra is named for its tenth chapter, in which a bodhisattva dreams of a golden drum that 'lights up the sky like the circle of the sun'. A holy man appears to beat the drum, which calls on those who hear it to repent. The ruler who copied this sutra could ensure that he would flourish and his realm be rich and peaceful; that there would be no sickness or disasters during his reign. In medieval Japan, copies of the Golden Light Sutra were hidden in ceilings to protect a house against lightning, and against bad luck.

The image of Benzaiten had her own tiny red and gold shrine just beside Dai-Anraku-ji, and across from the place where the condemned were executed. The shrine was shaped like a moon gate; the shrine was all door, and almost no building. In the darkness inside, electric candles flickered, picking out the gold leaf on Benzaiten's slippers, her spangled robes, the eyes of the dragon on her breastplate, the fruit in one of her eight hands. The goddess' eyes gleam, reflecting all the light there is.

'The color of the earth near the well was different,' the priest Nakayama said. 'Darker.'

It was the place where executioners once washed severed heads before displaying them on pikes at the southern and northern gates into the city. The well was used until 1964. Nakayama watched as the waters, and the capped stones above them, were sealed off.

We were sitting on the floor of a back room in the temple, and drinking tea from Kyoto. Nakayama had said that he might have made coffee, but 'it would take an hour to roast the beans.' He was sorry.

The room was empty except for a low red lacquered table, a

scroll and a pale wooden *go* gaming board. Paper screens filtered the light.

'In 1875 a priest passed by the old Tokugawa prison at Kodenmachō. The jail's prisoners had just been moved to Yotsuya and the place was being used as a storehouse for food.

'And at the exact spot where the condemned were beheaded, he saw phosphor rising.'

'Phosphor . . . ?' I asked.

'It's believed that phosphor arises from the souls of the dead.'

Nakayama was as still as the main hall's image of Kōbō Daishi, the monk who founded the Shingon sect of Buddhism. Nakayama appeared to have no trouble sitting in the *seiza* position, his legs tucked underneath him. Meanwhile I was trying not to squirm, and failing: my knees were stiff and my calves and ankles hurt. We had been sitting for more than two hours.

'Did the priest have any family who had been jailed in Kodenmachō? Did he have a connection here?'

'He was just a priest – from a temple near Azabu and Roppongi. He happened to walk by and saw the strange glow I told you about. He had no relationship with anyone who was executed.'

I asked if Nakayama thought what the priest had seen reflected his shock – that the old order had changed after two hundred and fifty years; that suddenly anyone could speak about what had happened inside the jail.

Nakayama paused. 'Well, people now don't understand what "phosphor burning" even means. Seeing it is a skill, like reading palms is a skill – although some can understand what is written on the hand, there are very, very few who still can.'

The darkness of Tokyo a hundred and fifty years ago, in the

last years before electric lights: every night the city would have been black. In the twenty-first century's dazzle of head-lights and streetlamps and LEDs and vertical neon signs and halogen bulbs, if phosphor drifted up from the asphalt, no one would notice.

The priest had gone into a restaurant nearby and asked two men he met there for a donation to found the temple. Nakay-ama smiled. 'One was Ōkura Kihachirō. The other was Yasuda Zenjirō.'

Both Ōkura and Yasuda created business empires which were among Japan's first *zaibatsu*, the influential business conglomerates that dominated Japanese industry before World War Two. The founder of Dai-Anraku-ji was lucky or canny or both.

'So you think the temple's first priest really saw some-thing?'

Nakayama toyed with the prayer beads around his wrist. 'I wasn't there. I can't say.'

The children's school opposite would be torn down soon, Nakayama told me. The district did not have enough children to fill its classrooms. The building that would be constructed in its place would be a nursing home.

During renovation, construction crews uncovered the foundations of the old prison. Nakayama wanted the stones listed as a World Heritage site.

'You could see where the prisoners got their drinking water and the tiny spaces where they slept. You could see the kitchens that fed them and where they took their baths – that's when they got a chance to bathe. The condemned were always executed in the same place. That spot was never moved. I wanted the connection – between this time and that – preserved.'

After the ruins were unearthed, the construction company pushed that the nursing home not just go ahead, but that its construction should speed up.

'I went to the Metropolitan Government to ask that the prison be preserved, but the government said they were powerless to protect what remained, that it was up to the district ward. Archaeologists came to study the ruins, and two Nobel laureates backed preservation, but when the ward held a vote, it went 40:1 in favor of the old folks' home.'

It was Nakayama who cast the lone dissenting vote.

'You were up against terrible odds!' I said, wondering how to say *crushing loss* in Japanese. There are many words for *defeat*, if not so many as words for time. The way you lose, and how, matters.

'Yes.' Nakayama said. 'Looking down at the ruins, you could see, in just one glance, how people lived!'

'I'm sorry.'

'I circulated a petition and the ward decided to preserve the stone walls. You'll be able to look down and see them through a glass floor.'

'How did you get the ward to agree to that?' I asked, thinking of Nakayama's 40:1 opposition.

He looked pleased. 'Well, the head of the ward wanted – really wanted – to retire at a certain rank, with certain honors. But if there'd been just *one complaint* against him, he wouldn't have gotten them.'

I looked across the lacquered table at Nakayama.

'Just one complaint?' I said.

Nakayama nodded. I looked away from him to his *go* board in the corner. I thought it was the most beautiful thing I had seen in Japan or anywhere else: both luminous and severe. *Go*, the game of strategy in which a player tries to surround an opponent's stones with his own.

'I'd really hate to play against you,' I said.

'That board is too good to use,' he shrugged. He was still smiling. I almost felt sorry for the old head of the ward.

'It's a board only to use when you dream, then.'

'It's a shame that we couldn't have preserved the old prison. You could see what it had been in the early 1600s. It burned twelve times, and after each fire, it was rebuilt, just as it had been, from a map.'

'Fires . . .' I thought of the guards, the walls, the iron locks. 'The people jailed there, did they . . . ?'

Nakayama stopped smiling. 'When the city was burning, the warders would open the doors and let everyone out. When the fires were put out, the prisoners had three days to come back.'

I raised my eyebrows.

'Oh, yes, they came back. Everyone always came back. If you didn't come back . . . they would find you. And they'd kill you. It was better just to turn yourself in.'

The nineteenth-century Kabuki playwright Mokuami grew up in Nihonbashi, only ten minutes' walk from Kodenmachō. In a late play about a samurai caught stealing from the shogun's vaults (*Four Thousand Gold Pieces, Like Plum Leaves*), Mokuami takes his audience inside the old prison. He interviewed men who had been inside as guards or convicts, and wrote about the inmates' secret language and their routines, about their hierarchies and their honor codes. The play's jail sequence opens with a poor country actor being forced into 'the naked dance', so the men around him can forget their hunger. With an extra stroke of cruelty, Mokuami has the man dance to the beat of a candy vendor's call from beyond the walls – Kodenmachō was famous for its sweet shops. 'Better things are coming! Better things are coming!' sings the actor, weeping.

For two hundred and fifty years, the prison had been a place of terror and mystery. Mokuami depicted newcomers arriving in the western wing ('the most infamous'), crawling through the door and then between another inmate's spread legs so every new prisoner would understand that, whatever his status had been outside, now he was nothing. Mokuami portrayed the room's boss overseeing the prisoners from a tower of tatami mats taken from the weaker among them, the less important convicts, who were mashed together into a space called the Far Road. He wrote about the illness and hunger, pretty boys seeking to defend themselves from the strong, old grudges being settled with beatings, new arrivals punished for failing to bring protection money into the prison. 'Your fate in hell depends on your *cash*', Mokuami writes, in one of the play's most quoted lines. 'This is Hell Number One. There is no Second Place.'

As Mokuami portrayed it, Kodenmachō was a distorted mirror of the city beyond its moat: its rituals and hierarchies and protocols. Inmates were separated according to class and status: samurai whose rank entitled them to an audience with the shogun lived in special quarters above the ground floor. Buddhist monks, Shinto priests and women were also housed in those upper rooms. But below, on the Far Road, an ordinary prisoner who had arrived without money might be forced to share a single tatami mat with six or seven other men and would often have nothing to eat at all.

In *Four Thousand Gold Pieces*, Mokuami's Vault-Breaker is admired for his daring, for his panache. The prison boss offers him a fine kimono and sash to wear to his execution. 'You must die in beautiful clothes,' the boss says. 'You deserve them, because of the brilliance of your crime.'

'It's very silent,' Nakayama said. 'Living here, we have no sense that we're actually in the heart of a city.'

I followed Nakayama along the corridor, where shadows muffled light and sound and the ceilings rose up so high that they might have opened out onto the sky, though it would surely always have been night, the wood was stained so dark. The corridor angled around a little rock garden – stones and sasanqua trees set around a pool of carp that glided and splashed through the water. It was more Kyoto than Tokyo.

'Before you enter into the sanctuary, you must purify yourself,' Nakayama said. He opened a small lacquered disc, and took out a pinch of incense, which he dusted into my hands, motioning me to rub my palms together. 'And this, please eat,' he said, passing me a little caddy filled with cloves. I took one tiny spike, and chewed it. I was surprised at how easy the clove was to swallow, and at the sweet bitter taste it left in my mouth.

We stepped up into the Buddhist hall, which though not beautiful, had the venerability of age; over almost a century, smoke has darkened the gold leaf of its rafters. Nakayama switched on a huge LED flashlight and let its beam play over the hall's sacred image, a Kōbō Daishi, whose face a thousand years of incense had turned the matte color of wet bark.

'During the 1923 earthquake, people from this area loaded the carving onto a wagon and dragged it to Tokyo Station.'

Crowds, screaming and shoving against each other; the believers piling the heavy wooden figure onto a wooden wagon, and straining with it through smoke, around abandoned cars and carts, around crevasses that had opened in the road surface.

'These *nenju* prayer beads. How old would you think they are?'

Nakayama passed the amber beads to me, and I cradled the rosary. I had thought the beads were made of wood, but they were too light even for balsa wood, each glossy sphere faintly pitted with white stipples. I looked at the white silken tassels, which had turned faintly gray. 'Meiji?' I asked. 'A hundred and twenty-five years old?'

'Very good,' he said, politely. 'But they are *four hundred* years old. They would once have been a light gold. Time flows and flows, constantly. It never stops, not even for a second. Sometimes we may think back, "I should have done this, I should have done that . . ." And it is through those regrets, those *reflections*, that we move forward . . .'

Above our heads stretched a yellowed scroll: *For The Repose And Comfort Of Those Who Died.*

'It's because we last only for a blink that our lives matter so much,' Nakayama said.

I stepped out, back into the harsh light of the Kodenmachō sun, opposite the bell that had survived even after the prison around it was erased. Nakayama bowed, smiling again, and went back into his temple. His footsteps were light.

In 2002 and 2003, as Omotesandō's bohemian enclaves gave way to developers and Moët Hennessy Louis Vuitton shops, my favorite coffee houses shut one by one: Café des Flores on Omotesandō dōri, Aux Bacchanales in Harajuku. Suddenly there were four Starbucks where there had been none. Only Daibo's was left, in the same place it had been since 1975; its ramshackle four-story concrete building a survivor among glittering steel-and-glass boxes. I brought people I loved, or people I wanted to impress, to watch Daibo roast coffee in the half-light; coffee poured over jagged ice shards in the summer, into porcelain bowls in the winter.

When the shop was quiet, I practiced Japanese with Daibo, who spoke very little English. I would try out phrases and words, but no matter what I said, Daibo was always laughing to himself. I'd call a *dictionary* a *bicycle*. Or say *cataclysmic catastrophe* when I meant the word for *minor inconvenience*. Daibo loved correcting me. 'Keep trying!' he said, convinced that my Japanese would always be awful. Daibo's wife, who sometimes worked in the coffee shop with him, spoke English to me. Like Daibo, she came from the snow country; they had met in a student production of one of Jean Anouilh's plays, in the 1960s when French culture was all the rage in Japan. Her family had not wanted him to bring her to Tokyo. Then Daibo persuaded Mrs. Daibo's grandmother to teach him to make soba buckwheat noodles, and she liked him.

Once the grandmother approved of the match, Daibo was allowed to take his bride to the big city.

Mrs. Daibo had a face like a flower: an iris.

When Daibo's wife wasn't there, Daibo's beautiful but forbidding assistant Maruyama took orders and settled the bills. If Daibo went out, or was busy sorting coffee beans, she would make coffee. Maruyama and I never spoke.

The longer I lived in Tokyo, the more Daibo Coffee became the place I went when anything was wrong.

I wasn't alone.

Once a Japanese madwoman appeared beside me at the counter, where she emptied her enormous handbag: she sifted through lipsticks, dirty Kleenex, packets of unused tissues, pencil stubs and papers and a hairbrush.

Maruyama glared at the woman as she desecrated the pristine counter. Her face looked like a Noh mask: Enraged Beauty. She said nothing, though, because Daibo said nothing. He just smiled.

'What may I offer you?' he asked.

'I wanna cap'ccino. Can you do me one of those?'

'No, I don't serve coffee with foamed milk,' he said.

'Whaddya mean you don't!' she gasped, raking the detritus – makeup, stationery, tchotchkes – back into her leather bag. 'No cap'ccino! Everyone in the world serves that!'

'We don't,' Daibo said, gentle. 'Would you like anything else?'

'Well, gimme coffee with milk, I guess,' she said.

Daibo turned and brought down a Bizen-ware bowl from the shelf behind him. He once told me that he loved that plain glaze, that it was his favorite, '. . . because you can see the way the bowl is fired. The clay tells no lies. It's just itself.' Of the Blanc-de-Chine bowls that I always picked – pure white, without any flaws – he said, 'They're beautiful, of course, but you never know what's underneath the glaze. I never quite trust them.'

Daibo pushed the coffee across the counter. As the woman drank it, she became still, quiet, thoughtful.

Then it was my turn.

Daibo put beans for my coffee in a battered old aluminum measuring cup. He ground the beans and put them into the flannel drip he had made himself with unbleached muslin cloth and a thick wire he had shaped around a whiskey bottle. He took up a stainless-steel pot and let the hot water fall in a shining thread, one drop at a time, onto the coffee grains. Except for his hands, Daibo was absolutely still.

Daibo poured milk into the coffee, straining it so no skin would form on the surface. The bowl was white like the moon.

Drink this. And heal.

浅

草

'Asakusa'

Sensō-ji demarked the border between this world and
another world – the one that separated death from life.

Nam-lin Hur

Asakusa: The Mythic Kantō Plain

The bar had glass walls. Many floors down, the districts of Hanakawado and Kaminarimon unfurled: pale gold head-lamps, gold streetlights, golden light under the eaves of Sensō-ji temple, gold on each uplit level of the red-and-gold five-story pagoda beside it. Gold, dappling the Thunder Gate leading to the temple. Philippe Starck's Flamme d'Or on Asahi Super Dry Hall, which everyone in Asakusa refers to as *kin no unko*, The Gilded Turd. The SkyTree and a few neon karaoke banners touched the landscape with electric blue. The Sumida River was too dark to see, flowing in blackness to the east.

I was sitting alone at the bar, reading *The Lotus Sutra*.

It is rare to hear this Law, and a person capable of listening to this Law is rare. It is like the udumbara flower which all the world loves and delights in, but which appears only once in many many ages.

I was wondering what an udumbara flower was, when someone touched my elbow, his fingers light. He was young, with a fine quiff and a good suit.

'Excuse me,' he said. 'Our . . . colleague would like to practice his English with you. Will you join us?'

He stumbled over the word *colleague*, gesturing to the three empty seats between me and an ancient, almost bald man in a pin-striped double-breasted suit. The man had glasses with enormous lenses; his left eye was closed so tightly that it might have been sewn shut.

'I'm fine sitting here,' I said, looking down at *The Lotus Sutra* again.

'You speak Japanese!' he said, eyebrows raised with an expression of exaggerated surprise. '*Wonderful!* May we come to you, then?'

I shrugged. The man gestured to the barman, who slid the grandfather's wine glass along the counter. A waitress brought me a small cocotte: meat and potatoes.

'You're not eating?' I asked.

'I never touch Western food.'

'Well, please forgive me for going first,' I said, falling back on one of those Japanese conversational formulae that fill in the blanks when you don't know what to say.

The grandfather handed me his name-card with a flourish: chairman and CEO.

His two young employees left the bar, snickering like small boys when a braver friend threatens to eat something inedible: a live snail, a frog, a jellyfish.

'Where are you from?'

'I live in England, but—'

'Piccadilly Shurkush! I love England!' He took a deep breath and launched into 'O Danny Boy'. The bar's other customers studiously ignored him. '*'Tis I'll be here in sunshine or in shadow! O Danny Boy! I lo—o-o-o-o-o-ve you so . . . !*' Then he sang a stanza from 'Love Me Tender' and finally a ballad in

Mandarin. I clapped after the ballad, impressed by his Chinese despite myself.

'I have a second wife in Taipei and a *huge, huge* . . .' he paused, smiling and raising his eyebrows, '. . . *house* here. Thirteen stories! You can see it from that window!' He pointed to the plate-glass observation window.

'You live near the temple?'

'Yes. In Azumabashi, for my whole life.'

'You weren't evacuated during the war?' I didn't know the word *evacuate*, so I gestured with my hands as if I were waving a bird away. From the bar top toward the ceiling. 'For safety?'

'No. I was in Tokyo the whole time. Bombs kept landing everywhere.' It was his turn to mimic something that he lacked words for: incendiaries whistling through the air, impact, exploding vectors. 'I like America, though. What happened was war. No one can do anything once it starts . . . The Americans weren't bad people.'

He gestured to the wedding ring glittering on my hand. 'You could never have a second man?'

'Never,' I said, sipping my wine. 'I like simplicity.'

He straightened as if I had insulted him, muttered a brief word to the barman, who slid his glass three seats westward again. He looked longingly at his name-card, as if he wanted to take that back, too.

I kept eating.

The grandfather produced an enormous magnifying glass, and examined his iPhone. '*Biji-ness*,' he said frostily, tossing back the last of his wine. Then he paid his tab, collected his briefcase and walked unsteadily past me toward the exit. 'Oh, this is no good! No good! I'm too old for you,' he said loudly, so that everyone in the restaurant looked over at us; as if *he* were refusing *me*.

He looked eastward, toward the thirteen-story house.

When he was gone, the young bartender frowned at me. 'He's a regular,' he said. And the next night, when I came into the bar for supper, the hostess was careful to seat me by myself, almost hidden behind the coffee machine.

The novelist Kawabata Yasunari once wrote that, standing on Kototoi Bridge near Asakusa, he could feel the wideness of the Kantō Plain eddying around him. The melancholy of the entire city flowed beneath that bridge.

Nihonbashi and the Kodenmachō jail are where Edo had its origins in 1590, when the first Tokugawa shogun Ieyasu began rebuilding a ruined castle. But Asakusa began at least a thousand years before that, as a village in a land-scape empty but for grasses and a labyrinth of rivers. One medieval traveler, a nun from Kyoto, described passing through vast fields where nothing could grow but bush clover, reeds and pampas grasses. The grasses were high enough that a man on horseback could pass through, invisible. 'For three days,' the nun wrote, 'I pressed on through the fields without getting where I wanted to go ... there was only the plain stretching into the distance far behind and far ahead of me.'

The great river, flowing one way before sometimes changing its course, in spate and in drought, was the single landmark.

The literati of western Japan liked the idea of the eastern badlands so much that, even as the plain itself changed – with settlements and farms – the rules for writing about it stayed the same. It was always a wilderness, always bleak, always almost empty.

The plain was not so much its own landscape as a foil for elegant Kyoto. Even its first name (Bandō) meant East of the Passes. A later name – Kantō – was East of the Barriers. In stories and songs, the eastern wastes were a place of bandits and exiles. No one actually wanted to visit, much less live there. Not even the thieves and renegades.

The beauty, and the murderer. These are the two faces of Asakusa.

Beauty was first, in the year 628. A small golden statue of Kannon, the goddess of mercy, which three brothers pulled into their fishing boat. In woodblock prints of the story, radiance blazes from the water, the weight of a mysterious object tugging down the hemp mesh nets. It is Asakusa before Asakusa: the broken ridge of Mount Tsukuba to the north, reeds, pagoda trees, the crosshatched waves of Tokyo Bay, which then didn't even have a name. It was just the Inland Sea.

The villagers built for the image a crude shrine. When a monk was blinded after looking at the image's face, monks created a receptacle to keep the dangerous face hidden. Then someone carved a wooden copy of the original statue, and put *that* away in another receptacle, which stood in front of the first image. The Kannon was doubly mysterious, doubly sacred.

No one alive has ever seen the original Kannon image. Its dimensions were never recorded. During great fires when the main sanctuary was threatened, the statues were moved to a boat on the Sumida River, and the receptacles were kept hidden in a palanquin. Buried deep under Sensō-ji temple, the image survived the firebombs of 1945, too.

The murderer was a crone who lived in the wastes near the river. No one knows exactly when. She had a lovely daughter whom she used to lure unwary travelers to her stone hut. The men would lie down with the daughter on a stone pillow. When the lovers were asleep, the crone would smash their skulls. What the travelers carried, the crone took, and then she dumped their bodies in a nearby pond. Nine hundred and ninety-nine men died that way.

One of the temples near Sensō-ji used to display the stone pillow for pilgrims to touch.

Kawabata later wrote this version of the story: the thousandth traveler heard a reed flute. 'It sounded like a voice, and sang: *When night falls, even if you have no place to lay your head, do not stay at the lonely house on the Asakusa reed plain.*' The next morning, the wanderer woke up in Sensō-ji temple, saved by the goddess of mercy. The reed flute had been the voice of Kannon.

In other variants of the story, the hag's daughter falls in love with the thousandth guest. Or: the daughter wants to atone for her part in the murders. She wants to die, and substitutes herself for that thousandth victim. In the dark, the hag kills her own child by mistake. In remorse and grief, the old woman then drowns herself in the same pond where she had disposed of her many victims.

Or: she becomes a goddess, and chooses to protect what she would once have devoured.

It is a single leap, in a single instant, from perfect evil to perfect goodness. The old storytellers saw no contradiction in movement from bestiality to enlightenment.

In Asakusa, the world of devils and demons coexisted along with the celestial world of Buddhas and petty deities. Asakusa was unique in Tokyo: history did not have to be a trap. Escape was possible.

By the early nineteenth century, Edo's townspeople had grown increasingly jaded, feeling that traditional Buddhas and Shinto deities had forgotten them. One contemporary writer complained: 'Today, all the spirits (*kami*) have ascended to heaven; the Buddhas have left for the Western Paradise; and all present and other worlds have fallen into disuse . . .'

New 'fashionable' divinities filled gaps of belief and faith, and the grounds of Sensō-ji were crowded with their shrines.

Benzaiten had been a water deity, dwelling in one of Asakusa's ponds. She was rehabilitated as the goddess of literature and music and given her own little shrine next to the Bell of Time, one of the oldest bells on the Kantō Plain. The bell was vast, heavy; a bell that could imprison a grown man alive like the bells in the old stories. Beside this one, other bells looked like toys. The tower's columns were woodworm-riddled and shearing away. Even the stones had cracked.

A placard read: RŌJO BENZAITEN. Old Woman Benzaiten, who was the third daughter of the Dragon King. The shrine's black and gilt doors were folded back. I was surprised; I had only ever seen the red shrine shut up like a box. But it was the Day of the Snake, and so the shrine was open: snakes are Benzaiten's messengers.

I had never seen an image so alive, so watchful. I looked at the Face, and then backed away from it. The Benzaiten stared outward, her skin shadowed, her hair a smooth sheet, white as a Yoshino cherry blossom. Incense drifting from the shrine burned my throat.

Behind me an old woman threw coins into a box before she prayed; she wore a silvery summer kimono with a black *obi* sash crosshatched with triangular fishing nets. After she had turned down the path back to Asakusa's main hall, her metal cane tapping the stones, a policeman came; he bowed to the Benzaiten as if he were saluting some dignitary.

I went slowly down the polished stone stairs, which a famous *koto* player had donated. I wondered what I had seen. I wondered what the policeman was worshipping. Benzaiten the goddess of knowledge and music, or the murderous hag?

By the square *ishigaki* stone wall, a woman was squatting in front of the shrine. She looked about seventy, although she could have been younger; maybe born during the first years of the war. She wore a thin dress the color of cherry-blossom liqueur. Her silvery hair fell to her shoulders and was pinned up like a girl's in an upswept bouffant, like Barbara Eden's around 1965. It was neatly, even expertly, done.

The White-Haired Benzaiten.

The man beside me had balanced his chin on his balled fists. He was what the Japanese call a *koffeemaniakku* ('coffee maniac') or coffee *otaku*. Both terms originally were rude, especially *otaku*, which appears in the 1990 edition of Japan's *Basic Knowledge of Modern Words* as 'a kind of fan discriminated against by others. They are reclusive, mentally unbalanced and obsessed with details. Nor can they communicate well. They usually do not care about their clothing and are not dressed well.' A nerd, in other words. A freak.

The cultural historian Jonathan Abel has tracked how *otaku* evolved in the 2000s to mean someone who was merely into role-playing games, or *anime* cartoons. The word lost its creepy overtones until it meant someone 'over-the-top, a hobbyist, an enthusiast of any sort'. There were train-spotting *otaku*, fishing *otaku*, wine *otaku*. Japan suddenly became a nation composed entirely of *otaku*.

The coffee *otaku* gazed at Daibo, intent: watching the thin thread of water as droplets fell into the cotton filter, becoming mahogany beads underneath; falling into the porcelain cup until it was three-quarters full.

'I'm writing a book about Tokyo's coffee houses. But this place' – he broke off and looked around, reverent – 'is in a class of its own.'

'You must have to drink a lot of coffee. For your research.'

'Yes.'

'I knew someone who studied the effect of caffeine on monkeys. Apparently caffeine didn't keep them awake longer than normal, but it did confuse their sense of time.'

Across the counter's long wooden wave, Daibo was listening. He looked blank. I tried to explain again, and again, in Japanese and finally – to the coffee *otaku* – in English. Both men looked puzzled, and even worried.

'But how,' Daibo asked finally, '. . . can a *monkey* tell time?'

I thought of the animals and their testing chamber with its computers and press plates and indicator lights for correct and incorrect answers; the banana-flavored pellets that were rewards, and how they would clatter into little troughs when the monkey got an answer right.

Time for the monkey would perhaps have been the gaps that elapsed between banana pellets.

赤
坂

'Akasaka'

Rat Mountain amazed no one for many ages.
Then the bull king appeared – Buddha's virtue triumphed.
Tigers and other beasts grew violent, and greed spread,
But stories, like horned rabbits, explained the dharma.
In the dragon king's undersea palace Buddha's bell boomed,
Snakes in their rooms woke and were enlightened.
A horse suddenly grew pregnant with a Buddhist prince.
Let the rumbling of goat, deer, and ox carts stop.
Monkey cries and frost in the pure moonlight,
The rooster-man still silent as visitors head home.
Dogs do not bark at night in sacred Rājagrha,
Wild boars touch Gold Mountain, making it even higher.

Inscription on the Entsūji Bell of Time
Translated by Chris Drake

Akasaka: The Invention of Edo

The smallest Bell of Time hangs in Akasaka. The bell has disappeared and reappeared twice, the last time during World War Two, when it was almost melted down for scrap in a junk yard.

Wandering through Akasaka just before his death, the writer Yoshimura Hiroshi experienced a sensation of vertigo; the buildings seemed to fly toward and away from each other at the same time. The hills below the buildings crashed into each other and fell back again. *If you talk about the mathematical concept of 'chaos,'* he wrote, *there have to be rules. But in Akasaka, you don't know where to start. It's unbelievable to imagine how remote this place once was.*

I wondered if Yoshimura wrote that as he was considering the graceless Tokyo Broadcasting Service headquarters, TBS Biz. When it opened, TBS Biz housed a fifteen-meter replica of the anime *Space Battleship Yamato*, which blazed away with its 'Wave Motion Gun'. Outside, giant yellow parakeets, made of resin, glowered side by side from a metal perch.

And, up a steep slope, at Entsu-ji temple, stands the Akasaka Bell of Time. Entsu-ji is hemmed in by office blocks and houses, by a parking lot and overhanging power lines. The bell is faint green in places and dark in others, where a poem is inscribed. There are twelve verses, one for each of the Chinese Zodiac animals. The words make up a labyrinth, a secret code.

The poem opens with Rat Mountain, a mythical place in ancient China, famous in folktales for nests shared by birds and mice. A wild place: the earth at its origins. The poem ends with Gold Mountain, a Buddhist symbol for perfect wisdom. In between the beginning and close of things are horned rabbits – creatures that do not exist in this world – and an underwater bell in the dragon king's palace; there are snakes that wake from dreams and into enlightenment. At last the world leaves time itself, after the keeper of the hours ('the rooster man') falls silent: the earth at its end.

The first description of Akasaka's bell, and the poem inscribed on it, appear in Toda Mosui's *A Sprig of Purple*, written in the late seventeenth century. Toda's political patron, the son of the second Tokugawa shogun, was forced to commit suicide by a jealous brother, and afterward Toda never held high office again. His connections were still good, though, and his family wealthy, so he was able to devote himself to literature. And since he knew the city 'inside out, down to its most intimate corners', he was perfectly placed to invent a literary identity for Edo. Earlier writers had mapped Kyoto landscapes onto the shogun's new city in the east; before Toda, no one had written about what actually existed there.

In *Sprig of Purple*, two friends wander through the great avenues and little alleys, getting into fights and visiting brothels.

Toda gives one companion – his alter ego – the pseudonym 'Iitsu', whose characters can mean 'passed over but not bitter about it'. Not a bad name for a writer.

Toda describes the Akasaka bell as 'an upside down, V-shaped gong, empty inside'. Its voice was a voice of shadows; that sound ebbed away like a setting sun.

Tokyo is a city of darkness, a city of light. Each melts into the other. At its center, the city of light blacks out, and at bridges and crossroads, at the margins around train stations, the city of darkness shines, gleaming.

In that other city are love-hotel rooms laid out like train carriages where men brush against women pretending to be commuters. And the (now almost extinct) No Panty coffee houses, which appeared overnight and disappeared as quickly, once Tokyo tired of their mirrored floors and the waitresses who served terrible overpriced coffee, wearing short skirts and nothing else. Before the New Public Morals Act outlawed certain excesses of bad taste (such as revolving beds and over-sized mirrors), there were cabarets near Shinjuku where women stood behind chicken wire as clients poked fingers through the mesh, straining to touch a rib, a wrist, or whatever they could reach. Rooms where adults could suck on a pacifier and wear diapers. And – most infamous – Lucky Hole, a bar where a man could push himself through an anonymous plywood board while someone invisible on the other side sucked or stroked him. 'I thought it was sex for the future,' wrote one aficionado wistfully of the time before the act came into force and the red light district's seedier establishments – including Lucky Hole – were shut down.

The two cities blend one into the other in Minato ward: at the Ritz, and in cheap karaoke bars. The American embassy, and the head office of the Tokyo Broadcasting System. The glass funnel of Roppongi Hills, and the towers of Midtown. The steel and glass ripples of the National Art Museum, and the hostess bars that cluster the crossing near where Expressway Number Three turns into Route One.

She was the most beautiful woman I had ever seen. She was lithe, her body like a wand, with silky blonde hair slipping over and around her shoulders in sheets.

She was dancing alone in Wall Street, a shot bar in one of Roppongi's long narrow basements; so graceful that no one would come near her because anyone dancing beside her would look clumsy. Empty space fanned around her legs, her arms. The other dancers shook themselves a few feet away. They were all a little off rhythm, watching her move.

'She's – radiant,' I said to the man beside me, almost shouting because the music was so loud. Indifferent, he looked over his shoulder at the dancer.

'That's a *prostitute*. From somewhere in Eastern Europe.'

The bar had walls of unfinished concrete. What lighting there was, was dim, except for a muted glitter under the bottles of vodka and whiskey and the massed empty tumblers and champagne flutes standing upside down on the bar. Like the glass, the dancer drew light to herself; to the lines of her shoulders and wrists, her hips.

I wondered if she had once trained at the Kirov or the Bolshoi. A tall girl, golden, who might have been a principal dancer in Europe, but who had ended up a few thousand kilometers to the east, a figure priced in yen on somebody's timesheet.

*

The Japanese language has a modest number of words for the English word penis. There's 'robust individual', and 'life-giving sword', after the spear used in the creation myth when the islands of Japan arose out of chaos. Blue-green snake and mythical serpent. Eel, turtle, cucumber. For monks, the penis was 'demon of worldly cravings'.

But where the words for the male member are either playful or grandiose, the Japanese vocabulary for female genitalia is whimsical, extravagant, and rococo.

The most common equivalent for vagina is *asoko*: 'there'. Female instrument, muscle, money box. For really large parts, 'the ultimate depth', and *soshiki manjū*, those sweet doughy buns served at Japanese funerals. There are terms imported from American English: rose, canoe, beaver, crevice, crater. Cherry blossom and the flower pink, for virgins. Secondhand for ones that are not. From the floating world of Edo's Pleasure Quarters, there is the antique language still sometimes used by older yakuza: teabowl, teapot, mortar, utensil, box. Inkwell. For loose vaginas: large basin, rice tub, bathtub, enormous plate. The garden has been scavenged for words (peach, watermelon, chestnut, fig), as has the sea (night clam, crab, and a wealth of different shells – raven, baked, freshwater, living, new). For monks who misbehaved in the so-called willow and flower world of Edo's pleasure quarters, religious terms in Sanskrit: sudden enlightenment. Lotus shell. And – harder to explain – 'straw sandals'.

Even if their lives were bound by strict ancient rules, the

monks' sexual vocabulary could run wild: solitary pilgrimage, copying out a sutra by hand, and whipping, which meant caress.

You need no passport or luggage.

Whatever the fantasy, whatever the desire, in Tokyo a love hotel exists for it and inside the hotel, a room. The themes change – merry-go-round carousel, medieval castle, galaxy far, far away, underwater grotto – but certain elements remain the same. A love hotel's entrance is always hidden and deep, a recess that turns back on itself; the start of a journey. The main door stands behind a screening wall, and opens in response to automatic sensors.

There will be no visible concierge, just a disembodied voice, saying, *Welcome.* A luminous wall of panels displays photographs of the available rooms. Choose REST (a few hours) or STAY (the night), and press the plate for the bedroom desired. Before magnetic cards, clear pneumatic tubes would deliver metal keys. Love hotels are designed so that guests never meet each other. In a hidden control room, glowing security screens cluster like an insect's prismatic eye.

Love hotels have variations on what the cultural historian Sarah Chaplin has called an 'ur-code'. Tiny traditional *noren* curtains to hide a guest's license plate. Enormous mirrors, everywhere. Ultraviolet lighting. Jacuzzis. Glass inner walls. The occasional cage. A costume rental service: Office Lady, Tart, Schoolgirl. A basic assortment of cosplay outfits.

To enter a love hotel is to depart from everyday life, to escape the crushing weight of society and its expectations. It is a fantasyland for grownups: the chance to reinvent yourself, to disappear, if only briefly. More than quick sex, that is the promise of the shimmering door.

In the heavy air, smoke from grilling eels. A shrine to the Seven Gods of Good Luck, pomegranates and pears ripening on trees by its stone gate.

I followed Kototoi dōri westward, through Matsugaya, Kita-Ueno; across Iriya and Shitaya, where the Black Gate of the old Yoshiwara district once stood. Yoshiwara, the nineteenth-century world of courtesans and Kabuki. At its height, a million men lived in Edo. Yoshiwara was the only legally sanctioned pleasure quarter: the nightless city.

I inspected my *Tokyo City Atlas*; the area between Ueno and Asakusa was blanked out. The atlas's mapmakers had severed Shōwa dori, the great arterial road that runs north to Nikko, and cut the thick weave of train lines that flow through Ueno Station. The missing crescent was crammed with love hotels; or would have been, if the *Atlas* had allowed it to exist. In guidebooks and atlases, love hotels are erased, absent. In Kabukichō and Shibuya, Gotanda and Uguisudani, love-hotel districts are shown as blank urban blocks on unnamed streets. The buildings of Tokyo's High City, with its museums and conventional hotels, its embassies and temples and shrines and theaters, always appear. And maps of Tokyo's Shadow City show love hotels, but not, for example, museums or even the nearest train station. The spaces that belong to the city of shadows exist only in the minds of people who visit, and know where to look for them.

I passed Xanadu and Hotel Sting. Hotel Next and Ya Ya Ya.

An old threadmaker's. Hotel Ramses Joy. Urban Castle Negishi. Petticoat Lane.

Once inside a love hotel, a guest can move only in one direction. A couple can enter as many times as they want, but they can leave only once. Further access is not allowed, so a guest must bring everything needed – food, clothes, toys – inside. Go out and the guest has to start all over again: the panel, the payment, the key. This is why foreigners are usually barred: Japanese guests understand the choreography, the protocols, where outsiders complain: what do you mean I can't come back in, why don't you have room service, can I have another room? A Japanese visitor knows that the love hotel is a theater of silence. Noise ruins fantasies.

A love hotel almost never has windows. Where they exist, they are always opaque.

Hotel Charme. El Apio. Hotel Crystal.

> Such an enjoyable place.
> You can spend wonderful time.
> Please enjoy your time.

Hotel Calico. Hotel Love.

A wall of blue fairy lights, and a tiny pharmacy stocked with soaps, unguents, tissues, foams, plastic razors, white cloth face masks.

Le Ciel, with a huge neon model of the planet Saturn shimmering over its entryway. Hotel Vogue.

> Rest ¥4500
> Stay ¥6500

A glowing blue circle over OPEN. FULL was blank.
Ribbon Hearts. Hotel Seeds. Hotel La Luna.

51

The street was almost empty. Under the expressway overpass, steel girders and floodlights; shadows and iridescent reflections off the green paint.

Invisible on maps is Uguisudani, 'valley of the nightingales'. Uguisudani, where solitudes intersect, before veering away from each other again.

The old man to my left was called Fukutani. He was a big man, with white sideburns. The rush-covered seats were too small for him.

I asked how long he had been coming to Daibo's.

'Thirty-five years,' he said. 'Since the place opened.'

'Has it changed?'

Fukutani thought, sipping his coffee: a tiny cup in his huge hand. 'Well, the counter used to be level.'

I saw for the first time that the wood was warped.

'I'm a copywriter. I first came here when I was just starting out. I used to work for American companies. Foreigners . . .' He glanced at me, twinkling. 'I hate 'em all.'

I pretended to look angry. Fukutani was pleased.

Over our heads stretched a collection of hard-boiled detective stories in a long row that had been yellowing year after year from the smoke of roasting coffee beans.

'Oh, it's not personal,' he said. 'I hate everybody.'

Across the counter, Daibo was laughing.

'Mejiro'

The city plan of Edo was orientated on a spiral aligned with the cosmos, thereby establishing a direct equation between Tokugawa rule and the order of the universe.

Naito Akira

Mejiro: A Failed Coup

On Tokyo's clock face, Mejiro stands northwest, at about ten. The city here is anonymous: parking lots, alleys, a four-lane stretch of Meiji dori. Apartment blocks and offices crowd the ridge and its downward slope. Each concrete terrace, each rusting fire escape, blurred into the next. The landscape was like an unfinished drawing.

Cherry trees in full leaf leaned down toward the Kanda River. The waters running through the concrete canal sounded like swimmers splashing each other.

A peloton of nursery-school children passed, wearing fluorescent orange caps. A policeman bicycled slowly along Meiji dori. I juggled an iPhone in one hand and my *Tokyo City Atlas* in the other, but couldn't find the temple's entrance: the high white wall followed the rise, and there was no gate.

An old man waved me up the hill. 'Konjō-in? Go up and then go down again. There's no other way to get inside.'

On Mejiro's main street, a kimono shop, a boutique selling shoes from Italy. Across Mejiro dōri was Gakushūin, the Peers' School, where the emperor once studied.

I followed an arc that ran parallel to the Kanda River, until at last Konjō-in's gate rose overhead, its name painted in gold: Mountain of the Sacred Spirits. The temple was new, although the upward sweep of its bronze roof gave it a gravitas that most of Tokyo's modern temples lack. The roof looked like it might crush the walls holding it up.

By the steps before the old gate stood Fudō: He Who Shall Not Be Moved, most powerful of the Wisdom Kings. Fudō had thin lips and high cheekbones; he looked more disappointed in the world than enraged with it. In his right hand he held a thick sword, the blade that slashes through ignorance; his left arm should have ended at his elbow in a burst of fire, though the burning arm had broken off, leaving only a stump. Behind Fudō's back, the sculptor had chiseled a sheer wall of flame. The stone eddied into billowing smoke, and arced outward like a great feather.

The temple's inner court was empty except for three ancient pilgrims. They were touring every Fudō temple on the Kantō plain. Rough stone stairs curved up the hillside behind the temple, past sensuous stone bodhisattvas and carving after carving of the Three Mystic Apes, hands clapped over eyes, ears, mouth. See No Evil. Hear No Evil. Speak No Evil. Moss had turned the stones green, and some of the monkeys had eroded so badly that their faces and tiny hands were almost invisible.

On the western ridge, above Konjō-in's roof, is a grave, a grave without ashes. The stone honors the rebel samurai Marubashi Chūya. In 1651, Chūya organized a force of masterless samurai in a plot to overthrow the Tokugawa. According to legend, Chūya himself betrayed the conspiracy, after raving about his plans during a high fever.

Chūya's history was retold in the puppet theaters and in novels, though the circumstances and character names were tweaked to get around the Tokugawa censors, who wanted the man forgotten as if he had never existed. But the story survived, somehow, and two hundred years later, just after the shogunate collapsed, the kabuki playwright Mokuami wrote Chūya's story: *Keian Taiheiki* (*The Keian Incident*). The production was wildly popular, and ran for years.

The Keian Incident opens with a child's song. Chūya longs for grandeur, for a chance to avenge his father, who was executed by the first Tokugawa shogun. The play ends when Chūya, betrayed by his wife's family and outnumbered, almost fights off an entire battalion sent to arrest him, before the shogun's men capture him. It is one of the most famous fight scenes in Japanese literature.

When Chūya was alive, the roofs of Edo Castle would have been visible even from distant Mejiro: the citadel was clad in gleaming white tiles made of lead. It was 'delicately sculpturesque in appearance, with multiple gables and rich gold-leaf decoration highlighting the eave ends and the ridge . . .' The lesser towers had copper tiling, which turned green, and dolphin finials made of gold. The entire complex was painted with black lacquer, which was – wrongly, as it turned out – believed to be fireproof.

The castle, which towered eighty-five meters above the plain, was the tallest structure ever built in Edo. The main keep had reception and residence halls almost past counting: the Thousand Mat Hall. The White Audience Hall. The Black Audience Hall. And a clock room, which set the official time for the entire city.

The castle evolved in a whirlpool design, with the main keep ringed by compounds radiating out to the east, north and west. A spiral of canals surrounded the citadel. Its perimeter was ringed by thirty-two massive fortified gates, while inside their walls the inner citadel had ninety-nine more gates, most at right angles to disorient outsiders and bottle up attacking forces. During the castle's entire history, no one tried a frontal attack.

Beyond the citadel, Edo itself was also laid out to confound invaders: the city had twice as many T-junctions and dead-ends as crossroads. Everything – from the number of bridges to the gates to the castle design – underpinned Tokugawa power.

It was this complex, this city, that Chūya wanted to burn. He calculated that in the chaos that followed the fires, his army of masterless samurai could depose the shogun. When he was caught, Chūya tried to kill himself but was prevented; his life was preserved so he could be tortured and crucified. Nor was death the end of Chūya's punishment: the grotesque stump of his body, all that was left of the man, was displayed so anyone else would think twice about challenging the shogunate.

Chūya's memorial was put up a hundred years after his torture and crucifixion. Konjō-in built a plain bronze roof over the stone marker, to stop the stone inscription from eroding.

Edo Castle lasted only five years after Chūya's execution. It burned to the ground during the Great Meireki Fire of 1657. It was never rebuilt.

In the courtyard below the pilgrims had rung for Konjō-in's monk, who was writing the temple's formal name in their *goshuin* books. His calligraphy was exquisite. The monk was young, and had a beautiful face. He raised his eyebrows when I leaned over the sill. 'Was there something you wanted?'

I asked if the temple had a Bell of Time.

The monk began speaking to me in *keigo*, the formal Japanese used for extremely important people. *Keigo* has its own distinct vocabulary, words almost never used in ordinary life. The monk talked for several minutes. I recognized the word *war. Transfer*. He suggested that I ask at a neighboring temple, Nanzō-in.

'I'm sorry,' I told him. 'I didn't quite understand . . .'

The monk smiled, faintly contemptuous, and answered again, briefly, quickly, enunciating each syllable in a clipped voice. I looked at him, blank. When he finished talking, the monk bowed with elaborate, disdainful courtesy. Then he slid the paper-and-wood door shut.

The pilgrims crowded around me, asking what I was looking for, and what the monk had said. I explained that I was looking for Bells of Time.

'I'm not sure . . . he said something about the bell being gone. Maybe that it was requisitioned for scrap metal during the war?'

'Ah, the war,' the woman sighed. '. . . I was young, then. We lost so much!'

'That's *not* what he said!' another pilgrim burst out. He had overheard the monk talking while he waited for his pilgrimage book to be stamped with the temple's seal. 'He *said* the bell has been gone – long *before* the war. All the monk knows is that it was *once* here.'

'So you're looking for the Time Tolling Bells,' the woman said. 'I bet the neighbors used to complain about those! What a racket they would have made! And such a gloomy sound!'

'You think they're gloomy?' I asked. 'Why?'

'Oh, bells make us think about death, and we'd really rather not, you know!'

'I wonder who makes those bells,' the third pilgrim asked, thoughtful. 'If they're even made at all now.'

'Nobody needs them anymore,' the woman said. 'After all, we have watches!'

I left the pilgrims, who watched me go, smiling to themselves. Opposite Konjō-in was an abandoned house. Wild strawberries and ferns grew in the cracks between its stone steps; vines grew over the porch and even on the roof. The ink tracing out the owner's name plate had almost eroded away: *Shimoda Katsujirō.*

I could hear cars and motorcycles and trucks passing along Meiji dori, and the sound beat at me like breakers on a great shore. I followed the Kanda River's north bank southward. I thought about Konjō-in's bell. It would have rung out here, and north past the rice fields that were not yet Zōshigaya cemetery, before the writers Akutagawa Ryūnosuke and Lafcadio Hearn and Nagai Kafū were buried there; a hundred years before the grave to Japan's wartime prime minister, Tōjō Hideki, was laid out.

The bell's absence somehow gave it a weight, a solidity, that the object itself would never have had, if I could have seen it or heard it ringing or even touched it. The bell had been melted down, maybe, and become part of something else – a car's engine, a radio. It might have become a hair pin, a pair of secateurs. Or an anti-aircraft shell.

I stopped walking, and looked around. I could no longer hear the traffic on Meiji dori. The waters of the Kanda River were loud.

Across the path I saw an old woman whose hair was dyed a rich, almost peacock blue, the blue of the Wisdom King himself, of the lapis parchments that ancient painters once used for copying sutras, or celestial landscapes. The old woman turned slightly away, looking down into the canal. I thought of a song about two lovers, popular forty years before.

> The Kanda River flowed past
> Our little boarding house.
> You looked at my fingertips –
> 'Are you sad?'
> At that time, we were so young
> There was nothing to be afraid of
> I was wary only of your tenderness

I walked blindly, happy to be lost.

Later I wrote to Konjō-in, asking about its history. The monk wrote back in that same formal Japanese, using the glittering cousins of simple words. I needed a dictionary even to read the word for *thing*.

The incendiary bombs of 1945 destroyed all records belonging to the temple and its neighbor Hase-dera, the monk wrote. Its most sacred object, the Fudō Myōō, survived, although the flames ate almost everything else, even the graves.

The current abbot, Onozuka Ikuzumi, says that in 1935, when he was a very young child, the bell had already gone. The monk wrote: *On the first shores of his memory, the bell no longer hung in Nanzō-in.* In 1895 it had appeared in a magazine called the *Arts Review*, under 'Famous Scenic Spots from the Old Capital'. The bell disappeared during the forty-year interval.

And as for Marubashi Chūya, *I think – and this is my own guess – the memorial was set up to mark the hundredth anniversary of Marubashi's death. We have no records, but it would have been erected discreetly, so as not to attract attention. And as for the man himself, you may think of him as a traitor to the Shogunate, or as a hero who had mastered his art: both views are correct. Be careful to balance each reality.*

And the Bell of Time – if it escaped the fires after the 1923 earthquake and the 1945 bombings, it may still exist. Somewhere it could ring again.

根津

'Nezu'

Those who watched never knew exactly how the clock's pieces worked; they were left with a sense of wonder at the seemingly magical quality of the movement. The insides were canny and opaque. The human heart is like this, too.

'Clock Metaphors in Edo Period Japan'
Timon Screech

Nezu: Tokugawa Timepieces

When the shoguns ruled Japan, a day had twelve hours. Each hour was named after one of the Chinese Zodiac animals, so dawn was the Hour of the Rabbit, and dusk was the Hour of the Rooster. Noon was Mid-Horse, and the Hour of the Tiger was just before sunrise, when journeys began and lovers left each other.

And in Edo the hours changed with the seasons: a winter daytime hour was much shorter than a summer daytime hour. A night hour was long in winter, and brief in summer.

Then, in 1872, the Emperor Meiji abolished the old clock and brought in timekeeping and the calendars used in the United States and Europe: 'Hereafter, day and night will be equal.' No longer did clocks adapt to the seasons, the weather, and the tides. The moon had no connection with the beginning of the month anymore. New Year's Day fell in mid-winter, not at the beginning of spring. *Nothing is the way it should be.* Time was torn away from nature.

The government announced that no longer would temple

bells sound the hours; that was forbidden. Time would be told with the noonday gun, fired from the palace.

There were riots over the changes, riots which the government quickly put down.

In northern Tokyo, just east of the university, there is an island of old clocks.

From Nezu Station I began climbing, past wooden shops selling *sembei* grilled over sunken stone fireplaces; old-fashioned cafes; a karaoke bar. I angled off down a side street that led past a shop selling wood and paper sliding screens, and crossed through the Dragon Erupting Mountain temple. Its courtyard was chilly and the garden in disorder; there was an ancient plum tree, its crooked gnarled trunk split into three, held together with coarse black twine.

A vast parking lot flanked the temple alongside houses where laundry fluttered on little plastic merry-go-round racks. One house was plastered with posters for the conservative LDP party; across the alley, another house was thick with signs for the Communists. The LDP candidates had fixed grins ('We're not crooks!'), while the Communist candidate looked worried ('We'll never be elected!'). Beyond the crisp poster portraits of the politicians was a faded metal sign advertising lessons for 'classical electric guitar'.

The hill got steeper. Beside the road, the whitewashed clay walls rose ten feet high on both sides: tarmac, stones, sky. Nothing else: no doors, no gates. Finally, beyond the hill's rise, there was a temple, and just before it a sign for the Daimyo Clock Museum. The museum's stone pillar gates, and even the walls, were fading into green: moss, ferns, vines.

Two motorcycles were parked at the gate: a shiny red

Yamaha Corsa and a grubbier white Yamaha Serow painted with blue and pink stripes. A Nissan Largo, its license plate ripped off, stood under a crude corrugated-zinc roof tacked onto an old-fashioned brick storehouse, built to outlast even the hottest fires. The path, part cobbles, part flagstones, curved past a stone lantern and a stand of dwarf bamboo.

The museum's sign read OPEN but its door was still locked. A handwritten note attached to a small buzzer read *If nobody answers, press this button.*

I pushed on the bell hard, and a woman arrived, flustered, smiling. She wore an oversized dark mustard quilted jacket and navy tracksuit bottoms. Her feet were bare, in plastic sandals. She might have been in her mid-fifties but she had a muted gaiety like a girl's.

I told her I wanted to understand how time was measured before factories and trains, before timetables. I said I was sorry, but I hadn't brought a name-card.

The woman smiled. 'Your face is your name-card,' she said.

She unlocked the museum door, switching on the lights. Inside, the room was cold, far colder even than the wintry garden. Fluorescent bulbs flickered into bleak, greenish light that flowed over the divans and the clocks behind glass panels.

The room was hushed, every sound muffled by the brown carpets and a long ruby velvet loveseat that faced the clocks. The place had the quiet of an airport chapel. Nothing moved. Even the dust was still.

All the clocks had belonged to her father-in-law, the woman said: the collector Kamiguchi Sakujiri. 'Guro' was his nickname: it was short for *grotesque*. In 1916, Guro founded a boutique, Kamiguchi's Ultra-Stylish Common Western Clothing Shop. He built a log cabin where he worked and fitted clothes for his clients; the neighborhood called the building

The Grotesque. The shop even had mail delivered under the name. What he made, Guro spent – not least on the old clocks that everyone else was throwing away, because they were hard to look after and couldn't keep the time.

Except for the ruby red loveseat, the room's only color was a framed, hand-painted letter, sent to Guro just before he died. Its author portrayed the collector with one arm thrown over a friend's shoulder; laughing. Both men wear indigo robes, with a cloudburst of ocher, leaf green and yellow spattered behind them; a cluster of characters crowds the paper, like a flock of birds startled into flight. *Get Well Soon.* Everywhere around the little painting, the dial faces were motionless.

Jesuit missionaries brought the first clocks to Japan; they were objects of wonder. Unlike temple bells, which sounded at intervals, the new clocks registered *permanent* time. The ceaseless and visible movement of the clocks' hands was something altogether new. The idea of time itself changed: it became mechanical.

Guro's oldest clocks are iron copies of clocks missionaries brought. Later clocks are brass. They are painted in gold, inlaid with mother-of-pearl, adorned with coral. The hands might feature a snail, or a crescent moon, or a monkey. A carp climbing a waterfall. The numbers on the night face sometimes glitter darkly, damascened. The numbers for day might be silver.

Clocks built for a temple bore lotuses etched onto their cases, and Buddhist *vajras* on their domes. Clocks for the nobility might be adorned with dewdrops or passion-flowers, which the Japanese called *tokei-hana*: 'clock flowers'.

On old Japanese clocks the hours were counted backwards. The clocks have no number greater than nine, which marked midday and midnight; then eight, seven, six, five and four counted off the following hours, then back to nine. Nine was the one moment of the day that never varied, when the sun stood at its zenith.

I asked Mrs. Kamiguchi if it were true that only nobles – *daimyō* – were allowed to own clocks. Were there laws that barred commoners from owning them?

'I have no idea,' she said. 'My husband . . . my husband could have answered anything you asked. When he was a child, these old clocks were all around him. But I just keep the displays, now. That's all I can do.' Tears welled up, but she didn't rub her eyes. The tears looked unable to fall; frozen, like the room itself. 'My husband died ten years ago. It was so sudden. We didn't have any warning. He hadn't taught me anything about the clocks, and he hadn't taught our children what they needed to know, either.'

She showed me her husband Hiroshi's favorite. It was made in the spring of 1816. The clock's face moves, but its hands are fixed. We looked at it through the glass.

'In the shoguns' time, the city was quiet,' Mrs. Kamiguchi said. 'So quiet, that when this clock chimed, you could have heard it from a long way off.'

Near the room's only door is the museum's oldest clock. It is made of iron, and has a lantern dome, and only one hand. The Zodiac animals, which would once have marked the hours, have all worn away. The hand's rotation had polished the face, and polished it, and polished it, until the mouse, ox, tiger, rabbit, dragon, snake, horse, sheep, monkey, rooster, dog and wild boar all disappeared.

'Does anyone wind these clocks?'

'Nobody. They're just . . . decoration.'

'What about that one? Why does it work?' I asked, pointing

to a small lantern clock on the floor. It was the only clock not behind glass. It had two foliot balances, which looked like see-saws.

Mrs. Kamiguchi considered the little clock. 'My husband thought that there should be one that actually showed the time. That way people would get the sense of what these clocks were really like, back when they were used.'

I got down on my knees to look at the case, which had a delicate pattern of grasses and rippling waters around a drifting skiff.

'Your husband knew how to make this run? All by himself?'

'He could.' She paused. 'I just keep it oiled.'

Mrs. Kamiguchi turned a key and shifted the cluster of iron weights on the clock's foliot arms. Her movements were abrupt, all gaiety gone. When she twisted the gears that set up the clock's striking train, I imagined her hands remembering other hands, his hands, showing her what to do – thirty, forty years before.

He would have stood behind her, his fingers over hers, his chin almost on her shoulder, his cheek next to her hair.

Wind it this way.

I don't know what I'm doing!

. . . You will.

The clock ground to life and the bells jangled, shrill. The room wavered, its air churned up like the surface of a pond.

When we stepped outside, it was like breathing after too long underwater. Mrs. Kamiguchi locked the door behind us.

In the final analysis, Guro wrote, *we humans are slaves, slaves to machines and to time. We get home every day after being harassed by clocks. But when you come to this place,*

71

don't remember time! If you can forget what hour it is, your life will be long.

In London, I heard a rumor. In all Japan, there was a single clockmaker who still made clocks the old way. Clocks that told the time by when light rose, and when dark came, instead of in fixed, unchanging numbers.

I was at the Japanese embassy to see the Myriad Year Clock, a huge golden timepiece built in the mid-nineteenth century just before Japan's traditional clocks were abandoned. A man called Suzuki Kazuyoshi was escorting the clock around Europe. He had a neatly clipped beard and was bald. Without his rimless spectacles, Suzuki might have passed for Ebisu, the god of fishermen and good luck.

'Everyone in Japan uses the modern clock now: it's a great shame,' Suzuki said. 'We never think about Edo time anymore. The temple Kanei-ji is the only place where the hours are still rung out the old way, like they were before Tokyo was Tokyo.'

The Myriad Year Clock has six faces. It shows not just the twenty-four-hour day of modern time, and the twelve-hour day of Edo time, but the phases of the moon, the twenty-four Japanese seasons and the days of the week. Another dial shows the ancient Chinese system, which combined the Zodiac animals and the elements: wood, fire, earth, metal and water. The monstrous golden clock can run for almost an entire year without rewinding.

Along with the Myriad Year Clock, Suzuki had brought a doll that served tea. It was about as tall as my knee, and after winding could glide in a straight line and stop, coy. The doll had a shaved head with a single glossy forelock, and the other-worldly, suffering face of a boy. While Suzuki and I talked, the doll moved back and forth as the embassy crowd drank champagne and clapped at its antics. It seemed to wince when its white and gold *hakama* skirt was removed and the red silk *happi* coat stripped away so everyone could see the gear trains that made it run. Despite its nakedness, the doll still carried tea on its tray, back and forth between spectators. It was stoic.

'But,' Suzuki said, speaking loudly over the applause, 'we are still less bound by clocks than people in the West. And we don't express ourselves the way you do. You come right out and say, "I love you!" In Japan, we never do that. We might say, "The moon is beautiful," instead. Which means you're seeing the other person in the moon. For us, the individual isn't central to anything. But because we believe that we are one with nature, we say, "The moon changes!" Which means, our feelings are changing, too.

'... Or think about how you consider stillness. Here, because originally you thought that God controlled nature, when everything is quiet, you feel peaceful. In Japan, it's quite the opposite. We feel happiest when there's a commotion, a racket. But when things are still, we get nervous, because quiet means *danger*. If it's quiet in England, that means your monsters and ghosts are sleeping. But for us, when we hear crickets or birds, we can relax. Our ghosts come out when everything is silent.'

'Like in 2011, before the earthquake,' I said. 'I knew someone who was in a park, and everything went quiet. The birds stopped singing. Nothing moved. She said, "Oh God! God! *Here it comes!*" And then everything started to shake.'

'... Yes. In Japan, silence can be sinister.' Beside us, the doll took someone's tea cup and then veered away in a stately arc. Everyone cheered.

'But there's one man who still makes clocks the old way,'

Suzuki said. 'His name is Naruse. Go talk to him. He lives in Nagoya.'

I'd expected Naruse Takurō to be old: a wizened craftsman. He wasn't. He was young. Small and graceful, like the tea-serving doll I had seen in London. He would have been another kind of doll, though. An archer, perhaps.

'What modern people don't understand about *wadokei* – old Japanese clocks – is that measuring time wasn't important,' Naruse said. '*Of course* those clocks weren't accurate! The point is *pleasure*, pleasure in the mechanism. Those clocks are all about delight.'

Naruse flipped open the side of a three-hundred-year-old tower clock so I could see its inner parts: the escapement, the striking train, the gears. 'Even when you fiddled around with the clock, you'd just be showing off for your guests, not actually fixing something. You'd be showing you knew how to run it.'

In the broad alcove where other people might have displayed scrolls, or art, Naruse had hung a profusion of wall clocks. They all read different times.

'We're really into pleasure in this country. The advantage of the old Japanese clocks was, they go *off* time, not that they keep it. Who needed clocks? Most people were farmers, and the sun was their clock.'

Naruse worked in a factory just after finishing school, where he learned to weld metal brackets. He invented a composting machine.

'That's like a clock?' I said, thinking of minutes and hours, shredded, crushed.

'Oh, the mechanism isn't so different,' Naruse said, his face straight. 'But the factory was dire. The work was so boring. I wanted to make music boxes and toys and I wasn't allowed to. But then I happened to go into a junk shop and I found this—' Here Naruse crossed the room and lifted a heavy 1960s Seiko radio clock off a low shelf. It was squat and gold and its weight rested on short knitting-needle legs.

I took it out of his hands and looked at the face.

'My grandparents had one like this!' I cried. '... *Natsukashii!*' I remembered the clock watching over everything in the flickering half-light of their TV room; the curtains and carpet smelling of the cigarettes my grandmother smoked. The games we would play there, and the plastic washing basket with my toys inside and the old decks of cards that were incomplete.

'*Natsukashii*,' Naruse repeated, laughing: 'it takes you back. I took the clock home and took it apart and rebuilt it and took it apart again. I felt a rush, just like I had when I was a boy and did the same thing. My father was furious, because after I took his clock to pieces, it didn't work again. But – I felt that finding that old clock was a sign, a message from the ancient craftsmen: *Create*. So I quit the factory and started my own company. I bet my life on the clocks.'

'You learned from old books?'

'No. I taught myself. I couldn't believe that no one had made a single *wadokei* since 1872. That's just wrong. Making clocks in the Japanese way is a return to identity; a return to who we are. When you copy someone else, even if the quality is good, the *feeling* is off. The clocks showed me how unique Japan is. Think about food. Compare Japanese and international food. Japanese food is very intricate. It's colorful, it's playful. You whiteys just eat hamburgers!'

'That's not exactly true.'

'OK. Potatoes . . .' Naruse said gleefully, his face straight. '. . . Coca-Cola . . .'

'*Maybe* your chicken is better than ours.'

'Nagoya chicken is the best, isn't it!'

'Delicious.'

'We have a long history with chicken. We really are the best, at chicken.'

'. . . Chicken and clocks.'

Naruse led me upstairs to the rooms where he assembles his clocks and hair-line polishes their parts, like a jeweler. The workshops were luminous white, and a pendulum and cogs and escapement wheels scattered over his work table like tiny silver galaxies.

I told Naruse about the clock museum in Tokyo, the widow who looked after her husband's things, though she didn't understand them. 'It's a strange place. Time has stopped for the clocks but not for her.'

'I've never been there,' Naruse said. 'But the clocks will teach you how you should live. A clock is more than just a machine.'

March, 2011

For a few hours after the Earthquake, Tokyo was a carnival.

Birds, which had been quiet in the parks, began singing again. Horses penned up in the Meiji stables calmed down. The trees, which had been whipping back and forth as if tortured in high winds, rested on their roots. The earth had rolled like a flapping sheet, and at last it was still.

In Omotesandō, people quit screaming and stumbled out of shops and stood on the pavement; lit cigarettes; laughed. It was a Friday and we thought the weekend had come early. The trains had stopped. An hour later, the crowds began streaming past, northeast to southwest, walking in their expensive Italian shoes and best suits, from central Tokyo's business districts toward the satellite towns where they lived.

No one in the capital knew about the vast waves that would break over Sendai thirty minutes later. Our mobile phones didn't work. We didn't know what had happened to the north for hours.

That night I watched video streaming of Kesennuma, a small city near the earthquake's epicenter. It blazed away in the darkness, and the Pacific Ocean reflected the shimmering fires. I couldn't understand what I was looking at. I thought it was another country, someplace far away.

Before noon on Saturday, the baker's shelves were stripped

almost bare. In the grocery store, instant noodles and flashlights were disappearing. The BBC reported that the Fukushima plant was having trouble stabilizing its reactors.

Fukushima Reactor-1 blew up at 3:36 that afternoon.

I fell asleep and dreamed a thin bubble was blooming north of Tokyo: radiant. Invisible.

On Sunday, a friend called. 'I've got tickets out. My husband couldn't get anything today or tomorrow . . .'

I phoned another friend. 'What are you doing?' I asked, before I'd even said hello.

'I'm already in Osaka,' she said. I hung up.

Sunday was a day of rumors and apocalyptic e-mails. You can't rent cars, or book taxis. The French ordered their nationals out and said to tape up windows and not drink the water. The airport road is damaged. The trains aren't running. There are long lines for petrol. There's no more food.

On Monday at 11:15 a.m., Fukushima Reactor-3 blew up. On Tuesday, the BBC announced that the fuel-containment pools might be on fire.

I bought tickets for Hong Kong. One-way.

I wanted to see Daibo before I flew. I'd called him on Saturday to find out if his family in Iwate were all right, but I wanted to meet him. The light was stale and milky and I licked grit off my teeth. Where had the wind come from, I wondered.

Daibo's was empty except for a man I'd never met before, a sleep researcher named Sasegawa. Like Daibo, his family came from a place the tsunami had wrecked.

Sasegawa was about to light a Cohiba cigar when I came in, but put it down, nodding to me. I stared at him in disbelief. 'You can't be worried about second-hand smoke *now*! What with everything else going on!'

Sasegawa and Daibo talked, but I heard nothing. I stared at

objects instead: the little iron bell from Iwate, the battered hand-roaster Daibo used; a camellia in a vase. I wondered if I would see them ever again.

'The Dutch and the Germans and the French have said their people should evacuate,' I said. Daibo and Sasegawa looked at me, their faces slack with shock. '. . . The British embassy just says, "Be careful." '

I wanted to tell Daibo that I would leave the next day for Hong Kong, but how? With what words? So I said nothing.

I knew Daibo would not leave Tokyo, no matter what. It would have been easier to move one of the trees rooted on Aoyama dōri below.

I paid for my coffee, bowed, and went slowly down the narrow stairs. And then I ran.

上野

'Ueno'

Sudhana said, 'Where has that magnificent display gone?'
Matreya said, 'Where it came from.'

The Flower Ornament Scripture
Translated by Thomas Cleary

Ueno: The Last Shogun

A huge glass box, in an almost empty room.

Inside was a purple costume that had been made in Paris, by the order of Napoleon III, as a gift for the last Tokugawa shogun, Yoshinobu, in 1867. The rich violet silk was stitched in brilliant crimson threads with the shogunal family's three-leaf paulownia crest. Its cuffs and collars and hem were trimmed with gold piping.

In the absence of any real knowledge of Japan, which had been closed to Europeans since the mid-seventeenth century, the royal couturier had invented an imaginary place of *luxe, calme, et volupté*. Napoleon's gift was for the ruler of that dreamed country.

In the 1860s England and France were playing out an East Asian version of the Great Game, with France backing the Tokugawa traditionalists (who fought for the shogun) and England backing the rebel fiefs of the southwest and their would-be modernizers (who fought for the emperor). Though the French and English were allies against Russia in the Crimea, they were rivals over Japan during the country's brief civil war.

'*Jimbaori*,' the monk behind me said, nodding at the glass box. '. . . War clothes.'

The empty suit hovered behind its glass like an archbishop's robes. It was nothing to be worn on a battlefield, unless somebody wanted it for target practice.

'It's not very Japanese,' the monk admitted, laughing.

His name was Kobayashi. He handled all enquiries about Kanei-ji, the temple the Tokugawa built to match the great 'demon gate' temples in the northeastern quarters of Kyoto and Nara. When the ancient Chinese planned their towns, the northeast was believed to be the region of greatest danger; the zone of bad luck. The Chinese built temples in that direction as spiritual firebreaks. The Japanese borrowed this formula for their own cities, but with Edo, the northeast really *was* a region of pollution, because that was the direction of Kozukappara and its execution grounds; the outcaste districts; and floods. Kanei-ji was built to keep curses and demons away from Edo.

Kobayashi's almost translucent black robes were too big for his thin body. Because the fabric was stiff, it floated around his arms and shoulders rather than hanging down off them. We were in the reconstructed apartments of Yoshinobu. Except for the French robes, the rooms were echoingly empty, even by the most austere Japanese standards. There was an incense burner, a lacquered table bearing the Tokugawa crest painted in gold. Nothing else.

'No one can just – take over Japan! By resigning as shogun when the emperor was restored to power, Yoshinobu helped with the transition. If he'd resisted, there would have been chaos.

'Yoshinobu resigned as shogun, and then he left Edo Castle for Kanei-ji. He was here for sixty days. He secluded himself inside just three rooms to show complete submission to the imperial throne. Around two thousand Tokugawa samurai gathered in Ueno when Yoshinobu was here. They wanted to protect him. And then, as he left Edo for exile, he told them, "Disband. Go home." But a thousand or so wouldn't leave.'

When the shogunate collapsed, samurai rallied first in Asakusa and then near the Tokugawa family temple in Ueno to challenge the Meiji emperor's soldiers. They called themselves *shōgitai*, 'the League to Demonstrate Righteousness'. Most were young, and responding to the anomie of their times. Many came from domains that the imperial forces had already taken over. Almost all were low-ranking retainers from the margins and fringes of Tokugawa society. They signed their names in their own blood to oaths promising to protect the shogun. The oath began, *During the past three hundred years, fighting spirit has declined until loyalty and patriotism are mere words . . .*

Ueno had seven gates. On 15 May 1868, the *shōgitai* massed near the main one, known as the Black Gate, where they faced off against the forces of Saigō Takamori, the era's most gifted general and – even more ominous for the *shōgitai* – his five British-built Armstrong cannons. The *shōgitai* answered Saigō's fusillade with flaming arrows that missed, soaring past the imperial troops and striking the wooden houses beyond. Despite heavy rain, block after block caught fire. The air turned white with smoke from the guns and burning buildings, and the soldiers could see almost nothing. Woodblock prints record the dense clouds from the bursting shells; the walls of fire.

Kanei-ji's monks had backed the *shōgitai*. On the morning the imperial troops attacked, the young abbot – the Rinnoji –

was saying his prayers, as if there were no screams and shouting beyond the Main Hall, no gunfire or barrage from the echoing Armstrong guns.

When the Rinnoji finished praying, he walked to breakfast. He drank a cup of tea, and then lifted his chopsticks. His monks – the ones who had not already run away – stared at him. Once he had finished eating, the Rinnoji called for an adviser and requested that he be appraised of events at the gates.

The adviser looked down, and said nothing. The monks begged the abbot to leave Kanei-ji, and eventually he agreed. He dressed in plain clothes and went north with his body-guards, who wanted him as far away as possible from the Black Gate. It had rained for days and the paths were streams of red mud. The men kept slipping, and the sludge soaked the abbot's white *tabi*. Yet the woodblock prints of the Battle of Ueno all depict his socks still white, pristine, as the abbot leaves his temple for the last time.

As the abbot and his entourage fled, an artillery barrage hit the Main Hall. One of the Rinnoji's companions later wrote about 'the unspeakable roaring' as everything inside caught fire, and the ancient wood began splitting and cracking.

At 1 p.m. Saigō's forces broke through the Black Gate, and by the time the Rinnoji reached the edge of Ueno, the *shōgitai* had scattered in defeat. The monks' faces, wrote one observer, went 'blue with shock' at the news. No one had foreseen that the *shōgitai* would lose so quickly. There were no contingency plans, even for an escape.

It is difficult to understand why the monks were so compla-cent. The *shōgitai* not only lacked modern guns, they lacked strategists and any vision beyond 'dying for one's lord'. To that extent, they succeeded in their aim. In contrast, the imperial troops had excellent generals and statesmen who knew that control of Edo meant control of the entire nation. A victory in Ueno would mean that the Meiji Restoration would become more than just a palace coup.

An English newspaper reported that after the battle, the emperor's armies were 'so completely masters of the situation that men are even afraid to bury the dead Tokugawa men, whose bodies are allowed to lie, the prey of the wild dogs and the fowls of the air, in the sacred precincts of one of the holiest places of the defeated clan. The Tokugawa men are literally swept out of Edo and no man dare harbor one on pain of death.'

At Kanei-ji today, a letter from the abbot is preserved. He is writing to friends in the northern city of Sendai. A few months have passed since the battle. 'I am coming, but plan nothing grand for me. I am no longer the abbot.'

The letter contains one of the earliest mentions of the city's new name.

Edo was now Tokyo.

Kobayashi slid back a wooden door depicting a baby in colored robes reaching up toward a sage and we went into one of the temple's inner rooms. The air smelled like wet tatami matting, the humidity all that remained of a typhoon that had clipped but not hit Tokyo the week before.

The door's inner panel was painted with egrets standing in a lotus pond.

'From another temple,' Kobayashi said.

We crossed the room and Kobayashi slid back another door, this one painted with peonies, waves, rocks and a green dragon whose body flowed and turned like a waterfall.

'These doors aren't from the original Kanei-ji, either,' Kobayashi said. 'I don't know where they came from.'

Every year, on 15 May, nineteen of Kanei-ji's most senior monks hold a requiem service for the spirits of the *shōgitai*. Passages from the *Lotus Sutra* are read aloud. The ceremony lasts about half an hour. No outsider may witness it.

In an antechamber, the senior monk was waiting. He was wearing dark blue robes and a surplice embroidered with golden chrysanthemums. Unlike Kobayashi, who looked fragile, like a mayfly, Takahashi was built like a kendo champion: hard shoulders and arms. A warrior monk.

Kobayashi bowed and left us.

Takahashi spread a map of Ueno on the table and traced out with a red pen all of Kanei-ji's former precincts. West, far beyond Shinobazu Pond. Around the statue of the general whose forces crushed the *shōgitai*. East, far beyond the huge train station. North, past what has become the thriving love-hotel district of Uguisudani.

I looked away from the new map to a woodblock print that Takahashi had brought out. It was a bird's eye view of Kanei-ji before 1868: its famous drum bridge arched between two temples. The Bell of Time. The Great Buddha and a scattering of pagodas. Ancient pine trees and wild cherry trees. Willows. Groves and gardens and golden mists.

But I couldn't see the precinct's heart, the central temple.

'. . . Where was the Main Hall?'

Takahashi tapped the National Museum of Art on the modern map. 'It was here. The abbot was always the son of an emperor. So no artist could show the Main Hall. It would have been disrespectful.'

'Does the Battle of Ueno still matter? Does it have any real meaning to modern Japanese?'

Takahashi shrugged. 'If anyone thinks about the Battle of Ueno at all, it's as a New Year's drama on television. No one really remembers what it was.'

'Even the great-grandchildren of these fighters wouldn't be alive now. Will you ever stop holding the memorial ceremony?'

'No.'

'Because of –' I thought of the concept that Daibo always said was necessary for being fully human '– *gimu*? "Duty"?'

'That word is close, but it's not quite right,' Takahashi said. 'We recite the prayers because it's our *job*. And because the connection between Kanei-ji and the *shōgitai*, and Kanei-ji and the shoguns buried here, is very clear. Even if there were no *shōgitai* descendants, we'll keep saying those prayers. For as long as Kanei-ji exists.'

Behind Takahashi's head, in vast letters, a scroll read

一 微 塵

I asked Takahashi what the words meant. I could only read the first character, 'one'.

'*Ichimijin*,' he said. ' "A single atom".'

The phrase comes from the Flower Ornament Sutra: *In a single atom, there can be untold worlds*. The sutra describes the entire cosmos and its many billions of universes through the eyes of the Buddha after he has attained enlightenment. It is an ideal universe, a perfect one.

'A single atom' was an appropriate epigraph for Kanei-ji, which is now a fragment of what it had once been. But for the writers of that sutra, nothing substantial had changed.

Reducing a land to atoms,/ These atoms are measureless, untold./ Boundless lands, as many as these atoms/ are gathered on a single hair.

'For Buddhists, the past, the future, and this moment: everything flows at the same pace,' Takahashi said. 'Every second is equal. The past and the future and what's happening now, aren't separate.

'You can say a lot about time: but time is also things that *don't* happen. I grew up in Hokkaido. On my route to school there was a crossroads and at the crossroads was a stop light. It was such a quiet place that my younger brother and I used to blast right through on our bikes without stopping. But one day, for some reason, I did stop. And a car whipped around the bend and zoomed through the crossing. If I hadn't held back a few moments before, I would have died. Right in front of my younger brother.

'Afterward I thought everything had happened in slow motion. For my brother, the moment went by like a flash. But time has the same flow: everywhere and always. How we think of it must just be a function of our brains. That sense is just the way we process our fear of death.

'Because no one comes back to tell us what happens after we stop breathing, we're scared of death. Time is the framework, the scaffolding, for how we experience that terror. Time lets us look away from fear. You might think of *time* as the life we have left.'

'And the dead?' I asked. 'What about the dead?'

Takahashi shrugged. 'The dead have slipped out of the framework.'

*

Kobayashi returned and led me to the temple's front entrance. Then, by a small votive tablet, I stopped so abruptly that Kobayashi crashed into me.

'What is *that*?'

Painted on the wood was a monster: with an amphibian's legs and arms and deer antlers and ribs picked out like a skeleton's; its eyes were pinwheel whorls.

Kobayashi smiled. 'Tsuno Daishi. He dispels bad luck.'

'*Dispels* it?' I asked. The thing looked like a demon.

'He was a monk called Ryōgen but during his training he took on the appearance of Evil, all the better to fight it.'

We stepped outside into the courtyard. Even in the sunlight I still saw Tsuno Daishi: those ribs, the antlers, the flipper-arms.

'Kobayashi san,' I asked, abrupt. 'What makes you think of time?'

He smiled, easy. The little tablet didn't bother him: he saw it every day. 'Waking and sleeping. When I close my eyes, everything stops. When I open them, everything is born.'

We walked in silence to what remained of the shogunal burial grounds. When someone in the Tokugawa family died, three bells would once ring from Ueno: not just the Bell of Time, but two others. One sounded a note of rest; the second of sadness; and the Bell of Time itself, a note of transcendence.

A train passed; the Yamanote Line's tracks ran below the bluff where we stood. Kobayashi gestured toward the rough *ishigaki* stone walls. 'Can you see how uneven they are? Not at all the standard you would expect. They're not like the ones around Edo Castle. Katsu Kaishū ordered them thrown up very quickly, because he was worried about robbers plundering the shoguns' graves.'

It was Katsu Kaishū who negotiated Edo's surrender to the emperor's troops when the shogun gave up power; who persuaded the emperor's generals to let the shogun live rather than commit ritual suicide. It was thanks to Katsu that only Ueno, and not the entire city, burned. If the *shōgi-tai* had listened to Katsu, Kanei-ji itself would probably have been saved. 'One sturdy pillar cannot support a decaying house,' Katsu wrote in his diaries, bitter but resigned. 'The wicked monks refused to negotiate with my emissary. All my efforts were in vain.'

The cemetery's outer ring was now crowded with other graves, like an ordinary graveyard anywhere in the city. We passed new granite and marble markers with *sotoba*, the long thin wooden boards with protective phrases written in Sanskrit. If these memorials are forgotten, the dead can become hungry ghosts: wandering, unappeased.

'The Tokugawa family supported this temple until 1946,' Kobayashi said, 'when the nobility was abolished. Then the family sold plots to help pay for the temple's upkeep.'

Kobayashi began pointing out the buildings that had disappeared. He gestured to the air in front of us and said, 'This was the Daiji-in. The feudal lords who came here to pay their respects to the grave of Tsunayoshi, the Fifth Shogun, would change their clothes in that place.'

I followed Kobayashi's gaze and looked toward a battered red bridge under a weathered bronze roof: nothing else was there. Kobayashi was looking calmly ahead, as if between us and the bridge were a bright procession of nobles. He walked on through the huge bronze gate's doors, smiling at a grounds-keeper, who bowed. We passed a vermilion *chōzubashi*, the stone basin where worshippers, before entering a sacred space, purify their mouths and right hands. Then we passed through a gate set between the high stone walls.

Kobayashi again stretched his palm out into the air in front of us – pointing, of course, would be bad luck and bad manners – toward enormous stone lanterns covered in moss that had turned an almost fluorescent green after the rains. 'And here is the pavilion where the Tokugawa would have moon-viewing parties. The shogun's tomb – it would originally have been enclosed inside a wooden building.'

I looked, but couldn't see what Kobayashi saw.

Kobayashi moved toward the eighteenth-century tomb of Tsunayoshi, the 'Dog Shogun'. Tsunayoshi became infamous for his edicts that penalized anyone who mistreated animals, especially dogs. 'For the sake of a single bird or beast, the death penalty was inflicted. Even relatives were given capital punishment or deported and exiled . . .' one contemporary account complained, after Tsunayoshi's death, and his so-called 'Laws of Compassion' were rescinded.

The weathered bronze of Tsunayoshi's tomb is the best preserved among Ueno's six shogunal tombs, though it is somewhat battered. Decorated with phoenixes, with dragon-horses and clouds, the stupa tomb soared over the river stones at its base, over Kobayashi, over me.

'The shogunate was rich when this was built,' Kobayashi said, nodding at the detailing. 'This tomb would have cost quite a lot of money. On the other side, in a place that only the abbot is permitted to go, is a tableau of the Western Paradise. You can't see it; but it's there.'

The writer Paul Waley once complained that although Ueno should be one of the most attractive places in the city, it isn't. 'It's a jumble of assorted buildings . . . all interspersed with promenades and dirty clumps of vegetation behind which one half-suspects some sort of lurking presence.'

There's a baseball diamond wedged among Ueno's art museums, and the district is ringed by pachinko parlors and love hotels. The zoo and the concert hall and the lusterless restaurants do not cohere; they are fragments that never make up a whole.

However luminous its great promenades with their cherry trees, however sublime the lights and shadows in the Hōryū-ji Treasure Gallery, Ueno feels disjointed, like a bone wrenched out of its socket. During the Battle of Ueno, Kanei-ji's vast temple complex almost entirely burned down. Photographs taken a few weeks afterward record a scorched plain without trees, and with almost no grasses; a place scraped down to the foundation stones and naked earth.

With the old regime's defeat so complete, the Meiji authorities were free to reinvent the shoguns' temple district however they wanted. They made it a showcase for everything new-fangled: electric lights, a trolley line, Japan's first zoo, and even a horse-racing track that circled Shinobazu Pond. It was the opposite of what had existed before.

And always, the sense of something lost. Ishikawa Jun caught this atmosphere, which was at its most intense in the years immediately after World War Two, in his short story 'The Jesus of the Ruins'. In it, Ishikawa describes how New Japan mauls Old Japan and gets away with the crime.

The story begins with a brutal sketch of the Ameyoko black market, which flourished right by Ueno's train station until 31 July 1946, when the occupying American authorities shut it down.

This is Tokyo's Ueno, the most pugnacious part of town,
where tempers and nostrils flare, and every inch of territory
– even the space under a train trestle – is guarded jealously:

a city in ruins, the burnt-out shell of a metropolis. Its
creatures have hatched out of the debris, and now they
survive by the sheer tenacity with which they came into
the world and by which they cling to life.

Everything is contraband and nothing is legitimate; money is
devalued, too. Ishikawa records the ugliness of this world; of
the market's hawkers and the spoiled food they are selling.

Into the post-apocalyptic landscape comes an urchin, a
young boy who incarnates the new order. He was 'black as the
sludge in a ditch, and it was impossible to tell at a glance
where the ragged edge of his clothes ended and the flesh
underneath began. He was so caked in dirt and filth, he looked
as if he were covered in scales.' Even the hawkers ('and surely
they had never been known to flinch at the thought of hand-
ling anything foul or rotten') shy away from the boy, who is
covered in crusted boils. He brings back unwelcome memories the city wants to forget.

Now that Tokyo's people had lost their way in a land
ravaged by war and fire, and wandered into the labyrinth
of the marketplace that grew out of the ruins, what need
did they have to think of the past, anyway? It was as if no
one had survived from the last century and, no, there had
never been an era in the history of modern Japan when
people had paraded about smugly wearing the look of His
Majesty's loyal subjects. No, not a soul from that day and
age appeared to be alive. They had all vanished – down to
every last man, woman, and child.

What remains, Ishikawa wrote, are errant seeds. 'They had
sprouted out of the ground, and with the force of a weed that
reaches maturity overnight.' The boy himself is 'the Jesus of

the Burnt-Out Shell of Japan', since 'he is to be the leader of a new breed of humankind that dwells in the place of ruin and sends out its tendrils to the earth.'

The boy follows a man as he leaves the market, and attacks him near the shrine to the first Tokugawa shogun. No longer the progenitor of a new race, he becomes 'the sole survivor of a generation of swine who, possessed by the devil, flung themselves over a precipice and perished in the waters below.'

The boy steals the man's food rations and his wallet, and then disappears.

When Tokyo dreams, Ueno never appears with a single face.

Inside Ueno Station an old man was squatting outside a Danish bakery chanting, in grindingly enunciated English, '*Monday, Tuesday, Thursday, Friday! ... Monday, Tuesday, Thursday ...*'

A wadded rectangle of thick cotton was taped against his jaw.

Out through the great pillars that support the Japan Rail tracks; past the caverns beneath them, with their clothes made in China, their dried fish. Up the stairs that lead into the Park itself. A chainsaw ground away somewhere in the trees. The slope was thick with Sunday crowds, with mime artists carrying lace umbrellas, acrobats dangling from steel hoops and magicians playing card tricks. A troupe of musicians from the Andes were playing pan pipes of various sizes. Wind stirred the cherry trees until their leaves sounded like water flowing over stones. And behind all these noises, was silence.

Some relics of Edo remain.

I once saw Zen musicians – *komusō*, 'monks of nothingness' – playing their *shakuhachi* bamboo flutes near Shinobazu

Pond. The monks wore enormous, tight-woven wicker barrels over their heads, hats that symbolize the death of the ego. When the Tokugawa fell, the emperor's new government outlawed *komusō*, because they had often acted as spies for the Tokugawa. After 1868, *komusō* temples were burned, and much of the sect's musical repertoire lost: notes that imitated the crying of cranes, or the beating of their wings; wind; petals falling; a bell. The Meiji authorities appropriated the beehive-shaped hat for convicts, who wore them into court. What had symbolized the ascetic's ascension toward the sublime became stigmatized, an object of shame.

On another visit I met a man who recites medieval Buddhist sermons for a fee. One begins, *There is a green willow tree in this world, and under it a gatekeeper, who beckons you to go one way, or the other.* And: *The wind from Heaven comes from the West. You can catch the wind, though it be cold, in your own sleeves.*

But there is something ersatz, something false, about these acts. They lack a connection with the present, the twenty-first-century city. The link between tradition and memory has been broken, and can't be spliced back together.

A brushwood barrier hid the bell-ringer's house from the street; the building was attached to the Bell of Time's stone tower. Yamamoto Makoto was waiting for me outside his door, smoking. He wore a Calvin Klein sweatshirt and pale jeans. We bowed. He gave me his name-card. I gave him mine. He opened the door to his house, which stood at the base of the bell tower.

Inside, an arbor: panels painted with grapes and berries. Silk roses and hydrangeas, and bowls full of plastic grapes. A grape vine with green silk leaves and plastic fruit twined itself around the ceiling lamp and its electric cable. Among all the silks and ceramic toys were model aircraft: a Flying Fortress, and a smaller, more delicate model that might have been a Mitsubishi Ki-67. At the family altar was a black-and-white memorial photograph of Yamamoto's mother, who rang Ueno's Bell of Time for almost forty years.

He gestured for me to sit at the table.

'You like collecting model planes?'

'I like building them.'

'How long have you been ringing the bell?'

'For fifty years. I first rang it around the time when Tokyo held the Olympics. My grandfather had been ringing it since 1947.' Yamamoto paused. 'The bell stopped ringing during the war. There was no able-bodied person around then who could sound it.'

'Were your family priests . . . ? Is that why your grandfather was chosen?'

'No. Because the bell rang the hours like a clock, not for religious ceremonies, anybody was eligible. My family were townspeople. My grandfather, who was the first in our family to ring the bell, had been a painter of bird and flower scenes before the war.' And *his* father made the thick *shironuri* powder that could make a woman's face glow like the moon reflected in water. Yamamoto smiled a crooked smile. 'They weren't *priests*.'

I asked if Yamamoto could show me one of his grandfather's sketches.

He shook his head. 'No. He sold every single piece he made, and later on he developed palsy. His hand shook so much that he had to give up painting. He was the one who taught me how to ring the bell. I first rang it when I was ten years old. He would say, "Do what I do." '

'Is it possible to ring it the wrong way?'

'You can forget a stroke. Then you say, "Ah! I was one short!"'

'But no one ever complains when you make a mistake.'

'No one ever complains.'

'Did you want to be a bell-ringer when you were growing up?'

'Absolutely *not*,' Yamamoto said, somber. 'I wanted what everyone wants. I wanted the life other people had. When you are the bell-ringer, you can never go away on holiday. You can never take time off to be sick. You have to ring it once, twice, three times, every day. Those restrictions made it hard to have a family.'

I wondered about whether his children would follow him and ring the bell, but his face seemed to anticipate that question and warn me against asking it.

'And your wife, how does she feel about the bell?'

'She . . .' He hesitated. 'She doesn't like it. She wants me to retire. But I can't.'

'Why not?'

'It would be wrong to quit. Not while I can still keep on going. I'll be the last of my family to ring it.'

At five minutes to noon, Yamamoto started to become uneasy. He kept craning around to look at a clock mounted on the wall behind him. It was round and framed in blond wood, with the white silhouette of a cityscape at night; near the 11.00 mark a tiny witch flew on her broomstick through a haze of stars.

'We still have a little longer.'

'How can you tell when it's time to ring the bell?' I asked.

'The mobile phone tells me.'

'. . . And before there were mobile phones?'

'The television.'

'And before the TV?'

'The radio.'

Yamamoto stood up and I followed. He opened a narrow door and we climbed up a flight of wooden stairs to a door that opened out into the bell tower. Above us the bell's green bronze dome shone with reflected sunlight.

'So, before the radio, how would people know it was 6 a.m.?'

'*Sono goro de ii*,' Yamamoto mused, climbing upward and skirting the huge bell. He stood beside an octagonal column that had once held up Kanei-ji itself, but which now, lying horizontal, was used to strike the bell. The column was suspended from two metal chains. Yamamoto placed his palm on the beam.

'In those days, they weren't so strict about minutes and seconds. But now we live in the Digital Age. And everything is different.'

Some Japanese never forgave the foreigners who abandoned the country after the Fukushima reactors exploded. I heard of a woman who told her British boyfriend: *Don't call me. Ever. I never want to see you again.* He was gone only a few days, but he might as well not have come back.

When I called my Japanese teacher to tell her that I was returning – after almost a month waiting in Hong Kong to see what would happen – I asked how she was. I didn't understand her answer. I had to ask her to repeat the words.

' "Unaltered", she translated. 'I'm *unaltered*. The situation is *normal*.'

An Austrian institute had just tested for radioactive particles in the air. Iodine-131 was already 73% of amounts released after Chernobyl. Cesium-137 was 60%. The foreign newspapers were full of horror stories: contaminated rice, contaminated tea, contaminated water. Bean sprouts, cabbage, broccoli. Certain things – like fish – no one ate at all.

After the earthquake, Japan had shifted five meters closer to North America. The seabed off Sendai had risen as much as ten meters and had moved fifty meters southeast.

Unaltered. The situation is normal.

'. . . Can I bring you back anything?' I asked, after a silence.

'I need nothing,' she said, formal in a way that she had never been before. 'Thank you for your kind concern.'

I had known my teacher for ten years. If she was so offended, what, I wondered, would Daibo be like?

I walked into the cafe and sat down at the counter. Daibo was laughing with a few customers. He turned away from them to face me. He said nothing, just looked at me. I slid a little package – a Chinese ink stick, wrapped in paper – across the counter. It was a *miyage*, a present from abroad.

Daibo took the block, glanced at it, glanced back at me. '. . . You ran away?'

'I ran away.'

He laughed. Then he thanked me for the ink. That was the last time we spoke about how I had left. If Daibo remembered, he never said.

鹿

鳴

館

'Rokumeikan'

The Japanese have their eyes fixed on the future, and are impatient when a word is said of their past. The cultured among them are actually ashamed of it. When I asked one man about Japanese history, he answered bluntly: 'We have no history. Our history begins today.'

Erwin Bälz,
personal physician to the Meiji emperor

The Rokumeikan: The Meiji Restoration

A doll's house in a glass display box, with a tiny plaque that read: ROKUMEIKAN. A mansard roof, a white colonnade; balconies and a portico. Chimneys and window panes; all perfect, all to scale. A Renaissance villa on the Pacific.

The Rokumeikan itself was built in 1883, a pretentious building financed by the Japanese government. It included a large dining room complete with a French chef; salons, parlors, games rooms with billiard tables, ballrooms and 'a corridor for promenading'. Its bars sold American cocktails and German beer and English cigarettes. Newspapers published warnings about correct behavior, for the benefit of those who were to attend events and functions there: 'Do nothing to make the foreigners laugh at us.'

The Rokumeikan gave its name to Japan's 'enlightenment era', and came to symbolize decadence and subservience to the West. In 1890, the Foreign Office sold the structure off to private investors, who turned it into a club for the nobility.

Rokumeikan means 'Deer Cry Pavilion'. The name was taken from one of China's most ancient collection of poems,

The Book of Songs. It is a convivial ode to drinking and toasting foreign guests:

> The deer call to one another,
> Eating the southernwood of the fields.
> I have here admirable guests;
> Whose virtuous fame is grandly brilliant.
> They show the people not to be mean.
> I have good wine,
> Which my admirable guests drink, enjoying themselves.

The Foreign Minister Inoue Kaoru hoped that if Japan copied Western culture – its canapés and polkas, its waltzes and card games – the imperialist powers might revisit the hated Unequal Treaties forced on the country in the 1850s when it first opened its ports to foreign ships. In this regard, the Rokumeikan was a failure. European visitors sneered at the design, at the dancers. The French author Pierre Loti attended a ball there, and dismissed it as 'hardly elegant . . . built in the European style, all fresh, white and new, it resembled a casino in one of our second-rate resort towns.'

Ultimately revision of the treaties came only in 1899, after the Japanese armies had defeated China, prizing away Korea, Taiwan and the Liaodong peninsula as spoils of war. What dancing with diplomats failed to achieve, big guns did. Berlin, Washington, Paris and London all signed new treaties with the imperial government in Tokyo; this time, the diplomatic agreements were established between equals.

The poet Arthur Waley translated part of the Rokumeikan ode this way: *Here is a man that loves me/ And will teach me the ways of Zhou.*

The 'ways of Zhou' meant how things are done in foreign places.

The optimism and naiveté of the Meiji Era is contained in those two lines.

From the 1930s onward, the Rokumeikan was destroyed piecemeal. In 1941, the wartime government ordered it razed altogether, embarrassed and resentful of the Meiji Era's wholesale embrace of what was foreign. And when the Rokumeikan disappeared, nostalgia enfolded its memory: the marble and magnificence of Meiji, and the beginning of Japan's short-lived empire.

Mishima Yukio, writing about the Rokumeikan with his usual combination of nostalgic romanticism and rage, wrote: 'The Age of the Rokumeikan, according to contemporary paintings and poems, was truly ridiculous and *grotesque*, a kind of monkey's theatre for enlightenment, in which bucktoothed midget Japanese men wearing ill-suited swallowtails bobbed their heads to foreigners.'

In Mishima's play *Rokumeikan*, a grand ball is planned to entertain foreign visitors. A government official – Kageyama – and his wife, an elegant former geisha called Asako, host the reception. Asako has abandoned her Japanese robes for a ruched bustle, crinolines, and a corset. She cries in humiliation, thinking of her loss of identity, of concessions that are expensive but meaningless.

KAGEYAMA: Look. The people old enough to know better
are slowly coming toward us, feeling bitter about the absurd-
ity of it all. They're dancing. Rokumeikan. These deceptions
are what slowly make the Japanese wiser, you see.

ASAKO: We have to put up with it only a while longer.
Fake smiles and fake balls won't last that long.
KAGEYAMA: We must hide our true feelings. We must
dupe them – the foreigners, the whole world.
ASAKO: Nowhere in the rest of the world should such a
faked, shameless waltz exist.
KAGEYAMA: Still, I'll continue to dance it for the rest of
my life.

The Rokumeikan's successor was the Tokyo Kaikan, where I
was standing. Inside and out, its looks were unremarkable. I
had never heard of the club, but when I had asked one of the
receptionists in its building, she exclaimed, 'But it's a fantastic
place! Sometimes the emperor himself is entertained there!'

I was waiting for Tokugawa Tsunenari, head of the main
Tokugawa family, eighteenth in a line that had begun in the
seventeenth century with the first Tokugawa shogun, Ieyasu. I
stood in the foyer of the Kaikan, which was empty except for a
scattering of chairs and low tables, and – of course – the little
Rokumeikan model in its vitrine.

I knew Tokugawa Tsunenari only from his book *The Edo
Inheritance*: in the little author's photograph on the dust jacket's back flap, he is beaming like a schoolboy. It is not a dignified
portrait. I was surprised, then, when the real Tokugawa Tsunenari entered the room. He was stately. He glided forward almost
like a Noh actor, stopping at the Rokumeikan in its glass box.

As I bowed, I thought of the first Tokugawa shogun: in creating Edo, Ieyasu had flattened mountains, reclaimed land
from the sea, moved rivers. He and his successors built the
city on a spiral aligned with the cosmos: illustrating the direct
equation between Tokugawa rule and the order of the
universe.

Lord Tokugawa was smiling. 'What,' he asked, 'is the condition of your stomach?'

'Sorry?'

'. . . Are you hungry?'

A maître d' materialized – out of the air, it seemed – and ushered us into the Gold Room, where he seated us by one of the plate-glass windows. On the opposite wall near the kitchens, staff craned their necks to see Lord Tokugawa. Passing waiters watched him from the corner of their eyes.

'All year I've been visiting places with the Tokugawa crest: temples and graves. It's a nice change to meet a Tokugawa who's still alive.'

Lord Tokugawa laughed. 'Temples and shrines are all very well. But what's heartbreaking is the loss of the core city. Shitamachi: the downtown where people lived and loved and laughed. That's all gone.'

'So when you look at modern Tokyo, you feel that Shitamachi is the great loss?'

Lord Tokugawa waved his hand, as if batting a flying insect away. 'It's just simple nostalgia.' He looked at me, level. 'I don't know how you can write a book about Tokyo, because in this city everywhere changes so fast. It's not like London. When I first came to the Kaikan in the mid-sixties, this was the tallest building around, but now look—' Outside the window, the skyline stretched away, blank with gray buildings, without any horizon. South and north, east and west, every direction looked the same. 'I'm always asking people, why the hell do you want to go up so high? And all these glass buildings get so hot in the summer!'

'You're right about Tokyo,' I said. 'It's a surprise, when I read about things and then find that they still exist. So much has gone.'

*

The waiters brought *coq au vin* served from silver domes and a silver *saucière*. While we ate, Tokugawa talked about studying in England during the early 1960s, visiting Confucius' tomb ('It's like a film set – new but looks old'), environmentalism, the proper way to eat soba ('You must always slurp'), wood-block prints, and the pendulum clocks in his grandparents' house. One was Swiss, the other English. His grandparents did not own any old Japanese timepieces. 'Those disappeared when Western mechanical clocks came in. They were very difficult to maintain.'

'When did you become aware of time?'

'When I was small, very small. It would have been the *o-yatsu*, the little snack I ate at 3 p.m., between lunch and supper. Sometimes my mother and our maid were very busy, and they would forget. But I didn't forget. I had to claim my little sweet.'

Lord Tokugawa was born into the Matsudaira family, raised, he said, in a frugal household staffed with servants from Aizu, the northern province that had suffered immensely during the brief but bloody Boshin War of the 1860s, when supporters of the shogunate fought supporters of the emperor.

Tokugawa's memoirs are full of the Confucian texts he copied as a child, the samurai sayings ('What a man shouldn't do, he must not do') he learned in the Aizu dialect, as well as popular comic books that treated the Tokugawa as villains. When he was a child, his mother's father – Tokugawa Iemasa, the seventeenth head of the Tokugawa's main branch – adopted him. Tokugawa Iemasa's only son had died, and he wanted a male heir. The line would otherwise have become extinct.

'When I was five or six or seven – I can't remember exactly – I met a very old gentleman, a friend of my grandfather's. He might have been ninety or so. And he'd actually lived through the Boshin War . . . the Meiji Restoration War . . .'

'Your civil war . . .'

'Our civil war, yes. And he picked me up and he held me. He'd been drinking with my grandfather, and he smelled *horrible* – not just him, but the entire corridor stank of sake. And if I hold my grandchildren, and tell them the story, there's a line, a *continuum*, of stories and memories.

'I know what World War Two was like. I know what Tokyo looked like in 1945 because I *saw* it. I was six years old. Most houses had burned to the ground and people were living in small nests that they'd built in the ashes. Everything was razed, and I could stand in Roppongi and see all the way to Tokyo Bay and the sea. We could see the sun rise and the sun set on that black plain. It was our playground. You'd be surprised at what's left after great fires. There were lots of metal rings made out of melted electric sockets and doorplates and – what's that called? When you open the door?'

'The "knob"?'

'. . . The children would dig through the ashes and there were so many things that came out. Hundreds of different rings, all different sizes. We'd play, whose ring could run the longest? Children can get into so many places. We played hide and seek, everywhere.

'Say I tell my grandson or my granddaughter about Tokyo after the war. They'll always remember, and then they can tell the story to *their* grandchildren. Time jumps . . . and jumps . . . like this—' Here Tokugawa sketched a graph. For people, he drew circles; for the movement of time, arrows. And stories and memories were arcs joining one circle to another.

'When that old gentleman held me, reeking as he did of sake, the abstraction of time became real.'

'Your grandfathers must have remembered a very beautiful city. Before the 1923 earthquake and before the war. Lord Matsudaira and Lord Tokugawa. Did they ever speak about Tokyo before the war? Or talk about what was lost?'

'They didn't say anything.'

'They said *nothing*?'

'Whatever they might have felt, they never talked about it. A lost thing is lost. If you try to chase it, that's a mistake. Being sentimental about the past leads to darkness.'

築地

'Tsukiji'

Tsukiji regulars call the marketplace the *uoichiba*, the fish
market, or *uogashi*, the fish quay; or simply *gashi*, the quay.
Only Tsukiji habitués (and only older ones at that) stroll
the *gashi*, mostly in golden memories. Tourists visit the
Tsukiji *uoichiba*, with the sense that a fleeting glimpse of
the *gashi* may be just around the next corner.

Theodore C. Bestor

Tsukiji: The Japanese Empire

This is the district of theaters – the Kabuki-za, the Enbujō, the Hakuhinkan, the Tōgeki – all built on reclaimed land. It is the Tokyo of interstices between the skyline and the Sumida River, between back alleys and the man-made islands of Tokyo Bay.

Japan's biggest fresh market was once here, famous for its fish but selling fruit and vegetables, too. Mornings at Tsukiji: men dragging carts heavy with squid; an auctioneer jerking and twitching as he invited bids; the zircon glint of ice blocks; blowfish; carp thrashing in black tubs; eels rippling in buckets; mussels, scallops, sea slugs, giant blue-fin tuna sparkling with frost. Bells and buzzers. Electric saws cutting into frozen tuna. Sun shining through the Art Deco skylights and flooding the wet pavements and the runners flying over them.

The market's elegant Bauhaus curve stood on what was once one of Edo's grandest estates: Senshū-kaku, the Turret of a Thousand Autumns, the home of Matsudaira Sadanobu, a man who might have been shogun. Matsudaira's garden was sublime but had a humorless name: Yokuon-en ('the Bower of Bathing in Obligation'). Like Edo's other great gardens,

Yokuon-en evoked travel; the landscapes of greater Japan and of China and India beyond. 'There were paths,' Timon Screech has written, 'that wound among trees and rocks designed to lead into spaces of mental remoteness.' There were waterfalls, beaches by lakes, cliffs. An hour-glass pond called the Lake of Autumn Winds, which faced Edo Bay and its masts. Another pond called the Lake of Spring Winds, which faced Mount Fuji. Guests would climb a bridge 'to be lost in the blossoms, as if floating, with only Fuji visible above.'

The Turret of a Thousand Autumns burned in 1829, and all that remains of the estate and its gardens is a single crude sketch.

To the northeast, the green bronze roof of Tsukiji Hongan-ji soars in an improbable curve. Japan's Buddhist temples are almost always made of wood, but Hongan-ji is white marble. Its arches and stupas echo the repeating lines of the prayer halls carved out of rock faces in southern India's caves and cliffs. Where Japan's traditional temples depict elephants and giraffes that the carvers, not having seen, had to imagine from imperfect descriptions in books, Hongan-ji's animals are perfect simulacra. No longer creatures of the imagination, the stone elephants look like the beasts that were housed in Ueno's Imperial Zoo. Somehow those correct shapes look more otherworldly than the elephant that is unrecognizable as an elephant, the giraffe that is cousin to the unicorn, the manticore.

Hongan-ji temple belongs neither to the glass and steel boxes of Ginza to its west, nor to the Sumida to its east. It is an anachronism that jars the viewer out of time and out of Tokyo itself.

The history of Tsukiji Hongan-ji is about the search for identity. Japan, having embraced the West in the late nineteenth century, rejected it in the mid-twentieth. Built when the imperial army was storming through northern China, Hongan-ji is a hymn to Japan's empire.

The white marble evoked the earliest Buddhist structures in ancient India; Buddhism unified an imperial Japan with its Asian colonies: 'Asia is One.' But the temple was not just a simple imitation of ancient Buddhist sites in India; it was cosmopolitan, too, built in the Indo-Saracenic pastiche that the British Empire employed everywhere from New Delhi's Secretariat Building to the Brighton Pavilion. In the same way, Japan's foreign policy was justified in Tsukiji Hongan-ji's stones.

Golden peonies and gilded apsaras. Gilt phoenixes and hollyhocks. Huge gold taiko drums, gold panels. Flat-screen televisions are bracketed to the columns, alongside speakers shaped like silver bento boxes.

On the sanctuary's north wall is a forlorn shrine to the glam singer Matsumoto Hideto ('hide' to his fans), who hanged himself in 1998. A few spent votive candles, brilliant origami cranes strung on a thread, wilting roses. A framed photograph of the star, with his fountain of scarlet candyfloss hair, the ice-white powdered face, the liquid eyes.

When hide's coffin left Hongan-ji's Main Hall, thousands of fans, shrieking and crying, surged against metal crowd-control barriers. Police on the other side threw their entire bodies against the railings to keep them upright. Teenage girls shoving against middle-aged men. *Otaku* Japan and conformist Japan crashed together.

The balance held.

*

In Tokugawa Japan, the metallurgical formulae for casting a temple bell were kept as a secret tradition; a master would teach his disciples, but no one else. Consequently, knowledge disappeared both by design and by accident.

Hongan-ji's architect, Itō Chūta, loved old bells. Because records were fragmentary or non-existent, Itō made a formal study of existing temple bells, trying to recover what was lost: how thick the best bells were, and the ideal distance between their striking point and the mouth. He also analyzed the alloys that made the finest sounds. A high tin to copper ratio meant a sweeter note, but a weaker structure: the bell might crack. Balance was all.

Itō wanted a bell that would have a velvet tone. He discovered the correct ratio was one *kamme* of copper mixed with 170 *momme* of tin.*

Itō found for his new temple one of Edo's old time-telling bells. The bell had once sounded the hours at Ichigaya, a northwest Tokyo shrine to Hachiman, the god of war. The bell rings out over a shore that once curved like a bow, one that's now broken into jigsaw segments.

'Where is the bell?'
　'In the tower.'
　'May I see it?'
　'No. Come back when we ring it at New Year's.'
　'But I won't be in Tokyo then.'
　'What a shame.'
　'Does the bell have an inscription?'
　The woman disappeared and returned with three photographs

---

* In metric terms, roughly 3.75kg copper to 637.5g tin.

printed on ordinary paper. 'It doesn't look like anything's written on it.'

The first photograph caught the bell from below: the image looked wrong, ugly. The lens and the shot's angle distorted everything: the stupa tower, seen from the inside, was paneled with varnished boards like a sauna. Its windows stretched upward like fun house mirrors. Seen from below, the bell was not a green dome, but a dark cavity.

I angled the paper one way and then another in the dim light.

'But – look! – words! What do they say?'

I traced the columns of characters, row after row. The writing was almost invisible.

'The photographs were only taken on a phone, not with a good camera. I can't read it.' The woman glanced up at me. 'Sorry.'

I stepped outside, looking toward the northern tower. It was shaped like a stupa and featured the ogee windows so beloved by architects of the British Raj.

The bell hung inside; invisible, silent.

I left the temple precinct, looking back until Hongan-ji's green bronze roof and the tower disappeared.

At an overpass, a steel signboard depicting an engraved landscape gave vital statistics of a vanished bridge: The Turtle Well – Kameibashi. Height, 36.2m. Width 15m. Walkway, 3.5m^2.

'The name probably originates with the man who built the bridge in 1872. It was renovated in 1928. Below is a sketch of what the bridge looked like in 1957. It used to span the Tsukiji River. In 1964, the bridge turned into a highway.'

On the engraving, a scattering of human figures are crossing the Turtle Well Bridge; frozen in the act of walking. A car from the late 1950s. Phantom trees and eddies in the river. And the three thick arches, with their coping stones and squat spandrels, of the demolished bridge itself.

Beyond Kameibashi is an old house the film director Kurosawa Akira's family have turned into a *teppanyaki* restaurant. Wooden panels, sliding screens; curving tiled roof and carved transom: flammable and fragile, it is surrounded by concrete boxes. The building is an orphan.

St. Luke's Hospital, with a delicate sky bridge linking its two towers.

Mammy's Paw Dog and Cafe: 'Relaxation and the Hand of Magic'. Mammy's Paw offered teeth cleaning (though 'without anesthesia') for pets. Yellow glass lined with chicken wire. In purple stenciling, a dog, a coffee cup, and twinkles without teeth.

On one of the backstreets of Irifune, off Shin-Ōhashi dōri – New Great Bridge Street – was an old rice cracker shop. A Noh mask of a demon, an old red lacquer water bucket. The *sembei* were ready to be sold, wrapped in crisp white paper and tied with silver ribbon. Printed sheets detailing the season's sumo matches were taped to the windows.

A shop selling pianos. A shop selling ribbons. Bars: The Black Dog. Jack Lives Here. One diner had set a tray of glasses half-filled with ice near the door. Each tumbler had a glittering meniscus of melted ice at its base.

Music seeped out into the street; luminous tanks were filled with tender whelks in their ancient battered shells.

North, past Sintomi, Hatchōbori, Hakozakicho. And – briefly – I knew where I was; near the site of the shogun's jail and Nakayama's temple Dai-Anraku-ji. I kept walking northeast, and in a few minutes, nothing was familiar again.

Darkness was falling. Suitengumae, Ningyōchō. Night deepened, and the windows of restaurants and bars became all the color that existed in the world. Vast scarlet paper lanterns that a grown man could almost stand up inside.

The streetlamps picked out a house surrounded by stone troughs where fish small as eyelashes swam beneath brilliant green lotus leaves. Ancient yuzu trees growing in wooden buckets ringed the house, unripe fruit clustering their branches. Orchard and ocean.

By Asakusabashi, the steel shutters had already come down.

One Tokyo was going to sleep while the other was waking up. The two cities share the same space, but never meet.

The year I moved back to England, Daibo invited me to his apartment for lunch. The rooms were as austere as the coffee shop: in Daibo's study, floor-to-ceiling shelves crammed with books. Six fedoras hung on one wall, arranged two by two.

The apartment was on the building's ground floor, and a green, almost marine light filled the rooms, flowing in from Daibo's garden: ferns, hydrangeas, moss on the flagstones. The summer's worst heat was still coming. It was May, the season of warm rains. Nothing had burned yet.

Mrs. Daibo served Japanese powdered tea – *matcha* – in a bowl, one of the ivory-white ones that Daibo knew I liked. She whisked an espresso cup's worth of hot water, and less than a thimble of tea, into a brilliant green froth that filled half the bowl.

The tea was light and rich and bitter and after I drank it all, a little ring was left at the bottom. The bowl looked like a peony: white petals and green at the center.

I wrote Daibo a poem, later, to thank him –

緑の縁
しゃくやくちゃわんを
ふきけさない

The circle of green
From the peony bowl
Will never be erased

It was half a joke ('Don't wash the bowl because the tea stain is pretty') and half a promise ('I won't forget you, ever'), because of the pun on the word 縁 (*en*), which means not just 'circle' but also 'connection', a tie that binds one person to another.

I wrote the words, but I never thought that what I wrote would be true; that the circle would hold. What circle holds?

横川本町

'Yokokawa-Honjo'

Of all Edo's beauties, the river is paramount; its face
changes from morning to evening.

Blossoms on the Sumida
Terakado Seiken
Translated by Andrew Markus

Yokokawa-Honjo: East of the River

I stood in a police box near Kōtōbashi. No one seemed to have any idea where the easternmost Bell of Time was.

'Never heard of it,' said a policeman behind the counter. He wore an official cap with a little pink flower embroidered on its brim, and carried a tiny nightstick and a holster with a walkie-talkie.

'She has a photograph, so it must be here somewhere,' another policeman said, flipping open a district atlas. His finger lingered on the neighborhoods north of Kameido. I tried to read the map upside down: the piano wires where the train rails passed through; the Yokojukken canal, whose waters run impossibly straight.

'It was supposed to be on the banks of a river,' I said. 'In a place where three rivers ran together.'

'Ages and ages ago, a river did run through here,' the policeman murmured. 'What was the river called?'

'I don't know. The story didn't say. It was just, "the bell stood where three rivers met".'

The policeman's fingers skidded off the paper, and he looked up. 'The place you want doesn't exist. Not on this map.'

*

The earth is without memory.

'The city called "Tokyo" is always destroying itself,' said Tsuchiya Kimio. 'Destroying itself and rebuilding again. That's what makes "Tokyo" different from a place like London.'

We were in Yokoami, on the Sumida's eastern bank, and though we couldn't see it, the river flowed around us; in the pale sunlight blurred by the water, in the smell of wet concrete and stones, in the hidden gutters under our feet.

Yokoami holds Tokyo's sorrows. The city's memorials for those who died in the 1923 earthquake, and in the 1945 fire-bombings, are both here.

Tsuchiya and I looked at the narrow oblong lined with white granite stones. He had designed the Air Raid Monument.

There was a shallow pool that kept everyone out, blocked any approach. For two days a year, the water is drained and a walkway stretches into the dark crescent beyond the door. Inside are printed volumes recording the names of people who died in the city's firebombing. Their ages. Where they had lived.

'The surface of Tokyo is so crowded with memorials that I wanted to put this one deeper into the earth, but I couldn't do it,' Tsuchiya said. 'If you dig below the riverbed, water seeps into the walls.'

Tsuchiya is a tall man, with a tenor voice and gold wire spectacles. When we first met, he was dressed like an English gentleman inspecting his estate: canary yellow waistcoat, white Oxford cloth shirt, jeans, battered but expensive brogues. He even had a neatly pressed handkerchief tucked into the pocket of his tweed jacket. But you could still see the strength of the welder he'd once been.

'When we started, we took Polaroids of the construction site,' Tsuchiya said, '– and I saw . . . faces.'

'Faces?' I looked up at Tsuchiya to see if he was joking, but he didn't smile. His face was intent, serious.

'. . . Of people who died, whose names we don't know. They were waiting. For the memorial. They wanted people to remember that they had existed in the world.'

A light rain began to fall; there was also the staccato of hammer blows. Incense drifted out of the Hall to Great Disasters, and then disappeared. In one breath, it was there, the next gone. Then the perfume was back again. It was November and wind pulled the gingko leaves from their branches, and their golden eddies filled the air.

Tsuchiya and I crossed the empty pool and went inside.

In its thousand years of written history, the Sumida has been moved and merged, its channels drained and diverted from one riverbed to another. Its waters were diverted so often – into canals, into gutters – that no one knows where the original channel once lay.

The river has had many names. What it was called depended on where you were. It was the Asakusa River near Asakusa, and Sumidagawa near the village of Sumida. The shoguns called the river the Ara, and the Meiji emperor retained that name, although his was an era for rebranding almost everything else, including the city itself. People living near Tokyo Bay knew it simply as Ōkawa: Big River.

The Sumida is not the river it was a thousand years ago, or when the first Tokugawa shogun turned the fishing village of Edo into a great city. It is not even what it was before World War Two, just as in English the same word – *water* – can describe a raindrop, or a lake, or an ocean. Every era has its own Sumida. The river's looks match its time.

Today the Sumida has concrete banks and the buildings along its banks turn away from the river, as if it weren't even there.

No one knows what the name *Sumida* means. One nineteenth-century gazetteer claimed that the word is older than the first Japanese settlements on the Kantō plain, that it is related to an indigenous Ainu word that means *rough waters. Almost drown.*

Or: *wash away.*

The city east of the river has always been a realm unto itself. Here the shoguns' city lived on longest and died last, in the 1923 earthquake.

Under the Tokugawas, the east bank was 'the equivalent of Greenwich Village or Montmartre . . . Restaurants, teahouses, gardens, and historical sites beguiled the wanderer for hours on end.' In the spring people would leave Edo for blossom-viewing on the eastern embankment. Cherry trees and flowering peaches and willows lined this stretch, which stood twelve feet above the river's marshes. When the trees were in bloom, the crowds were 'as dense as threads in cloth', according to the satirical poet Terakado Seiken.

The eastern districts used to flood every autumn. Very great floods happened roughly once every generation in the seventeenth century, but became more frequent, until by the nineteenth century they occurred one year in every four. The city's governors would then break the levees that protected the eastern bank, and let the water surge over the fields and farms near Minowa and Kameido. Farmers on this side of the river built houses on mounds of banked earth. They stowed 'boats beneath the eaves of their homes, and measured floods less by the bursting of levees than by how far above the floorboards the waters rose.'

After the fall of the Tokugawa, the eastern districts retained an atmosphere of melancholy dissolution, of dissipation. The writer Nagai Kafū remembered how, before the 1923 earthquake, the alleys east of the Sumidagawa still passed through open rice fields, groves and ponds full of lotuses blooming 'in rank profusion'. The earth here was dark and damp, its streets narrow; the place all 'mossy shingled roofs, rotting foundations, leaning pillars, dirty planks.' A soaring tiled roof would be a temple, but one almost always in bad repair. 'Moss flecked tombstones lay falling over into marshes that had once been garden lakes but had so decayed that it was difficult to know where the bank gave way to water.' The land was cheap and it was useful to be so near the river's wharves, so Mukōjima and Honjo became industrial zones; the old houses were pulled down and replaced with factories.

During the firestorms that swept Tokyo after the 1923 earthquake, more than thirty thousand people died just west of Honjo, in Yokoami. As one of the ward's few open areas, the police directed refugees running from fires on the river's western bank, here. It was a catastrophic mistake. The crowds were carrying papers, clothes, wooden screens. Winds carried sparks and embers across the river from central Tokyo, and the bundles began burning. Then tornados of fire swept through the park, trapping those who had come for shelter. Almost no one who went into Yokoami got out.

The Air Raid Memorial was supposed to have had its own space, separate from the 1923 Earthquake Memorial, alongside a lavish museum devoted to peace. Some survivors lobbied that the museum acknowledge Japan's 'invasion, colonization, and annexation of parts of the Asian continent . . . and the carrying out of numerous state-sanctioned atrocities by Japanese troops.' The museum's founders hoped it would mourn not only the air-raid deaths of 1945 but also 'worldwide victims of the war'.

Right-wing members of the Tokyo Metropolitan Assembly opposed the museum altogether, describing the plans as 'anti-Japanese', and 'masochistic'. They demanded that the air-raid memorial *not* mention other victims of World War Two, and that it be built in Yokoami, alongside memorials to the earthquake. Japan's property bubble had just burst, so the Assembly blamed lack of money for scrapping the museum. It was a compromise that made no one happy but right-wing bureaucrats.

Tsuchiya's simple monument was what remained of a grand design. It is also why Tokyo, where more people died than in Nagasaki or Hiroshima, has no central focus for its memories of World War Two. There is no equivalent of Nagasaki's A-Bomb Museum; nothing like Hiroshima's Peace Memorial.

'It's the Age of Mass Forgetting. We live with such a flood of news that we forget what's real,' Tsuchiya said. 'In a single day, we get ten years' worth of news. To survive, we have to forget things: we forget things we hate. We forget things we love. We forget who we are.'

Tsuchiya was not an obvious choice to design the air-raid memorial. He was an outsider, born not in Tokyo but in the northern prefecture of Fukui. And his earliest works were elegies for the living, not for the dead.

His first art memorializes the salaryman, the stoic office

worker who represented Japan in its richest, most confident era. Tsuchiya first began creating installations during the 1980s, when Japan's bubble economy was at its most frenzied; when the country was awash with money that fueled a blaze of destruction. Anything old, anything unfashionable, was thrown out. Furniture. Clothes barely worn. Blenders and irons and printers that still worked.

Maybe that's why Tsuchiya's work turns people into objects: strip lights arrayed in asterisks, books stacked into a helix, even office chairs – all stand in for human subjects. The line between what we own, and who we are, is so blurred that it dissolves. For the Air Raid Memorial, people were turned into flowers. Every spring, a hundred thousand are replanted.

While the Air Raid Memorial was being built, Tsuchiya also created a great rose made out of ashes. From the burned rubble of twenty houses, he made a single gray flower, whose petals splay outward in roulette curves, like a Spirograph.

'The rose was made out of houses built for salarymen. Each house was supposed to last only thirty years. To be *consumable*. So that ash is memory,' Tsuchiya said. 'And that's how Japan builds: our architecture has always been something that has to be renewed – think about the shrines at Ise, rebuilt every twenty years. Or that famous palace in Kyoto, the Katsura: have you seen it? It's three hundred years old, but the structure isn't original. Like our own bodies, which are always being renewed. We last *because* our cells don't last. – Nothing lasts.'

Working with ash is difficult. Ash is not solid. It is not hard. It has no fixed shape. But Tsuchiya has made it his signature medium.

'When I look at ashes, I'm seeing time. I'm thinking of my father. He made new clocks and he fixed broken ones. Whenever he finished with a clock, he would hang it on the walls of our house. *Kachi kachi kachi kachi . . .'*

'We say, "tick-tock, tick-tock, tick-tock"—'

'. . . When I was young, I couldn't get away from that sound. I almost went crazy listening to it!'

One of Tsuchiya's installations consisted of three hundred clocks hanging in a sealed metal room. 'It was a *flood* of clocks . . . after my father died, I thought of it as his portrait. He had been weak for so long, that after his cremation, everything he had been, turned to powder. And I . . . I *ate* some of his ashes. So that he could live on. In my heart.'

丸
の
内

'Marunouchi'

Imperial rule over the eight corners of the earth.

Prime Minister Konoe Fumimaro

Marunouchi: New Origins

Edo burned, and was reborn, many times. Tokyo, too.

The city's most beautiful incarnation was also its shortest-lived; the imperial capital of the early Shōwa era, a capital that existed between the fires of 1923 and the fires of 1945.

It was an Art Deco city, of new bridges spanning its old canals; of shimmering streetlamps, buildings picked out in sherbet-colored neons, a city of silhouettes and symmetries, of the geometries of shadow and light.

On 26 March 1930, the young Emperor Hirohito issued a rescript congratulating Tokyo on completing its reconstruction after the earthquake:

> Profoundly impressed with the splendid achievement of completing the reconstruction of the Capital, through the loyal cooperation of officials and citizens, in such a comparatively brief period of time, We hereby express the greatest pleasure and satisfaction.
>
> Yesterday, on a personal tour of inspection through the reconstructed portion of the City, We were rejoiced at the

marvelous transformation and restoration everywhere in evidence.

On this happy occasion, We express the hope that all Our subjects will continue to unite in heart and mind for even further development of the Capital.

No mention was made of the more than six thousand Koreans and the eight hundred Chinese who had been lynched in the aftermath of the earthquake, while the police not only looked on, but colluded in the killings. Kawabata witnessed the scripted anarchy that followed the fires, when Japan's colonial subjects became scapegoats for the disaster. 'You thought it was perfectly normal,' Kawabata wrote, 'to see people beaten to death with iron bars' among the 'burnt walls, fallen tiles, singed electrical wires, clouds of dust and ashes all over the place.' Tokyo's police and city authorities themselves put about rumors – which were completely unfounded – that seditious Koreans had been poisoning wells and setting off explosions; for days afterward, self-appointed vigilante gangs murdered anyone perceived to be an outsider. As the historian Gennifer Weisenfeld has shown, films of the massacres were confiscated and destroyed, and the memory of those deaths was erased 'so the city authorities could tell Tokyo's earthquake story as one of resilience, unity, and innocence.'

Alternative histories exist, but in the 1930s as now, they are histories visible only to the knowing eye.

The reckoning of time in Japan is tethered to the emperor's body.

For more than a thousand years, a special name has been given for an emperor's reign, which the Japanese call *nengō*.

Nengō always have aspirational meanings, like 'Original Happiness' or 'Prolonged Wealth' or 'Great Peace'.

In the pre-modern era, a new *nengō* would be announced not only when a new emperor took the throne, but also after disasters: an earthquake, a flood, a famine, or an epidemic. A comet could trigger the naming of a new *nengō*, or a terrible defeat in war. It was believed that disasters polluted time, and that time could be cleansed with a new name.

But from the Emperor Meiji onward, the *nengō* changed only when an emperor died. After Meiji ('Enlightened Rule', 1868–1912) came Taishō ('Great Righteousness', 1912–26), and then Shōwa ('Enlightened Peace', 1926–89). When Emperor Hirohito died in 1989, 'tens of millions of calendars were discarded and replaced as the nation literally went back to year one. Time had been renewed.'

Births, deaths and marriages are still registered using *nengō*, rather than Western dates. Since the late nineteenth century, Japan has used the Western calendar, but never the Christian system of counting years from the birth of Christ. So World War Two is calculated to have ended in Shōwa 20. The Berlin Wall fell in Shōwa 64. The end of the Cold War gave its name to the reign of Emperor Hirohito's successor, Emperor Akihito: Heisei ('Peace Everywhere'), because he ascended the Chrysanthemum Throne just as the Soviet Union was collapsing. The 9/11 attacks happened in Heisei 13. Under the old system, the emperor's astronomers might perhaps have restarted time by calling a new *nengō* after the so-called Bubble Economy collapsed in 1991, or after the 2011 earthquake and tsunami. But Heisei – Peace Everywhere – has continued on, while North Korea launched missiles into the Sea of Japan and the United States fought al-Qa'eda.

And Shōwa was always Shōwa, an era that folded up within

itself the aftermath of the 1923 earthquake and World War Two, as well as the country's years of wealth, and the post-war Peace Constitution, in which the Japanese people 'forever renounce war as a sovereign right of the nation and the threat or use of force as a means of settling international disputes.'

In 1940, the Japanese empire celebrated the 2600th anniversary of the mythic first emperor Jimmu and his 'Eastward Expedition' from the southern island of Kyūshū to Honshu, Japan's main island. The anniversary celebration was called *Kigen*, or 'Origins'. It was the beginning of time:

> The first emperor Jimmu's mother was the daughter of the sea god.
>
> Jimmu said, 'The gods gave this reed plain to our ancestors, who threw open the barrier of Heaven and cleared a cloudpath.'
>
> At this time, the world was desolate. It was an age of darkness and disorder. People's minds were unsophisticated. They roosted in nests or dwelt in caves. The remote regions did not enjoy the blessings of imperial rule. Each village had its own chief, and the lands were divided and strife reigned.
>
> The Salt Sea Grandfather said to Jimmu, 'There is a beautiful land in the East, circled by blue mountains. It is the centre of the world. Go there, and make it the capital.'
>
> Jimmu said, 'I am the descendant of the sun goddess, and if I march against the Sun to attack my enemy, I act against the way of Heaven. But if we keep the sun goddess at our backs, we shall follow her rays and trample our enemies.'

In the six years of our expedition, in the region of the Central Land, is no more wind and no more dust. Truly we should make a vast and spacious capital, and plan it great and strong.

The capital will be extended to embrace the universe.

The story acted as model and justification for Japan's efforts to conquer Asia. In one of the many histories of Japan published in 1940, the amateur historian Fujitani Misao scoffed that, when the Japanese empire was being founded around 666 BC, 'not one of the Western powers now struggling to gain the hegemony of the world had reached even the "quickening" stage yet.' Germany, Great Britain, and America were all parvenu civilizations. In contrast, Fujitani wrote, Japan 'has trodden a straight path of ascent, going ever upward step by step . . . History has not been a record of rise and fall, but truly a record only of advance. It is also worthy of note that this growth was not the result of either the maltreatment of other races in quest of territorial expansion or their oppression arising from the selfish desire of the strong.'

On Sunday 10 November 1940, across Japan's East Asian dominions, from the Kuril Islands off Siberia in the Sea of Okhotsk through Korea and Manchuria, southward to the Philippines, twelve thousand Kigen Anniversary nationalistic events were held. The main celebration was in Tokyo's Marunouchi, near the Imperial Palace, and that ceremony was broadcast throughout the empire by radio.

Tokyo itself was now sacred because the emperor and his family lived in the city. Preparations had begun three months before, during the heat of high summer: gold and purple chrysanthemums planted, a dais built for the emperor, stands constructed for fifty thousand guests.

During the ceremony, Marunouchi's many office buildings were completely empty, the American ambassador wrote in his dispatches. 'No one is allowed to look down on the Emperor, and I noticed how completely vacant the roofs and windows were.' After weeks of conserving electricity, however, the city was lit up for the anniversary, and those empty windows glittered and blazed with light.

At 8.30 a.m. on 10 November, guests began arriving at the Marunouchi plaza.

At 9 a.m., loudspeakers throughout Tokyo sounded:

EVERY CITIZEN SHOULD CELEBRATE! EVERY CITIZEN SHOULD CELEBRATE! EVERY CITIZEN SHOULD CELEBRATE!

At 11 a.m., Emperor Hirohito and his wife arrived. The national anthem was sung: *May the reign of the Emperor continue for a thousand, nay, eight thousand generations, until little stones become rocks and are covered with moss.*

The prime minister stood and, pausing every three or four words, read out congratulations on the 2600th anniversary of Jimmu's reign:

The sacredness of our national structure is unparalleled in all the world. This humble subject most respectfully considers that our present Emperor is wise, virtuous and brave. Under the present world situation, His Highness has dispatched forces to a foreign land, concluded an alliance with friendly Powers to establish the stability of East Asia and thereby promote the peace of the world.

This entirely coincides with the initial ideas of Emperor Jimmu at the outset of his task.

The 2600th Anniversary Anthem was sung. The prime minister threw his hands to heaven, and cried: *Long Live His Majesty the Emperor!* three times. The audience responded with perfectly synchronized bows and shouted, *Banzai!*

At 11.35 a.m., the emperor and empress departed, and the ceremonies were declared over.

On the Asian mainland, quagmire: by 10 November 1940, a hundred thousand Japanese soldiers had died in China, though less than a fifth of the country was under Japanese control. Six weeks before the Kigen celebrations, Japan had signed the Tripartite Pact with Germany and Italy, in the hopes, Japan's Foreign Office stated, that 'the spreading of world disorder could be prevented: the alliance contributes to world peace.'

The Tripartite Pact with Hitler and Mussolini infuriated the Americans, who retaliated by levying embargos against the export of scrap iron and petrol. America began advising its nationals to evacuate Asia, which outraged the Japanese. The American ambassador to Japan advised pro-Western Japanese that goodwill missions to Washington would be 'wasted' without policy changes. The Japanese pressed the Americans to stop funding Chiang Kai-shek's armies in China, and to respect Japan's sphere of influence in East Asia. Neither the American nor the Japanese government was in the mood to compromise.

But during the Kigen ceremonies, the two sides put on the appearance of affability, with the American ambassador offering congratulations on behalf of the entire Diplomatic Corps; he closed his remarks with the hope that 'Japan would contribute to the general culture and well-being of mankind'. The French ambassador later recalled that Emperor Hirohito, otherwise motionless throughout the entire program, 'nodded vigorously'.

Kigen parties lasted all week. Tokyo's citizens waved flags and sang songs and visited imperial sacred sites. Trams and buses were covered with brilliant lanterns and festooned with bright flowers. One of the emperor's poems was set to music, and a Shinto dance choreographed for it too:

> To the deities of Heaven,
> To the deities of Earth,
> I will pray:
> May the world be at peace, the sea calm
> as on a morning with no wild waves –

北砂

'Kita-suna'

Running
On the road of fire

Sō Sakon
Mother Burning

Kitasuna: The Firebombs of 1945

When I slid the paper-and-wood door open, the toilet seat levitated slowly upward.

The bathroom itself was as austere and pristine as a temple. Cypress wood covered its walls and ceiling; smoked bamboo concealed its panel joins. An antique woven basket hung from the wall; it held a single lily.

The polished concrete sink ran off a sensor, so – except for the door – it was possible to enter and leave the room without touching anything.

Back in the restaurant, I stepped onto a raised platform covered with straw tatami matting, and waited, kneeling, by my table. It had been carved from elm, and it looked as though it too belonged in a temple, rather than in a restaurant devoted to soba.

A waitress appeared. I asked for green tea.

'There's none!'

'Barley tea, then?'

'We have water,' she said, so I asked for that, and then sipped it, thinking. After lunch I would find the Centre for

Tokyo Raids and War Damage, a museum dedicated to preserving the memory of the Tokyo air raids at the end of the Pacific War. When the right-wing Tokyo Authority cancelled plans for the city's Peace Museum, private citizens set up their own space, on privately donated land.

On the night of 9–10 March 1945 alone, a squadron of B-29s dropped more than 700,000 bombs over Tokyo. Between midnight and morning, more people died than in either Nagasaki or Hiroshima. The true number will never be known, but estimates stand between 80,000 and more than 100,000.

The Centre was in Kitasuna, 'North Sand', a residential district on the eastern side of the Sumida River. I wanted to eat before I went, so I stopped for soba in Asakusa. I would not be hungry, I thought, after the visit. I was afraid of what I might learn in Kitasuna. I was afraid of what I would see.

I knew many people who talked about visiting Nagasaki and Hiroshima the way they talked about visiting Mount Fuji, or eating raw fish in Tsukiji Market. They visited the atomic museums because those things exist only in Japan, although some went to the A-Bomb Dome in Hiroshima, or the remaining wall of Nagasaki's Urakami Cathedral, as if they were on pilgrimages: to look at something unearthly, to acknowledge the horror that exists beside the world's beauty.

I felt ambivalent. I wondered how I could visit Nagasaki or Hiroshima. My grandfather had been in Europe with the ambulance corps of George Patton's Third Army, and had lost his leg below the knee after he walked out into a field seeded with *Splitterminen*. He was carrying a wounded soldier. My grandfather triggered one of those S-mines, which exploded, killing the soldier he had been trying to rescue. The blast ground black powder so deeply into my grandfather's skin that it never came out. The grains tattooed his temple, his ear, his neck, a Milky Way of dark stars. As a child I loved to inspect his left earlobe and ask him what had happened, and where his missing shin and foot were. 'In Germany, I guess,' he would say, calm, letting me study the particles and even try to rub them out. I was convinced that I could.

My grandfather's friends would also speak a little about what they had seen, in Sicily or Normandy. But the soldiers who had been in the Pacific kept silent. If they talked at all, it was just before they died, when they were old, old men; and then it was as if not even an afternoon had passed since the battles they had fought seventy years before. One distant cousin remembered a friend who had been killed beside him on Okinawa. They were crouching by a wall when he turned and saw that the top of his friend's head was sheared away, like a soft-boiled egg. The old man told me that, almost with wonder.

Another man, who had served in the air-force bombing runs over Japan, and who retired in the city where I grew up, remembered the stench that rose from the burning cities. 'It worked its way, like a living thing, through every part of our aircraft – the smell of burning flesh. As soon as we dropped our bombs, the anti-aircraft fire found us. We immediately climbed higher trying to get out of range; we changed course, then tried to dive into the darkness. If they couldn't see us, they couldn't hit us. All the time the smell of death followed us.'

Growing up, I was part of the old soldiers' *we*. I had never thought about what *we* had done to *them*, and I never thought about who *they* were, not even when I was no longer a child.

*

Robert Guillain, a French journalist who spent the war in Tokyo, described the inadequate equipment of Tokyo's fire-fighters, and the lack of public bomb shelters, the subway system that was too shallow to provide proper protection. 'Nor were any private shelters built, except for hurriedly dug holes in a few gardens. People did not dare to take precautions for fear of losing face.' Tokyo knew, he wrote, 'that it was an overgrown village of planks. In the streets at night one was, in a sense, enveloped in wood. All those dry beams, all this wood ready to burn, waiting for a spark. Behind those planks, millions of people slept on straw mats.' Then, in September 1944:

> The ground in Tokyo suddenly gaped with millions of holes, like bomb craters before the bombings and in anticipation of the bombings. Holes everywhere – in empty lots, in gardens, even in the streets, in all the sidewalks, holes every dozen yards. *Hole* is the only name these shelters deserve, for these pitiful trenches so feverishly dug on orders from on high one fine September day, everywhere at once, all over the city – these trenches were all the government had planned to shelter seven million people from the coming bombs. Each was a maximum of ten feet long and some two and a half feet deep. No roofs . . . housewives in pants squatted down in them, with their knees against their collarbones, and beamed satisfied smiles skyward; now the bombers could come.

Outside the soba restaurant, I hailed a taxi on Kototoi Bridge. I gave the driver the address and he set off east. 'Never heard of it,' he said.

We were travelling through Kōtō-ku, which has the strangest shape of all Tokyo's wards: photographed from a satellite, the district looks like a cartoon monster with huge jaws made up of reclaimed land, geometric oblongs that pierce Tokyo Bay. Kōtō-ku is Tokyo in miniature: golf courses, heliports, baseball grounds. Incineration plants and canals, wharves and power substations. A theme park in Odaiba recreates an Edo era hot spring resort on the sea, complete with fish that eat the dead skin off your feet as they soak.

The taxi skirted the vast base of the Skytree tower, and then cut across the Kameido Tenjin district, whose red drum bridge and wisteria arbors have been made famous by ten thousand woodblocks. Hiroshige's prints made the shrine intimate, dazzling after a snowfall, while his more famous, late work, *Wisteria at Kameido Tenjin*, distorts perspective so that a single violet cluster eclipses the radiant arc of Kameido's bridge, its water, an ancient pine, and even the sky itself. The shrine's human revelers are the same size as the wisteria petals. Ten years after Hiroshige sketched that drum bridge and the flowers clustering around it, the Tokugawa shogunate would fall; but Hiroshige's world is outside time. His vine does not wither, even though Kameido Tenjin itself went up in the flames of 1945. The new temple is made of iron and concrete. It was built to the scale of its predecessor, but looks dirty and small.

'Never heard of this place,' the driver said again, glancing at the address. 'Do you know where you're going?'

'No.' I paused. 'Just drop me off. I'll find it.'

I got out by a boarded-up Chinese restaurant and once the taxi drove away, listened to the silence of the street. I looked at my map and then began walking away from the museum. Anything to put off going inside. I passed one or two old-fashioned houses, with clay *kawara* roofs and maple trees, bamboo stands and gnarled pines, but most were concrete or tiled apartment blocks. I stopped in front of one old garden, and watched sparrows settle on a persimmon tree and peck at the orange fruits, which were bigger than the sparrows themselves.

The street was empty, but I could hear someone in another lot, maybe in a neighboring alley: hammering on corrugated metal. It was a flat sound. Somewhere a door slid shut, or open. I looked at the garden, past its sparrows, at the last gold fans on a gingko tree. Behind me someone pushed a baby stroller; I listened to the grit between wheels and the tarmac. The child inside must have been sleeping. More distant, there was the muted music of keys in a pocket, and then the neighborhood was quiet again. I turned, and the street was empty. I walked back the way I had come.

The Tokyo Air Raid Museum does not look like what it is. It is one unremarkable tiled concrete building among a sea of other tiled concrete buildings. It could have been anything – a doctor's surgery, a small company's office.

Inside the museum was empty, except for two guides – both old women – who were talking to each other on the ground floor. I bought an entry ticket, and then asked if someone could answer questions. Nihei Haruyo, a woman with feathery black hair, said she would show me around.

Mrs. Nihei reminded me of a small bird: she barely came up to my shoulder. She didn't look almost eighty, though she was. She was born in May 1937.

The other woman handed me a copy of Mrs. Nihei's testimonial, about the night Tokyo became a sea of fire.

> I was eight years old. My family lived in Kameido: Daddy, Mummy, Brother, Little Sister, & me. March ninth was a night like any other night. We ate a good meal behind our blackout curtains. We listened to the wireless. Then we went to bed.

The radio was playing 'Little Cedars of the Mountains'. I remember that.

I put my clothes beside my pillow; then I lined up my rucksack and air-raid hat. Next were my shoes. If you laid things out in order, you could dress even when it was pitch black.

I didn't know what time it was, but my father said, 'It's different this time! *GET UP! WAKE UP!'*

Outside it was freezing & the sky was still dark. There was no fire where we were. But the winds were incredibly strong. Toward the south, I could see a red stain spreading on the horizon & a whirlwind of fire.

My brother was volunteering away from home and my father was on look-out duty. Mummy, Sister & I got into a public bomb shelter, which had space for two families. I was shaking. Above us, we heard noises – people moving past, people shouting & screaming, children crying. There were explosions. Then I heard Daddy's voice: 'If you stay in there, you'll be steamed to death! Out! *Out! Fast!'*

Mummy & Sister climbed out and I was following them, but my neighbour held onto me: 'Stay inside! You're going to burn to death!' She tried to drag me back, but I slapped her hand away & got out. I ran up, up the embankment and onto the railway tracks. From that high place, I watched my house burning down.

The sky was on fire & the earth was on fire and there was a noise: GOOOOOO GOOOOO. Like the voice of a monster. The winds blew all the fireballs sideways.

The tornado of fire raging gulped houses down one by one with a roaring sound. People were in flames & running. Children were burning on their mothers' backs, but the mothers didn't stop running. Children on fire held their mothers' hands but kept running. The ones who fell turned into fireballs on the ground.

The fire engines came & fought the fires but the fires didn't fall back, not at all. Water ran out. In the end, the firemen got caught up in the inferno. One man was standing with a hose & no water was coming out & he was burned where he stood. I saw a horse standing next to me, pulling a cart crammed with things. The bundles were on fire and the fire had jumped onto the horse, but the horse just stood still. The man holding the reins was on fire too.

Then the fire started climbing the embankment. The dried weeds began to blaze. Daddy, Mummy, Sister & I ran down toward the station, right into the sea of fire. My parents screamed, 'Your hat – take it off!' I let go of Daddy's hand, to undo the knot. The winds flung me backward & I got separated from my family.

Fire was everywhere. Then suddenly: darkness.

There was a tall building, made of stone, & in the shadows around it a woman was standing and burning. The flame wasn't red. It was green & wavering as if the woman were wearing a gorgeous long-sleeved kimono. She stared at me & put out her arms, & I thought, I have to put out the fire! I was stretching out my arms to her, but then I realized, I didn't have anything to beat the fire down – no hat or rucksack or overcoat or shoes. So I was going to put the flames out with my bare hands. Then I heard a lady's voice behind me: 'Don't go there! You'll die!' I felt like she had slapped me, & I turned away.

Then I bumped into something red-hot. A lamppost. I came back to awareness. That's when I knew I was alone. No Mummy, no Daddy. I felt the heat for the first time.

I called Daddy over and over again but never heard an answer. I ran and kept calling, 'Is that you, Daddy?'

Finally I couldn't move anymore. I sat down where I was. My body felt heavier and heavier. I felt sleepy, suffocated. In the distance I could hear the fire bells. Then sometimes human voices. Two men were shouting at each other.

'We are Japanese! We can't die like this! Stay alive! Stay alive! *Yamato damashii!*'

The fires were burning out. It was dawn and then sunrise. I was pulled out from underneath the bodies. I was at the very bottom. My father had found me. He kept talking to me all night, so I wouldn't slip away. I couldn't even say 'Daddy'. I was wondering, Where am I? What happened? As far as I could see, there was Nothing. Just smoke the color of dirty water. It was rising like mist. No sound. Nothing moved. In some places, pale blue flames were dancing.

When I looked down, I saw that the people who'd been piled on me were dead, burned to black ashes. They had saved me.

I took the four pages of the testimony, and read the first line. 'Night of the Blaze: Till Tomorrow!' – 'Let's play tomorrow!' But I read Japanese very slowly, and I needed a dictionary, so I thanked the woman who had given it to me, and slipped it in my bag, unread.

Mrs. Nihei led me upstairs, and walked me through the exhibits. We might have been in her own house. The first floor holds mostly art: oil paintings and watercolors and a cinema for screenings, and taped interviews with survivors of the firebombs.

An upright piano, and a smoke-darkened 1943 edition of Schubert's *Impromptus & Moments Musicaux*. Beside the piano was a great calligraphic panel, painted on a rectangle cut like butcher's paper. The wide page was spattered, streaked, smeared with ash-colored ink. The artist, Inoue Yuichi, was a young night watchman who survived the holocaust only by accident: he was off-duty on March Ninth. That midnight, people who tried to shelter at his school were trapped inside it:

> The school buildings were full of fire. It was like Day. The
> refugees had nowhere to go. It was as if they were in a
> sealed kiln. Morning comes, and everything is burnt
> down. Silence. Emptiness. Only rubble. A thousand people
> had become a single lump of charcoal.

Inoue's letters cluster together like people trying to shove past each other, jostling each other in panic. Around each is a halo of ink stains: droplets, black rain, grains. Neither solid nor liquid. The butcher's page is crammed with markings, from the first word – *Amerika*, followed by a long, white blank – to the last: *life*.

The survivors, Inoue wrote, *couldn't feel anything or do anything. They just stood where they were. Voiceless and tearless.*

I asked Mrs. Nihei if I could have a photograph of Inoue's painting. 'Yes, go ahead,' she said. 'The only thing that you can't photograph are the pictures of the dead. Those ones are upstairs.'

We climbed to the second floor and again, Mrs. Nihei was as relaxed as if she'd been in her own house. She pointed to a glass case, containing two M-69 incendiary canisters balanced on their ends. The thick metal of one cylinder was torn, as if it were paper; heat from the phosphorus charge had sheared the steel away like a ribbon gathered into loops on an elaborately wrapped gift. The flaking metal looked dirty inside the crystalline display cases.

Mrs. Nihei nodded at the cluster bomb. 'That night those were falling like rain,' she said. 'You couldn't breathe, the smoke was so thick. Everything burned. Everything caught fire.'

Mrs. Nihei pointed out the interior of a recreated World War Two era house, with starbursts of tape pasted to the glass windows, the blackout curtain, and dark cloth draped around a lightbulb.

I looked at the neat little interior, and tried to imagine her inside a room like that, as a child, listening out for the air-raid sirens and planes flying overhead. '. . . Did you have any idea of what was coming?'

'We had no idea,' she said. 'We thought we would be safe.'

Mrs. Nihei moved to another glass case, which held a temple record listing the numbers killed in the bombings, the houses and buildings razed. *Namu Amida Butsu*, the monk had written. *I venerate Amida Buddha.* What remained of a life, of a family, of a street of families, a district, a city: single marks on a scroll.

More objects salvaged after the air raids: a perfect brass nozzle attached to the carbonized remnants of its hosepipe, which looked oddly graceful, like the bones of a hand, or a Giacometti figure. A fireman's widow had donated it to the museum. A child's tiny kimono, its blossom pattern blackened. A baby's hand-knitted vest of red yarn.

Above the displays were framed photographs: people dragging carts through an ocean of ashes. A wall of blackened bodies. And the most famous, most hideous photograph: of a mother and her baby; their bodies bare, but without contours, every part blackened, except for a white shadow on the mother's back; the place where the baby had nestled against her as they both burned.

I looked at the tiny kimono again, turning my face away from Mrs. Nihei.

'And how can you . . . how can you keep reliving that night? How can you work here? How can you look at these photographs again and again . . . ?'

'Of course looking at the photographs affects me . . . My entire body shakes, when I show them.'

Later, in Mrs. Nihei's statement, I read: *I saw a mother cradling her baby. Those bodies were like charred matchsticks, and they were everywhere. I didn't want to stand on any, so I kept weaving between them and stepping over them. I had to tiptoe. After my father found me, we passed a tiny, tiny baby, who was flailing her hands and her legs. She was on the road, crying like a little cricket. I stopped when I saw her, but my father said, 'No. No. Not now.' And he pulled me away. I was looking back, looking back, but I had to go. I could have saved that baby, but I didn't. I witnessed her life, but I killed her because I did nothing. That guilt stays with me forever. It will never go.*

We passed a clay *kawara* roof tile fused with a blue and white porcelain plate; coins that the fires had transformed into bubbling lava that cooled into a single lump that looked like black petrified coral, or a sponge. A bottle, tortured out of symmetry into a glistening mass.

Another case held objects that had survived. In that room of damage, those things had perhaps the weirdest shapes: their perfection was almost sinister. There was a complete dolls' set for the March *Hina Matsuri* Dolls' Day festival, which had been celebrated a few days before the bombing.

The tiny emperor was perfect, without a single stain or singe mark on his gold hat, his golden cloak or violet trousers.

The empress and ladies-in-waiting, too, were pristine, and their miniature sweets looked so fresh, ready to eat, even after seventy years.

'All my dolls burned,' Mrs. Nihei said, softly. She was standing behind me. 'And my friends died, and every single one of our neighbors. But my family survived. All five of us.'

> Our house was completely burned down, except for a single waterpipe. I turned on the tap, and water flowed out of it. We scooped it up with our hands, and drank, and drank, and I tasted grit in my mouth. The water was cold, and delicious.

'You found somewhere safe?' I asked.

'*Nowhere* was safe!' she said, fierce. 'You couldn't go anywhere *safe*!'

'But – *everyone* in your family lived?' I asked, looking at a map of Tokyo, which was spattered with red circles. The bigger the circle, the more casualties: Mukōjima, Honjo, Asakusa, were vast stains against a white background. '*All* of you? How was that possible?'

Mrs. Nihei was almost eighty, but when I looked at her I saw my daughter, who was only a little younger than Mrs. Nihei had been the night of the Great Air Raid. I saw my daughter weaving among the ruins of a burning city; looking for me, looking for her father. Lost.

'How?' Mrs. Nihei asked, her face crumpling. '. . . *How*? – I don't know. I don't know.'

The easternmost Bell of Time is gone, its three rivers under concrete.

The East Bank's teahouses and ferries, its shrines and its

carp restaurants, the archery stands at the Hall of Thirty Three Bays. The lantern-maker district. The network of canals and their pleasure boats, and the groves of ancient cherry trees. Yoshimura Hiroshi, in *Edo's Bells of Time*, wrote: *When everything else has vanished, even the name becomes precious.*

Today the Sumida's banks are scattered with new-fangled architecture from the 1980s Bubble and the so-called Lost Decades afterward. The Egg of Winds, a huge glowing metal capsule with liquid crystal screens whose images change when the wind blows. The Tokyo-Edo Museum, which looks like a giant walker out of *Star Wars*. And, to the north, the Skytree tower.

I walked along the narrow park where the bell had once tolled the hours for the craftsmen and lumberyard workers and drunks, for the eastern bank's prostitutes and musicians – when suddenly, up a few shallow tiled steps, was a monument to the Yokokawa-Honjo Bell of Time: a tower with a model bell inside. It was the size of my head and stuck in place. The bell couldn't move, much less ring. Its granite tower was shorter than I was, and not much wider.

The bell was there and yet it wasn't. Like Yokokawa-Honjo itself.

Back in England, the postcard fell on my doormat. It read: *Daibo Coffee will close, after thirty-eight years in the same place.* The postcard read: *Daibo has no hair.* The postcard read: *Daibo hadn't decided what to do next.* I studied the words and studied the words, and finally decided that there had been a mistake, that I must have misunderstood.

A friend visited Daibo Coffee, and phoned me. 'You were right. Daibo really *is* bald. He has absolutely no hair. And yes – sorry – but his cafe is shutting, too. Why are you so upset? Things get knocked down in this city all the time. The building doesn't even fit in with Omotesandō. It's practically the only place that's over ten years old.'

I wondered if Daibo was sick. I wondered what had happened. Daibo Coffee would close on New Year's Day, 2014.

Daibo had created a village inside one of the world's biggest cities and that village was like something built on a cliff by the sea. It was being washed away.

I bought a plane ticket for Tokyo, and rang Daibo before I flew.

'This is Daibo.'

'Daibo? It's Anna. Good morning!' It was night in Japan.

'I got your letter.'

'What do you want me to bring you?'

'Just bring yourself. And, Anna . . .' He waited so long that I thought we had been cut off. 'You understand that . . . ?'

He used a word I didn't know, though I wondered if I might have heard it before. And the last word: did it mean *died* or *didn't exist*?

'. . . When?' I asked, cautious, trying not to commit myself.

'Four or five months ago. And, Anna . . .' Again the long silence, the echoing line.

'Yes?'

'Don't be surprised.'

'I won't be surprised.'

'*Don't be surprised.*'

After we hung up, I realized that he had said, *The shop will close. Shut down* was the word I hadn't immediately understood. But why, I wondered, should I have been surprised about that? He had already said so in his postcard.

In the cafe, an assistant was pouring coffee. He was intent, and didn't look up; I didn't recognize him. Daibo wasn't there. The assistant finally motioned me to a seat at the counter's end. I had come straight from the airport. My eyes felt dry, as if the cavity behind them were filled with sand.

'Milk coffee,' I said.

Then the bathroom door clicked open and an old man came out. He might have been one of Daibo's customers; someone who had been coming to Omotesandō Crossing to drink coffee since I was born. Then the man looked at me, and started, and I saw he was Daibo. A Daibo who looked like an overexposed photograph. He had hair, but it had grown back pure white, a soft halo of down.

Daibo rounded the counter slowly until he stood beside my chair.

'Well, it's been a while since I last saw you,' I said, using the formula. When you don't know what to say in Japan, there's almost always a script, words to plug into almost any gap.

He ignored set phrases. 'Aren't you jetlagged?'

'I'm OK.'

Daibo pointed to his luminous corona of hair, wincing. 'My hair,' he said. 'It's . . .'

'You always look great to me.'

'I got these glasses . . .' He took them off and without the horn-rimmed frames, I thought his face reflected blurred light the way stars do in photographs. He put them back on. 'It gives an *accent* to my face.'

'I like your spectakers . . .'

'Specta*cles*.'

'. . . You look like a Taishō intellectual.' Daibo winced again. If the 1920s meant glamor to me, to him the decade meant old. I wanted to say *edgy*, but I didn't know the word.

'I have to go home now,' he said. 'Because I have a cold . . .'

'Because of the winds?' *Flu* and *winds* sound the same in Japanese, though of course you write the words differently. A typhoon was moving toward Tokyo, and I thought he meant *weather*.

'No, because I'm *sick*.' He paused. 'Will you come in tomorrow?'

'I'll keep coming back until you're here again.'

Daibo stood, bowed to me, and took his fedora off its hook on the wall. He snapped it over his bright hair. Then he left.

For my last milk coffee in his shop, Daibo chose a dark bowl, one I had never had before. It was matte black like a *go* piece, the colour you take if you're the weaker player.

Fifty days later, the cafe shut, and then the next year, bulldozers pulled down its walls and rolled over what had been the ceilings.

That Daibo Coffee closed was not a surprise in a city of new places and novelties. The surprise was that it had ever existed at all.

芝切通し

'Shiba-kiridoshi'

At Zōjō-ji in Shiba Park is the largest of all the bells in
the capital. It was cast in 1678. It was originally called
'the One-Ri Gane' because people believed the sound
that followed each stroke would linger for the time it
took a traveller to cover the distance of one *ri*: that is,
for two and a half miles.

S. Katsumata
Gleams from Japan

Shiba Kiridoshi: Tokyo Tower

A vermilion gate. A warped pine tree in the rain. An undulating swell of lotus leaves and flowers crowds a wooden bridge; there is no earth, no sky, only the flowers opening out.

Kawase Hasui, whose six hundred woodblocks invented an idealized mid-century Japan, was an unlikely artist: near-sighted and raised to be a shopkeeper, he began formal training only when he was twenty-five. His prints, too, are reveries at odds with an age when firestorms burned the capital twice. Kawase's Tokyo is a city of cherry petals, willow trees, stone embankments reflected in water. The charred wreckage of the twentieth century is entirely absent in his work.

Born in 1883 to a family who lived in the temple district of Shiba near Zōjō-ji, where six of the Tokugawa shoguns are buried, Hasui was expected to follow his father in the family business, crafting and selling *kumihimo*, the fine braided cords used in traditional Japanese dress. Hasui's father forbade him to attend art classes, and insisted that he study accounting and English instead. Unable to take up an apprenticeship with an established artist, Hasui taught himself to sketch by copying illustrations serialized in the newspapers and tracing over old prints.

When his sister's husband took over the *kumihimo* shop, Hasui was at last free to concentrate on sketching; he made a living designing magazine covers and advertisements. He also worked on his own woodblock prints: *Twelve Months of Tokyo* and *Selected Scenes of Japan.* When the 1923 earthquake hit, he had filled 188 sketchbooks, all of which burned in the fires that followed the tremor. Hasui's Shiba, too, is gone: its green spaces and temples replaced by the Prince Hotel, a golf driving range, a bowling center and an 'Eiffel' Tower. Hasui's sentimental prints are what remains of his old neighborhood.

In Roppongi, I passed a stump painted blue, and buildings shaped like Tetris blocks built to fill in the space. A beggar with a blue towel tied around his head was dragging his belongings toward the bars and clubs of Roppongi Crossing. There were signboards: for Chinese soba, for the Hard Rock Café, for the Roy Building. A bar called Glass Dance, and vending machines packed with Natural American Spirit cigarettes. The logo featured a Plains Indian crowned with eagle feathers.

The scrappy verge beside the road smelled like urine. In a flower shop, a crowd of ice-white orchids packed the space, almost wall to wall.

I flagged down a taxi; a woman was driving. She had long, long hair tied neatly back. 'I want to go to Zōjō-ji,' I said.

'Would you like to hear my voice teacher sing?' she asked, jamming her foot down hard on the accelerator. We streaked down Torii-zaka.

'His name is Koga Hisashi . . . he's really amazing.' She fumbled with her iPod: a man's countertenor voice filled the cab.

Ave Maria! Koga launched into *bel canto* trills until I thought the taxi's window glass would shatter. The piece he was singing is an artful if overwrought fake, written in the 1970s by the Soviet guitarist Vladimir Vavilov. Vavilov thought audiences would appreciate a lost Renaissance composer more than a contemporary Russian one, so he pretended his own version of *Ave Maria* belonged to the repertoire of the obscure sixteenth-century composer Giulio Caccini.

'I love this song,' the driver said. 'I'm practicing my English before the Olympics.'

'This is Latin.'

'Really!' she said, shocked. '*Latin!* Where do they speak that?'

Four white vans, with the imperial gold chrysanthemums stenciled on their sides, passed us. They were playing martial music from loud speakers riveted to their roofs: 'Pray at Dawn'. 'Encampment Song': *Stroking the mane of my horse, I wondered what tomorrow would bring. Among bullets, tanks and bayonets, we rested on pillows of grass in our field barracks. In a dream my father appeared to me, calling me to return to him when I fall.* The war songs and the ersatz Renaissance harmonies struggled for supremacy.

I left the taxi in front of the Triple Gate, the vermilion entrance to Zōjō-ji. Its three doors strip visitors of the three sins – stupidity, hatred and greed – that trap us and keep us from enlightenment. Called Sanmon, it was built to erase the world of illusion. Walk through it and know: nothing in this world has a distinct character. Nothing has a distinct form. There is nothing to be sought.

The great Tōkaidō highway, which connected Kyoto and Edo, began and ended near Zōjō-ji. The temple was defined not only by its spiritual role, and its association with the

Tokugawa, but by its proximity to the execution grounds at Suzugamori; to the pleasure quarters of Shinagawa; and the outcasts' flophouse district. On the avenue down from the temple's bell tower were drinking and snack bars; the music of *jōruri* ballads, the calls of street magicians and whores. The air was steeped with the smells of grilled rice, of incense drifting from temples and from the tea shops. This flimsy Shiba was thrown together at dusk, the hour called *kuremutsu*, and then taken apart again at dawn.

Zōjō-ji purified and dissolved the social evils and defilement from the inner city.

On the concrete steps in front of Zōjō-ji's main hall a film crew was set up, its cameras trained on a manikin wearing a hat that looked like Mickey Mouse ears swathed in gold tissue. The statue's breastplate was gold, and it had a red cape. The crowd were ignoring the proscription against taking photographs, and angling their phones at the impassive white face.

Pink joss sticks blazed away in a bronze cauldron; I went into the Hall for the Safety of the Nation, where the Tokugawa genealogy, from the first shogun until the last, was inscribed on the wall. After the last shogun left the city, the sacred objects that had belonged in the shogun's private temple were once collected here: sixteen statues of the *arhats*, beings who have achieved nirvana; paintings of hawks; and an eighteenth-century bronze image of Amida Buddha sitting on a huge many-petaled golden lotus.

Monks were selling charms – for wisdom, for good health, for success in exams. The most expensive charm was for driving, at ¥700; wisdom was cheap, only ¥300. It came in a tiny sachet of purple and gold brocade, cinched with a white silk cord.

Outside the main hall stood a Lilliputian shrine to Jizō, one of Amida Buddha's attendants and a bodhisattva of compassion. It is Jizō who oversees life's transitions, and the borderlands of life and death. For anyone traveling between those worlds, he is not just the guide to hell, but also the possibility of return. The shrine's doors were shut, so whatever was inside was invisible. Chain-link rain gutters – *kusari-doi* – ran from the shrine's eaves to the earth. Into each of the gutter's links were angled little pinwheels; yellow and red, stamped with pink flowers. They spun wildly in the wind, clicking.

The red-metal frame of Tokyo Tower loomed over the trees, the temple, the Tokugawa graves. It is a small quiet corner of what was once a vast space, the graves banished here in the 1950s. An old woman was selling admission tickets – ¥500 each – at a booth in front of the nineteenth-century gate, a construction of wood and hammered weathered bronze: sinuous Chinese dragons climbed through scrolled clouds. The woman handed me an entry ticket and a packet of ten black-and-white postcards: a bell tower and colonnades; gilt peonies and phoenixes. The old photographs had been overexposed, and the monochrome prints were flat, lusterless: the stone stairways, the raked pebbles and roof tiles bleached almost white, the shadows without depths.

To see Shiba as it would have appeared in the middle of the nineteenth century, the letters and journals of foreign residents are invaluable: they describe what existed without the desire either to restore the buildings and the dynasty that built them, or to tear those places down. For the newly arrived Europeans and Americans, old Edo might have been mysterious, its ruins picturesque, but the castles and temples had none of the emotional significance that they held for the soldiers and townspeople who had lived through the civil disturbances that preceded the country's opening up to the West and the Meiji emperor's restoration. And in some cases, restricted sites were opened for the first time; before the Meiji era, only the shogun himself could enter Zōjō-ji's main hall. But after the last shogun left Edo for exile, anyone who could pay the entrance fee might visit, though foreigners were reminded to 'leave your boots at the door'.

In the first foreign guidebook to Japan, the British consul Ernest Mason Satow described the Tokyo of the 1870s. He began by setting out the limits within which the treaty allowed foreigners to travel: the Shin Tone-gawa (Yedo-gawa) from its mouth as far as the guard-house at Kanamachi, from Kanamachi to Senji, by the Mito Road. From Senji along the course of the Sumida-gawa to Furuya no Kami-gō. 'From the latter place by a line drawn through the following villages . . .'

Satow detailed passport requirements, gave advice on shooting licenses ('This covenant expressly stipulates that the holder of the license shall not shoot beyond Treaty limits'). He listed clothes that would be required, beginning with a light flannel coat, made to hook up, and with pockets to button, 'so that when you take off your coat and give it to someone to carry, the contents are not in danger of falling out' and ran through everything from singlets, stockings and handkerchiefs to slippers and air pillows. The traveler should also remember notebooks and writing materials; pencils; cigars; flask; requisite medicines; knife; shoehorn; extra boot laces ('hippopotamus are the best'); compass; traveling thermometer; books and maps, including a Japanese dictionary; and Persian insect powder.

It should be clearly understood that it is practically impossible, Satow wrote, when travelling in most parts of the interior, to obtain anything in the way of foreign food, and 'those who cannot eat the native fare should therefore take with them their own supplies ... As a rule, the innkeepers object to their kitchen utensils being used for cooking foreign food. A frying-pan, and perhaps a gridiron also, will therefore be found extremely useful.' A finicky foreigner should therefore pack copious stores of Liebig's Extract of Beef, German Pea-soup Sausage, Chicago Corned Beef, Tinned Milk, Biscuits, Jam, Cheese, Salt and Mustard, Bacon, Tea, Sugar, and Worcestershire Sauce. Do not forget your corkscrew and a tin-opener.

After listing the locations of telegraph offices found throughout Japan, details of the best insect powder ('Keating's is indispensable') and instructions on how to take a bath ('No foreigner should remain more than five minutes in a bath of 110° and upward') Satow opened with a description of Tokyo itself: 'Owing to the shape and the vast extent of the city, it is impossible to combine all the chief sights in a single round.' He offered a perfunctory description of the emperor's palace gardens, of Yasukuni jinja, newly built to worship the spirits of those who had died fighting for the emperor during the recent civil war, and a brief sketch of several government offices ('A day may be profitably spent in making a thorough inspection of the various departments'). Then Satow turned to Shiba. The description is almost half as long as his account of the rest of Tokyo combined. It would have been tactless to have begun a guidebook with praise of the old regime, recently overthrown; so Satow diplomatically began with the emperor's palace, and the bureaucrats' offices. But then he turned to the city's real glories: these *go-reiya*, or tombs, he wrote, are among the chief marvels of Japanese art. No one should leave Tokyo without seeing them. Or, as another European diplomat said:

'We will see the Shiba temples undazzled, sober still, if possible, but we shall want no more sights, afterward.'

We shall want no more sights, afterward. Because in all of Tokyo, there was nothing finer to see.

When Satow wrote his guidebook, only fifteen years had passed since the last shogun departed into exile, and the temple was surrounded by black scaffolding to keep out thieves, who 'are gradually stripping the exterior of all the Buddhist buildings of Tokio of some of their handsome metal ornaments, and even mutilating the bronze lanterns.'

Zōjō-ji's association with the Tokugawa made the temple a special target: before the Battle of Sekigahara, when the first Tokugawa shogun cemented his authority over Japan, he asked that Zon'ō, the head of Zōjō-ji, curse the opposing side. The Tokugawa did not just bury their dead at Zōjō-ji, but credited it with the founding of and then upholding their power. The new authorities therefore made an example of the temple to underscore the defeat of the old regime.

All figures of Buddha were removed from the main hall of the temple. The final appearance was bizarre: statues to Amaterasu Ōmikami and other Shinto gods appeared in the main hall, and a large *torii* was placed in front of the main gate. At the opening ceremony, Shinto priests sat on one side of the hall in their tall black hats; facing them was a line of bald-headed Buddhist priests in their flowing robes. The Buddhist priests who had become national priests had to wear Shinto ceremonial hats, make offerings to the Shinto gods and preach from the Three Doctrines.

Arsonists burned down the main temple on New Year's Day, 1874; the shoguns' mausolea, and the courtyards, survived. A new building, smaller and much less beautiful, replaced the temple, but it looked out of place behind the grandeur of the Sanmon gate.

After the Meiji emperor displaced the last shogun, the Tokugawa tombs were converted into public gardens. For twenty-four *sen* – which at the time could have bought about a kilo of rice – a priest would guide visitors up a red and black lacquered gallery into the tombs of the seventh and ninth shoguns and the temples that held their wooden images, though the images themselves were never shown. A traveler would find his gaze swimming in golden arabesques, which on a clear day were almost too bright to look at directly.

By the main altar, bamboo blinds tempered the brilliant red and gold colonnades and their menageries of carved birds and flowers. Beyond was the Gate of the Heavenly Spirits and then the Middle Court crowded with two hundred old bronze lanterns. Out through the Gate of the Tablet, with its pillars famous for their carved red dragons. Stare hard at each dragon, and it would change under your eyes. Or glance away, and then look back; the dragon would have shifted in its place. Beyond the dragons stood the Outer Court and its two hundred huge stone lanterns.

Here stood the Oshi-kiri Mon, the beautiful Dividing Gate, which led into another court of lanterns inside a colonnade 'whose soft red colouring charmingly contrasts with the deep green of the trees that surround it . . .' The monument over each grave was of simple stone, in marked contrast with the lavish temples.

Retrace your steps, Satow wrote, and see the tombs of the twelfth, the sixth and the fourteenth shogun. Beneath the coffered ceiling and its golden dragon, flying against a midnight-blue sky, were wooden peacocks and pines, wild ducks and chrysanthemum floating on water, white lilies and tree-peonies. And under rainbow phoenixes, the burial places of the second, sixth, eleventh and thirteenth shogun: gilded gates, gilded walls, gilded paneling, huge gilded pillars – everything sparkled with gold.

Before the court of the second shogun stood the bell that 'boomed out the hours all over Shiba, but whose sound was spoilt by the New Year's fire of 1874.' There were gilt brass lotuses, a bronze incense burner cast in 1635. In the wood at the back was the Hakkaku-dō, the Octagonal Hall. 'It is the most magnificent gold lacquer to be seen in Japan, and one which no tourist should fail to visit,' Satow wrote. The tomb was painted with scenes of the Eight Views of Xiao-Xiang and Lake Biwa. With lions, with peonies. Underneath the pavement lay the second shogun Hidetada, buried in a mixture of vermilion and charcoal powder to preserve his body from corruption.

Outside the tomb stood two stones, dating from 1644: on one, five-and-twenty bodhisattvas welcomed the souls of the dead. On the other was carved a scene from the Buddha's entry into Paradise.

On the night of 24–25 May 1945, American B-29 Superfortress bombers dropped their M-69 loads over Shinagawa, Gotanda and Hamamatsu, near Zōjō-ji. Dropped in 'amiable clusters' of thirty-eight, or loose clusters of fourteen, every pipe was packed with gasoline jelly, which would afterward be called 'napalm', each finless oil-bomb exploded by a time fuse four or five seconds after landing. A 1945 article published in *Time* magazine described what happened next:

> The M-69s become miniature flamethrowers that hurl
> cheesecloth socks full of furiously flaming goo for a hun-
> dred yards. Anything these socks hit is enveloped by

clinging, fiery pancakes, each spreading to more than a
yard in diameter. Individually, these can be extinguished as
easily as a magnesium bomb. But a single oil-bomb cluster
produces so many fiery pancakes that the problem for fire-
fighters, like that of a mother whose child has got loose in
the jam pot, is where to begin.

During those hours, 8,500 tons of incendiaries were dropped:
more than 2.5 million bombs.

The walls and roof tiles of Zōjō-ji catch fire. The Main Hall
on its granite foundations burns down; the colonnades, the
dragons, the Tang-style gates of gold and red. The second shogun's gold lacquered tomb. The Octagonal Hall. The Temple
of Benten blazes at the center of the lake of lotuses.

After the war, Kawase Hasui created few new prints, mostly
reissuing images from his sketchbooks of the 1920s and 1930s:
art its critics dismissed as 'emotionally vapid, creatively
stunted.' Hasui's prints were sold wholesale to the Occupation
authorities and then retailed at US Army base post exchanges
for a few dollars: Hasui had reinvented the politically charged
places of Japan as charming tourist spots. American soldiers
brought Hasui's woodblocks home, and in this way late Meiji
Japan survived in the foreign imagination, years after the
landmarks themselves had disappeared from the capital.

In 1953, after a day traveling around Tokyo, searching for a
new subject to sketch, Hasui returned to the neighborhood
where he grew up, where his father had once owned the
thread shop; where his two houses had once stood before they
burned. In his diary, Hasui writes that he had wanted to sketch
the tram stop in front of Zōjō-ji, but that heavy rain stopped
him, so he went back to his old notebooks, and drew the gate
from those, and from his memories. Rain became snow.

In *Zōjō-ji no yuki*, an image of the temple's Triple Gate in a snowstorm, Hasui transcended the trite prettiness that had limited his earlier work. Here he created an elegy for his neighborhood, and for all who lived and worked and died there. Beyond the incalculable human losses remembered, is an elegy for the era. The Sanmon looms over the print's three figures as they wait 'for a tram that never seems to come'. Electric wires and the tram tracks divide the print into asymmetric slices: Hibiya dori, the tram platform, the hipped gables of the Triple Gate, the trees. Only the sky escapes those black lines; snow falls angling downward, giving the print a sense of depth, of movement within stillness. The great red gate, with its promise of release from anger, stupidity and greed, towers above the commuters. A Tokyoite of 1953 would have looked at that print and known that nothing but rubble and emptiness lay beyond the Gate.

The human figures look away.

Daibo's wife worried about him. Something was missing. She looked in her dictionary, and I scrolled through the Kotoba dictionary app on my iPhone. At last we found the word she wanted: *serenity*. Daibo had no serenity anymore, she said. It had always been a part of him, even when he was young, but with the shop's disappearance, that thing, whatever it was, had gone.

I said to Mrs. Daibo that if her husband were suffering, she must be, too. ' "When one weeps, the other tastes salt." It's an Arab saying.'

'Will you write that down for me?'

Mrs. Daibo understood the English words; I translated the phrase roughly, but I promised her something better, something artful. I had a friend, I said, who was a professional translator. He would write something brilliant.

I met Arthur in Asakusa's Crown Cafe, and asked if he would turn the little phrase into Japanese. If he could read the classical language of *The Tale of Genji*, I thought, a single line couldn't be that hard.

But I was wrong. Arthur looked at the words and frowned. He held the paper away as if he needed glasses. 'This saying doesn't work in Japanese. It's something that would make sense in a very dry climate . . .'

'. . . Where water is precious,' I finished. 'I can't imagine "licking tears" in Japanese. People here would think it unhygienic.' I was frowning, too, but at the coffee, which was bitter battery acid. I wished, devoutly, that we had gone to Starbucks, where I could have drunk an espresso.

'In classical Japanese, you would talk about "wetting sleeves".'

'What, you ducked your head so no one would see you crying?'

Arthur ignored me, and scrawled a sentence in red ink, and then crossed it out. He wrote another, shorter one; then crossed that out, too. I laughed.

'Japanese is such a hard language,' I said. 'When I first came to Tokyo, I always thought I could learn it. That if I really tried, it wouldn't be impossible. But I *did* try, and now I know I'll always be at the level of like for like, point for point. Like those toys that we grew up with in the 1970s, the ones with an electric bulb in a box behind a plastic grid. You'd put construction paper over the grid and then stick clear plastic pegs inside and you'd make a picture. That's what Japanese is like for me. But you, you really *live in* the language.'

'You'll get there.'

'No. I won't. I *think* in English. I *dream* in English. And with Japanese, it's like, I'm playing on a beach and then bam! The land drops away. You fall off the continental shelf, into the deep sea—'

'And it's dark down there—'

'— No lights at all—'

'— And the fish are bigger—'

'*What* fish? There's nothing. Just the floor of the sea.'

Arthur finally wrote –

相手が涙
を流すと
その塩味が
こちらのしたに
伝わる

He read it out to me. I shook my head. 'It has too many syllables – too many *words*.'

'I know.' He slid the foolscap across the table and drained his cup of bitter coffee. 'I give up.'

サマータイム

'Daylight Savings Time'

The sun is simultaneously at noon and declining.

Hui Shi
'The Sorting That Evens Things Out'
Translated by A. C. Graham

Daylight Savings Time: The Occupation

During the seven-year Allied Occupation of Japan, Tokyo was recast as an American city. The Tokugawa shogunate had constructed Edo as a labyrinth, a place that would confound insiders and invaders alike. The Americans tried to impose order on that anarchy of unnamed streets and cul-de-sacs, and to that end renamed whatever had survived the air raids.

Avenues radiated around the Imperial Palace, running from A to Z counterclockwise, while streets numbered one through sixty rippled outward in concentric rings. There were new landmarks in the sea of ashes: the Ernie Pyle cinema, the Nile Kinnick stadium, and the Washington Heights housing complex. US Eighth Army cartographers created a map for the Occupation's soldiers, a map that detailed the city's essentials: typewriter shops, motor pools, ice plants. The Supreme Allied Command Headquarters.

Language, too, reflected the new order. Reformers wanted to replace Japan's complex syllabaries and Chinese characters with Roman letters. Pointing to the blackened ruins of Tokyo, one writer said: *This catastrophe happened because the Japanese*

people lacked the words to criticize the military government.
Language must now underpin democracy: the new constitution, and all laws, would be written not with the archaic
grammar and vocabulary of classical Japanese but in a simple
vernacular that an ordinary citizen might read and understand. Difficult and obsolete *kanji* were struck off the list that
schoolchildren were required to learn: old-fashioned characters – for words like *palanquin, inkstone*, and *desire* – were no
longer deemed necessary. And with the Occupation came a
new vocabulary, English loan-words written in the katakana
alphabet: *Quiz. Body-building. Leisure. OK.*

But some imported ideas were rejected outright. In 1948,
the Japanese, still recovering from the war and the lingering
exhaustion that followed years of starvation and despair, held
noisy protests against American-style Daylight Savings Time.
The Occupation authorities were surprised: bringing the
clocks forward an hour had seemed a minor innovation, when
more drastic ones – granting suffrage to women, abolishing
the hereditary rights of the nobility – drew fewer and less
vehement complaints.

Daylight Savings Time became *sanmah ta-imu* ('summer
time') in what the historian John Dower has termed 'the marvelous new pidgin terminology of the moment'. The Japanese
felt summer time drew out the difficulty of their daily lives,
and when the Occupation ended, it was one of the first things
to be scrapped.

People wanted darkness to come earlier.

During midsummer in Tokyo, the sun rises at 3 a.m. By
4 a.m., the day is already present, as if night never were, as if it
never had been, as if darkness and shadows were fairy tales
not even the smallest child could believe in. Some people tape
black bin liners over their windows, and everyone buys what

the Japanese called 'sunlight cut' curtains. It doesn't matter. The beams seep through every barrier.

Early summer mornings are as bright as if the clock has already struck noon. Noon arrested; noon not ticking over, but noon forever.

Daibo Coffee still exists, but on a screen as small as my palm. We were in Daibo's apartment, in a corner that he'd converted into a coffee room, with the old pine counter cut to fit the space along his wall. We were watching a documentary (*A Film About Coffee*) on Daibo's portable DVD player.

'In the land of Japan, is a master of coffee . . .'

A stringed *koto* plays in the background. One string is plucked, and then another, as Daibo pours roasted beans onto his scales; checks the weight and reconsiders. He puts a few beans back in the jar.

When Daibo lets the water fall, one droplet at a time, over the grounds, the *koto* goes crazy, twanging wildly.

'. . . Do you like this kind of music?' I asked.

'Not really.'

'I guess the producers wanted to play something so foreigners would know we were in Tokyo.'

Daibo's hair was now silver, and he had grown it out. It shone over his skull. His merriment had almost vanished. He watched with detachment as another self made coffee.

'When was this filmed?' On the little screen, Daibo's hair is still cropped like a Zen monk's, and mostly black.

'About five years ago.'

I looked at the DVD player, and remembered the coffee shop's light, its bamboo blinds, the cigarette smoke, Fukutani complaining, the yellow glass globes enclosing old-fashioned electric bulbs. One globe shattered and Daibo could never find a replacement.

Daibo was looking away from the screen. 'Sometimes I can't sleep at night, and I think, *There's no such thing as time*, and I feel at peace. But then the next morning when I wake up, and it's day, and everything is the same as it ever was. Then I feel such despair . . . We're only lost when we think about time in terms of planets, and stars. If you count it out in heartbeats, an elephant's is different from a mouse's. Each living creature has its own time.'

'Maybe we make it up in our heads,' I said. 'Maybe time isn't real. Maybe there's no such thing: *Jikan ga nai*.'

'Thinking that way is what it means to conquer time. *Hitori . . . Hitori . . . Hitori . . .*'

Japanese has different words for numbers. What the word is, depends on a thing's shape: counting little objects like toy marbles, or dice, is different from counting machines, which is different from candles or plates. There are distinct number words for books, for birds, for bells. Daibo was using *hitori*, which means *one human being*.

'If each of us has our own timeframe, it's the same as time not existing. We would be so much happier if we did things by our own clock. Being forced to conform to what works for somebody else, well, that makes you crazy.' Daibo smiled, faintly. 'But when I think, "One instant is the same as eternity . . ." – When I think that, I feel alive.'

'Ichigaya'

The Jetavana Temple bells
ring the passing of all things.
Twinned sal trees, white in full flower,
declare the great man's certain fall.
The arrogant do not long endure:
They are like a dream one night in spring.
The bold and brave perish in the end:
They are as dust before the wind.

The Tale of the Heike
Translated by Royall Tyler

Ichigaya: Postwar Prosperity

A city always keeps part of itself back.

If Tokyo had been a clock, then the hours between ten and midnight – the arc running from Shinjuku through Ikebukuro to Tabata – and I were strangers.

These are the city's northern wards, in what was the old High City. The gardens of Rikugi-en and Koishikawa. Remnants of the great estates owned by temples and the nobility: now university enclaves and 'soaplands' – red-light districts – and apartment blocks for salarymen.

I went once to Ōji, for the annual kite festival. If the Imperial Palace stands at the centre of Tokyo's dial face, then at 12:00, almost due north, lie Ōji and its shrine to Inari the fox god, patron of rice and sake.

The shrine was crammed with stalls selling paper kites, thick painted papers stretched over bamboo frames. Kites shaped like Japanese chess pieces. Kites painted with the faces of legendary warlords. Magical kites that could stop fires from starting. Some smaller than my hand, others wide as a hang glider. Each kite was luminous, colored with vivid, unearthly blues, vermilions, golds, imperial blacks.

The crowds were so thick around the shrine that in some places passing was impossible, and I found myself jammed against a stall where an old monk was selling not kites but Buddhist prayer beads. The table shook.

'Sorry!' I said.

The monk laughed. 'It doesn't matter.'

A cone of incense was burning in a little tray arranged on the monk's table, with a domed pilgrim's hat made of woven rice straw slung alongside it. Six cups were lined up with rings scattered around them. Jade and agate prayer bracelets circled a small wooden Benzaiten.

'Your hand,' the monk said. 'May I see it . . .'

I was carrying a camera bag. I shifted it from my left to my right hand and held out the left one, but the monk shook his head.

'Give me *both* hands,' the monk said, so I put the bag down and stretched my left and right hands out toward him. He came around the table and stood beside me.

I'd seen fortune-tellers before – women sitting at velvet-draped folding tables on Aoyama dōri in the early evenings. The fortune-tellers came out in the summer, and always looked like office ladies, or somebody's mother, even the one who had a hollow where her right eye should have been. Not one looked like she could read the air for things that had already happened, or that hadn't happened yet.

The monk ran his fingers above my skin without touching it, glancing over the creases of my palms, my fingers, at the seam where the heel of my hand met the wrist. He might have been reading a newspaper. His look suddenly sharpened. He looked up at my face, then back down again.

'. . . Interesting!' he cried. 'So interesting! Here! *See* –?'

He said *mother*. He said *father*. He might have said *strength*. I had no idea what he was saying. I had never felt so locked out of the language, not since I first arrived in Tokyo and knew not a single word. The monk saw that I had not understood him; that I had not wanted to understand him. He was amused: not just that I was ignorant, but that I chose to be.

I wondered if he could see deaths. I didn't want to understand the words not because I thought the monk would lie, but because he might have told the truth. And because, whether he invented my life's history, or whether, like a child reading a manga storyboard, he could really see everything I was and all the things I had ever done and ever would do, I couldn't tell the difference between what might be real, and what was a lie.

I pulled my hands away. The old monk went back to his table, still laughing.

A natural amphitheater. A circle that drew the sky down and threw the earth upward.

In Ichigaya, I had passed concrete office block after drab office block – Sumitomo Insurance, Snow Brand Milk, the Salvation Army, the Vogue Building – when suddenly the landscape cracked open. I came to a halt on Yasukuni dōri and rocked backward, as if I had almost tripped at the edge of an abyss.

A place for performances, for high theater, for cinema.

What it was, I didn't know, and my map was blank, showing only a few scattered rectangles and unnamed roads that looped into each other and out again.

I crossed the wide stretch of Yasukuni dōri and found a district map engraved on a metal signboard. The atlas's empty space was Japan's Defense Ministry.

On 25 November 1970, the writer Mishima Yukio took a four-star general hostage here. Mishima then stepped out of the general's window onto a parapet to address the base's soldiers, thirty feet below. He threatened to kill the general unless the soldiers were assembled to hear him speak.

Mishima called on the men to rise up and overthrow the constitution that the Americans had put in place after 1945, the peace constitution that 'renounced war forever' and made the emperor a symbolic ruler, a ruler without any real powers.

Mishima was heckled and jeered, with the soldiers shouting at him to quit acting like an idiot, to shut up, to get down from his impromptu stage. Three helicopters clattered away in dizzy arcs overhead; between the rotors and the yelling, the audience could hear almost nothing Mishima said: he had miscalculated the acoustics of his stage.

Mishima began, 'Japanese people today think only of money! And politicians don't care about Japan: they're just greedy for power!' He had planned to speak for half an hour, but gave up after just seven minutes ('True men and samurai . . . Will no one join me? . . . Rise and die! Rise and die! . . .'). Finally, he climbed back inside the window of the general's office. Then he knelt, drawing a short sword, and stabbed himself in the gut, slashing downward and to the left. The general, still gagged and bound to a chair, watched in horror. One of Mishima's acolytes cut off Mishima's head, and then was himself beheaded by another conspirator. It was a medieval death in the late twentieth century.

I looked at the silent ring of buildings curving around the Defense Ministry's gatehouse. The avenue was quiet as if it were late night, not almost noon. Standing on Yasukuni dori, I knew: it was not Mishima the would-be warrior, but Mishima the artist, the actor and director, who wanted to die in Ichigaya. He imagined a death broadcast live after he had addressed crowds scattered across the concrete fan below.

There was space for thousands of listeners.

The 1930s building where Mishima addressed soldiers of the Self-Defense Force still exists; its broad parapet and wings are titanium-white, and overshadowed by the ministry's newer reinforced-concrete blocks and a telecom turret studded with satellite dishes.

James Kirkup described Ichigaya in the mid-1960s as a district of 'willow-hung streets of neat shuttered houses, small hotels, and gardens round the little fox shrine.' There was a coffee shop dedicated to the French writer Jean Cocteau; musical instrument repair shops for *shamisen* and shops selling *go* boards. Grilled chicken restaurants and blowfish restaurants and 'girlie bars' with names like Pleasure and Chanel. Akebonobashi, the Bridge of Dawn, which spanned a river that now flows beneath concrete. On one bank stood the Hon-jin, a love hotel rigged up like an ancient Japanese castle. Its tiered eaves were 'strung with electric lights and its horned roofs outlined in delicate white and green neon.'

On the bridge's other bank were the Ichigaya Barracks, which during World War Two housed the Imperial War Ministry. After Japan surrendered, the victorious Allied powers used the site to convene the International Military Tribunal for the Far East. A military court, the Tribunal prosecuted individual military and civilian leaders on counts of crimes against peace; murder; and crimes against humanity.

The trials were conceived primarily as history lessons for the Japanese public, an arena for disclosing facts about the war. The prosecution stated: 'This is no ordinary trial; for here we are waging a part of the determined battle of civilization to preserve the entire world from destruction.' The underlying symbolism of the trial's staging in the old War Ministry was blunt: Japan's old order was finished. Defeat was real.

The poet James Kirkup, who lived in Ichigaya during the 1960s, claimed that the trials still haunted the district. *Over this part of Tokyo hangs a dismal aura of perpetual execution.* The court sat from 1946 until 1948, while Mishima was a law student at Tokyo University. He would have followed the judgment and sentencing of prime ministers and generals, admirals and diplomats.

It was victory as spectacle, victory as theater. As a stage, Ichigaya was unrivalled.

What was wanting, Mishima might have thought, were different actors. And another script.

There are various theories about why Mishima chose that particular death, from the purely political (it was a right-wing protest against the post-1945 constitution) to the aesthetic (he wanted to die at the height of his physical and intellectual powers, before any decline set in), or the psychological (one of the co-conspirators was his lover, and it was a double suicide). Mishima burnt his diaries, and after his suicide people who had thought themselves closest to him realized they had only known what he allowed them to see. Mishima was a man of parts that added up to more than one whole.

The decade before Mishima killed himself was an era of ferment. In 1960, Tokyo was rocked by massive demonstrations against Japan's security treaty with the United States. In May and June of that year, the capital's streets were crowded with protesters every single day. In 1968 and 1969, university students took over their campuses, sometimes taking their professors hostage. The disputes were, in essence, over Japan's post-1945 values and the intellectuals who defined those values: what was the 'peace' constitution worth if the country's prime minister, Kishi Nobusuke, was a rehabilitated Class A war criminal? And did Japan have no future beyond blind economic progress on the American model?

Mishima's contemporary and sometime adversary Terayama Shūji responded to Japan's cultural crisis of the 1960s by arguing that only art could transform the world. The only real revolution, he said, was in the imagination. Mishima disagreed with this view profoundly. To back up his ideas, he formed a private militia – which he called the Shield Society – made up of university students who shared his right-wing values and his vision of a prelapsarian Japan. At the end of his life, Mishima claimed that writing had little value for him: he wanted to leave the world of words for a world of action. Mishima left instructions that he should be buried in his Shield Society uniform 'with white gloves and a soldier's sword in my hand. Then do me the favor of taking a photograph. I want evidence that I died not as a literary man but as a warrior.'

The suicide embarrassed the Japanese political establishment, especially the right-wingers. It came just as the country was being recognized as a modern industrial power that could compete with the West on its own terms.

Nor did Mishima's death please the artistic establishment. The screenwriter Oshima Nagisa complained that his suicide 'failed to satisfy our Japanese aesthetic' because it was 'too elaborate'. The writer and film director Terayama Shūji's only

comment was, 'He should have killed himself at cherry blossom time.'

Not everyone got the joke.

A year before he died in Ichigaya, Mishima began saying
goodbye to his friends, though no one understood what he
was doing until after the spectacular public suicide.

The writer and film critic Donald Richie remembered his
last meeting with Mishima, at the Tokyo Hilton a few months
before the latter's death. Mishima, Richie wrote, talked about
'purity' (a subject which bored Richie), and then mostly about
how much he admired the nineteenth-century general Saigō
Takamori. Saigō had wanted to re-establish Japan's ancient
virtues by deposing the shogunate and restoring power to the
emperor; he killed himself after coming to believe that the
revolution he led had failed, because the new Japan was full of
rationalizing, pragmatic, conciliatory ways.

Saigō's suicide was, Mishima told Richie, 'beautiful': a single
superb gesture in response to a country that was drunk on its
post-war prosperity. The country was rich, yes, but had fallen
into spiritual emptiness. Mishima told Richie that Japan in the
late nineteenth century and Japan after 1945 were the same:

— Japan, Mishima said, has gone, vanished, disappeared.
— But, surely the real Japan must still be around, if you
look for it?
Mishima shook his head sternly.
— Is there no way to save it, then? I asked, probably smiling.
Mishima looked past me into the mirror: No, there is
nothing more to save.

*

East of the Ministry of Defense, the waters of the palace moat flowed silent and unseen, muffled by the great cherry trees that overhang the canal banks. The buildings around Ichigaya were anonymous, interchangeable: built to be wrecked, built to be ephemeral.

Hachimangū, shrine to the Shinto god of war, rose abruptly from the flat spaces around it. The hill was so steep that it might have been a perfect cone. In Japanese medieval towns, temples often stood as defensive lines around castles: Hachimangū guarded the western approach to Edo. Looking down from the highest stair, the stone lanterns on the first step below appeared close and distant at the same time, separated only by a vertiginous drop. One leap and the distance would close very fast.

Under the Tokugawa shoguns, Ichigaya was crowded with tea shops and food stalls, a sumo ring, and Kabuki stages. During the great festivals at Hachimangū, there would have been fire-eaters, dragon dancers. Performing monkeys, acrobats, conjurors.

In the office at the top of the stone stairs I met Kaji Kenji, a priest of the Hachimangū shrine. He looked like an extra from an old black-and-white film about wandering samurai.

'Yes, there was once a bell here,' Kaji said. 'Its tower was right where we are standing now. But during the early years of Meiji, an edict separating Shinto shrines and Buddhist temples came into force and we gave up the bell then. I have no idea where it is now.'

Kaji showed me around the grounds of the shrine. A stone celebrating the accession of the Taishō emperor in 1912. A stone memorial for the great sword-makers of Edo, men whose blades were so sharp that they could cut leaves falling through the air.

'So what was around Ichigaya, back when your bell tolled the hours?'

Kaji glanced over my notes, reading them upside down. I had scribbled, *Red Light District. Brothels.*

He laughed. 'Not much. This area was like the places you find in Ikebukuro now. Or Shibuya. There were many soaplands, it's true . . .'

'I read that the shrine had a sign that said, *When you enter the precinct, all your ills will be taken away.*'

Kaji shrugged. 'We probably lost that during early Meiji.'

When the last Tokugawa shogun left Edo, and imperial forces took over the city, Hachimangū suffered more than almost any place except for Ueno. The shrine's Noh stage was ripped apart, its new belltower torn down; the Buddhist temple beside Hachiman's shrine was razed. The new imperial authorities made it clear that Tokugawa time was finished: temples were forbidden to sound the hours. There would be the noonday cannon, fired from the palace, instead. And by 1862, for only five *ryō*, anyone could have his own pocket watch. No one needed the melancholy notes of temple bells, lyrical but imprecise, like the world that had just passed away.

The raucous spectacle around Ichigaya disappeared almost overnight. The area was replanted with trees.

Time fascinated Mishima.

The world was like a leather bag filled with water, he once wrote, and at the bottom of the world was a puncture: time seeped out of it, drop by drop.

Time was like a whirlpool.

Time could be stopped if you stood between the sun and a sundial.

The present moment could be sometimes like the Mekong or Bangkok's Chao Phraya: a vast river. The past and future were tributaries that sometimes overflowed their own banks, and spilled into each other.

Time was like a palace's great hall, with partitions that could be taken away. Every instant that would ever be, or had ever been, might be seen all at once.

Sand pouring from a woman's shoe: the most enchanting hourglass in the world.

Kaji and I were standing under Hachimangu's copper *torii* gate, the metal streaked and weathered to green, looking toward the Ministry of Defense. The *torii* was inscribed with the names of people who had given money to rebuild the shrine in 1804; the copper has survived every fire, every earthquake. During the 1945 fires, it would have glowed white-hot.

'Mishima Yukio,' I said. 'Was he here before he died . . . ?'

'The Ministry of Defense is just next door: lots of soldiers visit us,' Kaji said. 'Mishima came here too. I still remember all those helicopters making a great racket overhead the day he killed himself.'

'Did you understand what had happened?' I asked. 'You must have been very young then.'

'My parents explained . . .' Kaji looked down at me, smiling faintly. '. . . That Mishima had slit his belly open.'

Silent, we both looked off toward the screen of cherry trees and the backdrop of buildings that hid the place where Mishima had died.

'He was a beautiful writer,' I said at last.

'He was.'

In his novel *Runaway Horses*, Mishima writes about a young extremist who is planning a coup in the 1930s. 'He himself had become a character in a romance. Perhaps he and his comrades were on the verge of a glory that would long be remembered.' The man prays but has no revelation as to what he should do; the gods will not speak to him, and provide no indication of the date or time he should choose. It is as if 'the gods have abandoned the decision'. The would-be assassin decides to act anyway.

Mishima planned his own coup in a Roppongi sauna bath house called the Misty. He acted with four young students who belonged to the Shield Society, the group that he had formed on the pretext of guarding the emperor from left-wing radicals.

The Misty was an odd setting for Mishima's plans to restore 'purity' to the Japanese state: somewhat louche, based in what then and now was a district of nightclubs and hostess bars. But it was at the Misty that Mishima asked his co-conspirators, on his signal, to swear that they would cut off his head. And it was here that he drafted the Manifesto that he distributed to the Ichigaya soldiers and the press the day he died: 'We will restore Japan to her true form, and in the restoration, die. Will you abide in a world in which the spirit is dead and there is only a reverence for life? In a few minutes we will show you where to find a greater value. It is not liberalism or democracy . . . Are none of you willing to die by hurling yourselves against the constitution that has torn the bones and heart from that which we love?'

At the bath house, Mishima and his students precisely chore-ographed their movements for 25 November 1970:

10.50 Arrive at the Eastern Army Headquarters.
11.20 The base commandant gagged and bound.
11.35 Soldiers told to assemble below commandant's office.
12.00 Address Self-Defense Forces.

If the Self-Defense soldiers agreed to join him – though he privately told his Shield Society acolytes that he didn't expect any to – Mishima planned to march on Japan's Houses of Parliament at 12.30. But no one could hear what he was saying, or if they heard, no one agreed with his vision, and at 12.07 Mishima abandoned his speech.

By 12.20, he was dead.

Mishima didn't need fortune-tellers. For some men, nothing is written. Mishima wrote his own story, and he wrote it in blood.

新宿

'Shinjuku'

Shinjuku sits at the intersection of perception and reality. What you have been experiencing for the last twenty-four hours is not supernatural, nor hallucination. It is the intersection of parallel dimensions. Perception is all that separates these parallel worlds.

Christopher 'Mink' Morrison

Daibo and I got out of our taxi on Yasukuni dori, near the Isetan Department Store.

In a shop selling artists' paints on the second floor a crowd of white plaster casts – heads, torsos – floated over the crossing.

I was telling him about my pilgrimage between bells.

'"Stars and frosts"! "Light and shade!"' Daibo cried, jubilant, reeling off different words for *time*. 'Beautiful! Of course, your grammar isn't perfect, and you don't know as many words as you could. Those things matter less, though, than you thinking about, really thinking about, such words.'

Daibo was laughing, and pointing his heavy umbrella at the sky, the pavement, the stoplights.

'Stars and frosts!' he shouted. 'Light and shade!'

It was as though he were summoning Shinjuku itself into being: its neon banners, its streets, the taxis that moved past like comets burning up in the atmosphere, the crowds of drinkers and wanderers.

Time! Time! *Time!*

The Clock of the Future

Albert Einstein's theory of General Relativity predicts that time slows down near anything heavy.

On earth, clocks run more slowly at sea-level, which is nearer the earth's massive core, than on mountaintops. Clocks on satellites run faster still.

In 1922, the publisher Kaizōsha invited Einstein to lecture in Japan. When the liner carrying him docked in Kobe, an Einstein frenzy seized the entire country. The German ambassador wrote Berlin: 'When Einstein arrived in Tokyo, such multitudes thronged the station that the police could only look on with folded arms at the waves of humanity which made one fear for one's life. The whole Japanese populace, from the highest dignitaries down to the rickshaw coolies, participated spontaneously and without any preparations or compulsion . . .'

Einstein's car couldn't leave Tokyo Station; it was mobbed.

There were fierce arguments in the government Cabinet Council over whether the Japanese public would understand Einstein's lectures on relativity:

Mr. Kamada, Minister of Education, rather rashly said, of course they would. Dr. Okano, Minister of Justice, contradicted Mr. Kamada, saying they would never understand. Mr. Arai, Minister of Commerce, was rather sorry for Mr. Kamada, so he said they would perhaps understand – vaguely. The Minister of Justice insisted that there could be no midway between understanding and not understanding. If they understood, they understood clearly. If they did not understand, they did not understand at all. He had ordered a book on the theory of relativity when it was first introduced into Japan, and tried. On the first page, he found higher mathematics, and he had to shut the book.

Whether most Japanese understood his theories or not, Einstein was received with adulation. An epic poem was composed to celebrate his equations. Academics wanted to call him *Father*. And confusion over how to pronounce the word for 'relativity' (*sōtai-sei*) meant that it was mixed up with a word for 'sex' (*aitai-sei*). In the pleasure quarters that year, many versions of the song 'Einstein Aitai-sei Bushi' were played over and over again: they were all love songs. 'Working out the Aitai-sei theory' meant being in love.

The rapturous reception embarrassed Einstein himself: 'No living person deserves this.' When he left the country six weeks later, there were tears in his eyes.

At Tokyo University, Katori Hidetoshi builds clocks that demonstrate Einstein's idea that space–time warps near massive objects. The atomic lattice clock: an instrument accurate to within a second of the birth of the universe.

Katori's clocks are housed like animals in cages; like the menagerie in a mechanical zoo. In his labs, each zone has its own taste; its own music, the bass thrum of its cooling systems. In a single clock, trellised black jumper-wires vaulted between breadboards, a small colony of blue lasers, an oven where the atoms are trapped. Inside the porthole window, which was the size of a human heart, a violet blue haze: strontium atoms, fluorescing.

The day I met Katori, he was wearing wire-rimmed spectacles, a cream knitted waistcoat over a pin-striped shirt, jeans, and trendy New Balance trainers. I noticed the trainers as I bowed. I studied them for some time.

Inside Katori's office a print of Salvador Dalí's *The Persistence of Memory* hung opposite the door: pocket watches drooping – one over a withered branch, another over a block of stone, and a third over skin-covered bone. A fourth watch faces downward, spattered with jet-black ants. Katori gestured toward a round table, where we sat. His secretary poured tea from a Royal Albert porcelain service.

I had brought a diagram of a cesium fountain clock (also known as 'the single ion clock'), the instrument that is still used for setting the international definition of time: the 'second' is currently defined as the time it takes for a cesium atom to move between two energy levels.* But cesium fountain clocks rely on a technology that dates back to the 1950s. Even the best fountain clocks are slower, and far less accurate, than the optical lattice clocks Katori is building.

Katori frowned at my diagram.

'In the abstract, the single ion clock is excellent, but in reality *it takes ten days to tell the time.*' Katori paused, delicately, raising his eyebrows. 'That's not so impressive. But when we can measure relativistic time within a minute, then we can *feel time as it is actually happening,* not ten days later. With optical lattice clocks, I get millions of atoms ready, and I measure them in a single second.'

'Are you nostalgic?'

Katori seemed to feel that question made no sense; I had to repeat it several times. 'But I *want* to surpass old technologies! I've never wanted to chase somebody else's ideas.'

Katori twisted around to look at *The Persistence of Memory.* 'We're on the brink of realizing Dalí's vision.'

I glanced up at *The Persistence of Memory*: the eroded

---

* 9,192,631,770 cycles of radiation.

escarpments, the barren plain, the ants swarming over a watch's case. The watch's face, if the watch even had a face, was invisible.

'The way those clocks droop is sinister. They don't scare you?'

Katori laughed. 'No! I *want* people to have a new way of seeing reality. Right now nobody cares about relativity: only scientists understand how gravity can change time and space. My dream is to change that, to make everyone understand Einstein's concept of time.'

'How would you do that?'

'If you put two of my clocks, far apart from each other, and something heavy moves, the two clocks could detect it—'

'Because the clock nearer the heavy thing would run slower—'

'Yes! Or think about the magma chamber under Mount Fuji: if lava moved, my clock could see what was happening. It's like how radar works, but in this case, we are observing disturbances, the distortions, of space–time.'

I glanced back at Dalí's print.

'So in the future, one of the two clocks would be able to tell time *before things happen*; but yet, that clock would still be a *clock*, just . . . not a clock . . . of the present moment . . .'

Katori smiled. 'Today's clocks show us how we share time. But *my* clocks will show that we *don't* share time: my clocks show that every person's space–time is different.'

'Your clock doesn't sound like a clock anymore!'

Katori grinned. 'I want to put my clocks in gas stations, and in antennae for mobile phones . . .'

An invisible web stretching like ganglia all over Japan, over Asia, the world. The clock would become one vast organism, something almost alive.

Shinjuku: Tokyo Tomorrow

In Shinjuku, the viewer and the view are one. What you see is what you are.

Shining in Shinjuku's eye, the port city of Yokohama in the distance, the mica glitter of Tokyo Bay, mountains to the northeast and Fuji to the west, and the great three-dimensional circuit board of Tokyo itself, with its white legend of avenues and alleys.

Shinjuku is a fragmented mirror. What it reflects, looks back outward.

Shinjuku is a monster, a chimera, a storm of light.

The woodblock artist Honma Kunio once said that at Shinjuku's crossroads, and in the nearby red-light districts, *Color is a different shade than at the center of Tokyo. Shadows are paler here.*

Shinjuku was originally famous as a collection point for nightsoil and horse manure, which was shipped out to the farms around Edo. When Hiroshige painted the district in *One Hundred Famous Views of Edo* in 1857, he chose to foreground a pack horse's backside and its dung. The animal and its droppings dwarf the graceful line of background shops. The stink of excrement almost rises off Hiroshige's print. But by the early 1900s, a thriving rail station had made the area rich. After the 1923 earthquake, Shinjuku became avant-garde, even fashionable.

Shinjuku is vertigo, and always has been. In the 1930s, Hayashi Fumiko described the view from the famous Naka-muraya curry house, where over lukewarm tea and mediocre pastries, the intelligentsia gathered to write and to argue with each other about socialism:

> The bookshop opposite used to be a black shop selling
> coal. It was once completely dark. The coal shop was one
> sort of space, but today that space has become white, and
> divided itself into two. You can't believe your eyes at the
> transformation: black to white, small to big.

Tokyo is always and everywhere destroying itself, and then creating new landscapes out of the empty lots and ruins, but in Shinjuku that process is extreme.

Shinjuku is a hot-air balloon, floating upward, Hayashi wrote. A clock shop, a jeweler's, a bakery, a launderette, a bank: each shop had its own background music. In front of Shinjuku Station, a store narrow as an eel's nest, selling records: a clerk, his head ringing from the cacophony of sounds. *Whenever I want to calm myself down*, the clerk told Hayashi, *I go up to the roof of Mitsukoshi Department Store. I look out at the open spaces in the far distance.*

I was lost in a train station so vast that I began to think that the station had only entrances, but no exits. A space that by the laws of geometry shouldn't exist, but somehow does.

The British artist Raymond Lucas has created a schematic diagram of Shinjuku Station, mapping the stages of disorientation: Locate exit sign. Move in the direction indicated. Find an open space. Move in the direction indicated – move in the direction indicated. Move away from the crowd. Does this exit lead out? Have you tried other options? *Does this exit lead out?*

After almost an hour of going the wrong way though I was always in sight of the station, I found a walkway that led over the tracks of the Chūō Line, and the Times Square shopping complex, toward Shinjuku Park. I took one of the open-air escalators down to Meiji dōri, with its parking lots and tanning salons and Chinese medicine shops. Past the Antik Nook, a subterranean bar whose cold air seeped out into the humid street. The stairwell was plastered with flyers for indie bands: Gold Joke. Snatcher. Hot Apple Pie. Loyal to the Grave.

Tenryū-ji lies near the Antik Nook, standing on a narrow triangle of land wedged between Meiji dōri and the old Kōshū-kaidō Road, which led northwest out of Edo.

The temple had only one entrance. It is wealthy, wealthier than any I had seen in Tokyo and maybe even in Kyoto. A Jaguar was parked just outside the main hall and hand-crafted bamboo mud guards arced between the walls and the street. The Tokugawa family crest blazed on its heavy wooden gate, the three paulownia leaves thickly painted in gold.

The temple priest's wife was standing in the thin strip of garden between the graves and the walk under the eaves of the main hall. Some tourists had wandered into the precincts, and she was showing them a musical stone resting in a shallow well. She took a bamboo dipper and let water fall in a thin stream onto the rock. Its sound came low and faint, like notes plucked on the strings of a *koto*. The priest's wife passed the dipper to the tourists and then turned to me.

'Yes, that's the Bell of Time,' she said, nodding to the bell hanging by itself among the graves. 'Our bell was different from the other bells, because it rang half an hour before the other ones did. That way the samurai who came to Naitō Shinjuku to play around in the pleasure quarters could get back to Edo Castle before the curfew sounded. It was called Oidashi O-Kane: the Get Back Home Bell.'

'Is it the original bell?' When the priest's wife nodded, I asked, 'Did you have to hide it during the war?'

'Yes, we have the original!' she said, indignant. 'And *no*, we didn't hide it! Of course lots of metal things were requisitioned during the war. But not *our* bell: it was too famous, too fine. No one dared touch it.'

Shinjuku is like a scroll painting of some Chinese mountain: the stony peaks visible, and the earth and sea, but the air between erased, hidden behind clouds.

From the atrium of the Park Hyatt Hotel, I watched twilight settle over the city, and the lights opening their eyes. On the peaks of Shinjuku's skyscrapers, the red glow of aircraft-warning beacons blinked on and off, on and off: systole and diastole.

A thousand feet below is the little district called Golden Gai, a grid of streets filled with concrete cubbyhole bars that look like ancient barracks. The Blue Dragon, Orange, Pickles, WHO, Golden Dust. Lonely.

Ceramic dwarves perch over entrance signs alongside Buddhas, polished pebbles, porcelain bodhisattvas, collections of miniature cacti and money-beckoning cats made of plastic gold. The canvas screens that once shielded doorways from rain and sun have burned or rotted, or been torn off, and the folding metal arms that held the awnings have rusted. Weeds and wild ferns grow in the balconies.

Beside each door stood crates crammed with last night's empty wine and beer and sake bottles.

Shinjuku the city of reflections, of ladders on water tanks and antennae on top of buildings, blanked-out windows, rusting fire escapes. The tangle of wires, graveyards crowded onto narrow terraces, zebra crossings, the huge columns of a post-Bubble atrium. Filmy curtains and what's beyond them, a lighter someone dropped in the street. Mirrors and clocks in love hotels and the time they tell, the translucent sheeting over building sites, the streetlamps, the slopes, the signs I can read and the ones I can't. Entrances to underground parking lots and station exits. The chain-link fences and crazy paving outside bars, the vacant lots, the circle and slit of DO NOT ENTER signs and TV screens. The city of shadows.

Shinjuku is the lives played out in the clubs of Kabukichō's quarter mile by quarter mile; in West Shinjuku's towers midway between peak and pavement; in the bars of Golden Gai.

Shinjuku is the limit of my knowledge, the future city where I am already a ghost; unknowable and unknown.

帝国ホテル

'The Imperial Hotel'

At every turn, it is possible to leave the major spaces for minor ones. There seems always to be another turning into a farther space; volumes interlock, and short runs of steps lead up to new outlooks. There are constantly changing perspectives of the interior, and through openings at unexpected places come views of the gardens.

To enter this hotel is to become involved in space whose very nature is limitless and unending: there is no certain point to be called beginning; there is no ending either . . . The shape of the Imperial's space is the shape of life, without origin and without end.

Cary James
Frank Lloyd Wright's Imperial Hotel

Hibiya: The Imperial Hotel

Art, Mishima Yukio once wrote, is a colossal evening glow. The burnt offering of all the best things of an era.

Mishima put those thoughts into the mouth of a grubby Japanese tour guide eking out his living in Bangkok just before World War Two, but the words, detached from their speaker, have a weight and symmetry:

> Even history, apparently destined to endure for ever, is abruptly made aware of its own end. Beauty stands before everyone; it renders human endeavor completely futile. Before the brilliance of evening, before the surging evening clouds, all nonsense about some 'better future' immediately fades away. The present moment is all; the air is filled with a poison of color. What's beginning? Nothing. Everything is ending.

I remember that passage whenever I look at Miyajima Tatsuo's art installations. I dreamed about Miyajima before I met him, or saw his face. I had the dream just after I saw his 1997 show *Time in Blue*, with its scattered glowing networks of red and green and blue LED numbers that counted down

9 8 7 6 5 4 3 2 1

and up

1 2 3 4 5 6 7 8 9

The countdowns finished and restarted. Finished and restarted. Finished and restarted. Restarted and finished.

Some of the LEDs were mounted on toy cars that veered in arcs around a room; others twined in spirals that rose from the floor to the ceiling; or were fixed into lattices. And there was a clock that changed its number just once every seven days.

Inside the glassy darkness, the LEDs glimmered and ticked away to themselves. Radiant vertigo: I was a number.

I got lost in blackness, unable to see anything except for the lights, which wavered and vanished, then blinked on again. There were no stable bearings, and no sense of why the countdown began or why it ended; why some numbers ran faster than others.

And there was no Zero. Not ever a Zero.

In a dream I had after seeing the show, I was kneeling in a wooden boat. The boat was drifting through an ice field, and I was pushing floes away from the prow. Overhead the stars were LED counters. I watched the counters rise in the east, although crumbling seastacks eclipsed them while they were rising. A man was reclining there, among the stones. *The keeper of the gate*, I dreamed. *Miyajima.*

Later I thought that vision – the numbers arcing across the sky, the oceans, the seastacks – was an electronic portent, a premonition of my move to Japan.

One critic has said of Miyajima's LEDs that 'the fusion of extreme electronics with extreme sentimentality is typically Tokyo', and in the city, Miyajima's creations are everywhere:

his numbers are embedded into staircases, or curved around Roppongi skyscrapers, or stuffed in coin lockers.

Miyajima has said: *Time is not what we think it is. We are alive, therefore time exists. We animate time. We invent it.*

Miyajima had in some way brought me to Japan, so I wanted to meet Miyajima before I left Japan.

The question was how to find him. In London, I might have rung his gallery, but in Japan, even more than elsewhere, introductions are everything, so I sifted through people I knew, wondering who would know someone who would know Miyajima. Unlike the near-infinite labyrinth of Tokyo itself, the city's expatriate community is small. I finally asked Caroline Trausch, a Frenchwoman who introduced Japanese artists to Parisian galleries. Like Miyajima himself, she worked in the chasm that lies between Tokyo and the West.

I asked Caroline at a drinks party for a young artist, Nishino Sōhei. Nishino makes cityscapes from contact sheets he cuts up by hand and then pieces together, creating vast dioramas that are true, yet not correct: an imaginary city that doesn't exist in the world.

Together we looked at Nishino's *Tokyo*. An azure sea ringed the city, and the tiny torn squares overlapped like scales on a sea serpent. Close up, I could see a traffic sign, a tower, a miniature person small as a brushstroke. It was like looking at Tokyo with the prismatic eye of an insect, or an angel.

'Why don't you just phone SCAI the Bathhouse? The gallery that represents him?'

'I can't just call them! That's crazy! That would *never* work.'

So Caroline introduced me to an art collector who, she said, would know how to find Miyajima. He knows everybody, she said cryptically. And everybody knows him.

The Collector was a tall man, and most of the room, even the artists – especially the artists – was in awe, even afraid of him.

I tried small talk, asking how many generations his family had lived in Tokyo. To be a true *Edokko*, or child of Tokyo, you have to go back three generations.

'Seven generations,' the Collector said, pleasantly. 'My ancestors ran soaplands.'

I laughed at the old-fashioned word for 'brothel'. 'That is patently not true.'

'They were in the business of bathhouses.'

I raised my eyebrows to show that I wasn't taken in. The Collector laughed.

'. . . My great-grandfathers were samurai doctors for the shoguns.'

The Collector's ancestors had acquired Dutch texts on anatomy, during a time when contact with foreigners was forbidden. For over two centuries Japan closed itself off from the West, with the sole exception of the small Dutch trading post on Dejima, the artificial island off Nagasaki, in the far southwest of the country. Edo's doctors taught themselves medicine in defiance of the shogun's restriction on Western books, and also despite the hostility of Nagasaki's doctors (who wanted to protect their monopoly on the so-called 'Dutch learning'). The Edo doctors had to work in isolation, entirely from books, like codebreakers. It was, one scholar has said, 'one of the most extraordinary chapters in cultural interchange in world history'.

The Collector's great-great-great-grandfathers translated the Dutch medical text *Ontleedkundige Tafelen*, known in Japan as *Tafel Anatomia*, with its charts displaying and identifying the parts of the body. One eighteenth-century doctor wrote: 'Gradually we got so that we could decipher ten lines or more a day. After two or three years of hard study, everything became clear to us; the joy of it was as the chewing of sweet sugar cane.'

The Collector had a steeliness about him, a scrutiny, which fitted the descendant of men who had acquired first-hand knowledge of the body's machinery. His people were mavericks, driven – to learn and to heal – by intellectual hunger.

I asked the Collector if he knew Miyajima, or knew how I might meet him.

'I know the work, but not the man,' he said, fixing his gaze on me. He smiled. 'Call SCAI the Bathhouse.'

Finally, with my days in Tokyo running out, and no other options – the weeks I had left dropping from four to three to two – I rang the gallery. I offered references, explained why I wanted to meet Miyajima, described my ideas about time. But in the end, for all my scheming, nothing mattered but that I loved the LEDs. That was enough.

The manager of SCAI the Bathhouse arranged for me to meet Miyajima the day before I left Japan. She asked that I go to the Imperial Hotel, in Hibiya. I should wait for Miyajima in the lobby's Rendez-Vous Bar.

The moving company came and packed everything away: books, papers, clothes, plates and cups. Our beds, chairs, tables. Almost nothing was left. In my empty closet, the clothes I would wear to my interview with Miyajima floated alone, animated even without my body inside them: a dark cotton skirt, an organza shirt the color of a seashell.

I had visited the Rendez-Vous Bar my first night in Japan and then never again. I remembered almost nothing about the place.

The lobby's inner wall soared two stories upward. Thousands of tiny tesserae crossed that wall almost like strata in an eroded canyon: gold, sand, opal and one thin line of celestial blue.

I was looking at the wall when Miyajima appeared, suddenly, next to me. He didn't look like a magician, a crafts-man or an artist, but like someone I might have walked past in Omotesandō, or sat beside on the Yamanote Line without really seeing: a man reading a manga, or playing a game on his phone, or sleeping on the train. He had rimless spectacles and wore jeans and an Oxford cloth shirt. There was a stillness about him; a lightness.

I had expected an ascetic, a wizard; at the very least, some-one gloomy. The art critic Waldemar Januszczak once wrote that Miyajima is driven 'by a set of surprisingly glum motiva-tions . . . his obsession with flashing numbers is ultimately an obsession with death. The way it keeps coming. The way you cannot escape it.'

But the man seated on one of the lobby's little couches did not look sorrowful. I remembered that his earliest works in the 1980s were mischievous one-off performances: in Ginza, he folded his own body into a cube, pretending to be a rock. In Shibuya, he stood in the center of the famously crowded Scramble Crossing, threw his head back and howled as the commuters around him scattered. In Shinjuku he lay down on the asphalt and waited for rain; when it fell his body made a dry silhouette on the ground. He stood up and photographed the outline as the shower erased it. Whenever he performed, he always wore the salaryman's uniform: a black two-piece suit and a white shirt.

Miyajima ordered a Darjeeling tea and, when the waitress left, asked what I wanted. I told him about *Time in Blue*, but not the dream that I had had about it: 'Your work was . . .' I said, halting, '. . . my doorway to Japan.'

'*Time in Blue* was fifteen years ago! And you've kept thinking about it!' he said, gleeful. 'Incredible!'

I wondered why Miyajima had chosen tea made with a teabag rather than something from Shizuoka or Kyushu; in a white cup, those teas shine an almost unearthly green, as if the cup itself is glowing inside. I wondered if paying a lot of money to drink bad tea was a cultural experience for the Japanese, who could pretend they were somewhere else without actually leaving the country. The foyer of the Imperial didn't even look like Tokyo. We could have been anywhere.

'What was your first memory of time?' I asked.

'I was twelve years old. That was when I first understood that time existed.' Miyajima sipped his muddy tea, smiling. 'I was very ill, hard sick, after a stomach operation, and spent three months in the hospital. I read many books while I stayed there – books about why and where people came from. Like that Gauguin painting: *Where do we come from? What are we? Where are we going?*

'. . . I had caught fear,' he said, so quietly that I could barely hear him over the room's echoing noises: the clatter of silverware and cups on saucers, the thousand voices. 'I had nothing to do but think about my life, and on my ward, the friends I made kept dying.'

Miyajima leaned back, and looked toward Hibiya Park, where taxis were arriving, with almost monotonous regularity, to drop guests off and take others away.

I'd assumed Miyajima chose the Rendez-Vous Bar because he wanted somewhere anonymous, somewhere formal, and it was true, the Imperial was nowhere you would meet a good friend, or anyone intimate; but it was a place that preserved within itself the city's modern history. Even the name was a relic of a time when the country was building an Asian empire.

The hotel's glory years came after the Russo-Japanese War of 1905, when Frank Lloyd Wright was invited to build an edifice that would proclaim Japan's place as an equal to the European powers and the United States, countries that had tried to dominate and subdue it. Then came World War Two, and the firebombs, which the hotel mostly survived. And in 1967, Lloyd Wright's ōya tufa blocks and bricks, the infinity pools and the Peacock Room and the heavy Chinese lanterns, were all razed to give way to a seventeen-story block that no architect would admit to designing, the one where Miyajima and I were drinking tea.

But if you wanted to think about time and Tokyo, the Imperial was a good place.

'What I decided was,' Miyajima continued, '*I am training for death, every day.* Just now – this moment – is very important. Many people think, "I have time. I have twenty or thirty years left." But what if you *don't*? What if *this is all there is*?'

Beyond Miyajima the tesserae rose glittering toward the ceiling's distant lights. I noticed a thin band of emerald green among the layered sand and stone colors. Five hundred years before, the place where I was sitting would have been under the sea. Hibiya was just an inlet of Tokyo Bay, a place where fishermen harvested oysters and seaweed.

'And you?' Miyajima asked. 'What's *your* first memory of time?'

I looked away from the wall and back at Miyajima, startled. I had never thought of that, and no one had ever asked me. 'My first memory of time was . . . I'm not sure. When I was growing up, we had no working clocks in our house.'

Miyajima looked shocked. 'Amazing! Not a single one?'

'Not one,' I said. 'In the early eighties you could call the bank and ask for the time and the temperature. At first, a real person would answer the phone. They would tell you how hot it was, or how cold, and then what the hour was. When I was older, a recording replaced the person. I used to call the bank a lot to hear what time it was. It was a habit that annoyed my mother. Especially when she got the phone bill.'

'No wonder you think about this question,' Miyajima murmured.

I poured more tea into Miyajima's cup. It was stewed, and looked muddier than ever. 'When you think of "time", what word do you use? . . . Your language has so many.'

'I'm not thinking of "clock time" at all,' Miyajima said. 'I'm thinking of an abstraction. Something from the language of physics, of mathematics.'

'But your word for it is . . . ?'

'. . . *Ta-imu.*'

'From the English word.'

'Yes, but my sense of it isn't Western. In the West, time is a line. In Asia, it's a circle.' Here Miyajima gently took my notebook, a small one covered in grey canvas, and drew a dial on the page, with numbers running counter-clockwise from Nine to One. He scrawled a swirling halo around the dial until rings danced around it. Between the Nine and the One he scored a black circle.

'. . . The Zero!' I cried.

'The Zero.' Miyajima smiled at me. 'The Zero is Death, yes, but not Death as an *ending*. Death as the moment when we become our perfected selves. As the filmmaker Terayama Shūji said, *We are growing into our deaths.*'

'So the Zero is a joke?'

Miyajima laughed hard, a delighted bark. 'It's not a joke! It's *very serious*!'

I laughed too, uncertain. 'Does that mean that for you, Zero
. . . Zero is a *joyful* thing?'

Miyajima once remarked that Zero originally meant not
just nothingness but also plenitude, increase, expansion.
'Avoiding Zero is a deliberate inclusion of a void – a rejection
of the idea of nothingness . . . Taking out Zero focuses attention on Zero.'

Miyajima handed me back the notebook. 'Life is movement
and color, while Death is darkness and stillness. I *use* that
darkness . . . It may *look* like nothing, but energy is brimming,
waiting for the next life. That's the Zero. Just as sleep restores
us for the next morning.'

'How can you still feel like that, even after the 2011 earthquake? A priest near Ishinomaki, that village where so many
children were washed out to sea, said, "The flow of time has
completely changed. Clocks have stopped." '

Miyajima took my notebook back again, and traced a horizontal line at the Four, the word that in Japanese sounds the
same as the word for 'death.'

'Wars and natural disasters cut our natural spans . . .'

'. . . which leaves a mark . . .'

'. . . which leaves a mark. It's never the same, but what's lost
can be recovered.'

I thought of the people dragged by the 2011 tsunami out
into the northern Pacific; those whose bodies were never
found. 'Can be recovered'? I wondered. What exactly can be
recovered? The idea was, I thought, a joke; like Miyajima's
howl at Scramble Crossing thirty years before, or the vanishing silhouette of his body, erased by the falling rain. Shioda
Junichi once said that the twentieth century was an era of
revolution and war, of the massive exodus of refugees. 'It is a
period when all things were considered measurable and

countable, and individuals were reduced to numbers. Production and consumption, the life and death of human beings, and everything else were reduced to numerical terms. Miyajima's digital counters, coolly ticking away their numbers, seem perfectly suited to this twentieth-century context.'

But no, I thought, no. The counters are – must be – Miyajima's own joke. I thought of him painting random numbers on people's faces in LED font, for his *Deathclock* series of photographs. His numbers repeat because nothing is repeatable. He turns people into numbers to prove that they are *not* numbers, that nothing can be counted. There are billions of stars in the galaxy, Miyajima has said, just as each person is made up of billions of cells. So the scale of the person and the universe is similar. 'One person can represent the universe and the universe is not bigger than one person.'

The earthquake's dead are not numbers, will never be numbers.

Miyajima looked at his watch and said goodbye. Then he left, still smiling.

After he had gone, I sat alone, sipping my own muddy tea, which was cold. I was surprised that the *andon* floor lamps were on. They radiated in ordered rows throughout the vast Rendez-Vous bar. I called the waiter and asked when the bar switched the lights on. 'At three o'clock? Or was it four . . . ?'

The waiter looked at me as if I had asked a question of sinister simplicity: *What country are we in? What year is it?*

'From eleven in the morning, when we open.'

The lights had been burning from the moment I came into the Imperial, and I hadn't noticed.

Edo was imagined as a place that could not be entered, or might not be left.

Katō Takashi

The rooms where I had lived were empty. Not even a coat hanger was left. There were marks on the walls – great gashes where a bookcase had sheared away to the floor during the 2011 earthquake – but except for that scar, nothing remained.

Outside my windows stood what was left of an old green-wood: maples and gingko trees. There was the appearance of stillness, indolence, an unbreakable pause. But the leaves are opening out, growing, and even the stones are disintegrating, slowly.

Nothing ever rests.

Light and Shade.

Time.

Notes

The Bells of Time

1 **Across Japan, the tunes vary, but Tokyo stations usually play the song 'Yūyake Koyake'** I have adapted this translation from Hector Garcia's 'A Geek in Japan' blog ('Yuyake Koyake', 9 May 2007).

1 **the Bell from Zōjō-ji** For temple bells and their origins, see Eta Harich-Schneider's *A History of Japanese Music* (Oxford University Press, 1973): 'Temple bells were imported from China and Korea. They are large bronze bells, masterfully cast and adorned with decorative reliefs, frequent motifs being musical instruments and music-making Bodhisattvas. These bells, called *tsurigane* (hanging metal), are suspended in a separate wooden building, called *shōrō*, to the side of the temple. The note is produced by pushing the bell from the outside with a wooden pole. The oldest of these bells, and also the most perfect in form, is in the Kwanzeonji, Kyūshū, and dates from 698. The material of the wooden striker is *shuro-no-ki*. The tone is extraordinarily pure and rich, with an incredible range of harmonics, and with the fundamental note clearly discernible . . .' (pages 67–8 and plate 8b).

3 **He could build an entire universe** Yoshimura Hiroshi, *Ō-Edo toki no kane aruki* (Shūnjusha, 2002). The passages quoted come from the Introduction, pages 4–5. For '*kinpo*

shohatsu, the lotuses' first opening, pages 6–7. For the preservation of Edo's 'soundscape', page 11.

4 **A circle has an infinite number of beginnings** See Judith Ryan's essay ' "Lines of Flight": History and Territory in *The Rings of Saturn*', in *W. G. Sebald: Schreiben ex patria/ Expatriate Writing* (Gerhard Fischer, editor, Rodopi, 2009), pages 45–60; in particular its reference to Gilles Deleuze and Félix Guattari's *Kafka: Toward a Minor Literature* (University of Minnesota Press, 1986): 'We will enter, then, by any point whatsoever; none matters more than another, and no entrance is more privileged even if it seems like an impasse, a tight passage, a siphon. We will be trying to discover only what other points our entrance connects to, what crossroads and galleries one passes through to link two points, what the map of the rhizome is and how the map is modified if one enters by another point.' The journey becomes what W. G. Sebald called an 'extensive, disorderly, fragmented web' (' "Lines of Flight",' p. 56).

5 **Daibo Katsuji was famous** See Daibo's *Coffee Manual*, translated by Eguchi Ken and Kei Benger (Nahoko Press, 2015). This thin little book is less a how-to than what the Japanese call a *zuihitsu*: an essay on Daibo's philosophy of coffee.

For a history of Japan's urban coffee culture, see Merry White, *Coffee Life in Japan* (University of California Press, 2012) and Marilyn Ivy, *Discourses of the Vanishing: Modernity, Phantasm, Japan* (University of Chicago Press, 1995). See also Eckhart Derschmidt, 'The Disappearance of the *Jazz-Kissa*: Some Considerations about Jazz Cafes and Jazz Listeners'. Derschmidt writes that in mid-1960s Tokyo:

Jazu-kissa [jazz cafes] began more and more to resemble temples, as the jazz following began to resemble [Neil] Leonard's notion of 'cult,' by which he means 'a loose group almost without organization not so much a brotherhood as a transient, fluctuating collection of individuals drawn together by ecstatic experience . . .' The darkness, the tremendous volume of the music, the motionlessly listening guests, and the frequently strict and authoritarian master, who not only placed the records on the turntable but also checked that his shop rules were being obeyed, all added to the impression that one entered a very special, almost religious room, a completely different world.' (*The Culture of Japan as Seen Through its Leisure*, Sepp Linhart and Sabine Frühstück, editors, State University of New York Press, 1998, page 308.)

Hibiya

7 **Hibiya contains relics of all Tokyo's eras** Edward Seidensticker, *Low City, High City: Tokyo from Edo to the Earthquake: How the Shogun's Ancient Capital Became a Great Modern City, 1867–1923* (Allen Lane, 1983), page 123.

9 *setsuna* See Bjarke Frellesvig's *A History of the Japanese Language* (Cambridge University Press, 2011), Section 4.2.3, pages 148–9. See also William LaFleur's essay, 'Shunzei's Use of Tendai Buddhism': 'The act of observation comes to an end at the same moment that it begins – in the unit of time the Buddhists called *kṣana* (*setsuna*); thus, the observer is no more permanent than what he or she observes' (*The Karma of Words*, University of California Press, 1983, pages 42–3).

9 **Japanese time is told in animals, in the Zodiac**   The Zodiac sequence runs: Rat (11 p.m.), Ox (1 a.m.), Tiger (3 a.m.), Rabbit (5 a.m.), Dragon (7 a.m.), Snake (9 a.m.), Horse (11 a.m.), Sheep (1 p.m.), Monkey (3 p.m.), Rooster (5 p.m.), Dog (7 p.m.) and Boar (9 p.m.).

See Yulia Frumer's 'Translating Time: Habits of Western-Style Timekeeping in Late Edo Japan', for commentary on this so-called 'Zodiac': 'Twelve animal signs designated the hours – with midnight associated with Rat and noon with Horse – as did numbers, to allow bell strikes to mark the hour.' A pre-modern Japanese hour was a double hour, so there was no direct equivalent with our 'midnight' – that spanned 11 p.m. to 1 a.m. Noon was the moment the sun was at its zenith: the one incontestable moment (except on cloudy days).

Frumer adds that 'although the twelve animal signs are often mistakenly referred to as "signs of the [Chinese] zodiac," they have no relation to constellations on the zodiac belt.' During the Edo period, 'The day in Japan was divided into two parts: daylight and darkness, defined by dawn and dusk. (As both dawn and dusk are naturally continuous processes rather than clearly distinguishable moments, astronomers made the decisions as to which moment to consider to be a turning point. Criteria changed throughout the period and varied by region.)

'Each of the periods lasted six "hours", but since the relative length of light and darkness changed throughout the year, the relative length of these "hours" changed too.' (*Technology and Culture*, volume 55, #4 (October 2014), pages 789–90.)

See also J. Drummond Robertson: 'It has been suggested that, as certain hours were lucky whilst others were unlucky, a glance at the clock would at once show whether the time for an action was propitious or not.' (*The Evolution of Clockwork: With a Special Section on the Clocks of Japan*, Cassell, 1931, page 199.)

Philipp Franz von Siebold wrote that dawn and twilight were defined as 'that moment when one begins or ceases to be able to recognize a printed character held in the hand, or when in the morning the stars disappear; and when in the evening they appear once more' (*Nippon* (Leyden, 1852), vol. iv, part iii, page 117). Quoted in Robertson, *The Evolution of Clockwork*, page 276.

In Tokugawa Japan, the animal signs also indicated directions on maps. '[T]here was also a spatial association between hour-digits and directions . . . In ancient Chinese cosmology, the animal signs were identified not only with months and hours . . . but also with directions. Thus, the sign of the Horse, associated with the summer solstice and with the noon hour, was also associated with south . . . the Rat represented winter solstice, midnight, and north.' (Yulia Frumer, *Making Time: Astronomical Time Measurement in Tokugawa Japan*, University of Chicago Press, 2018, page 42.)

For the origins of this framework, see 'The Concept and Marking of Time', in *Sources of Chinese Tradition*, volume 1: *From Earliest Times to 1600* (William Theodore De Bary and Irene Bloom, editors, Columbia University Press, 1999), pages 351–2. 'Dates in Chinese history are customarily recorded in terms of the years of the reigning monarch. But by Han times, there was already in use an additional system of cyclical signs for designating years, days, and hours. The origin of these signs, one a set of ten known as the "ten heavenly stems," another of twelve called the "twelve earthly branches," remains today a mystery, though it is apparent that they are very ancient . . .'

10 **the hour of the cow** For an early example of the Hour of the Ox, as that time of night is more often known, and its appearance in ghost stories, see *The Tale of the Heike* 4.15,

'The Nightbird' (Royall Tyler, translator, Viking Press, 2012). 'Night after night His Majesty was assailed by crushing fear. By his order, great monks and mighty healers worked the most powerful and most secret rites, but to no effect. His suffering came on him at the hour of the ox ... A black cloud would rise, approach, and settle over His Majesty's dwelling. Then his agony always set in ...' (page 242).

11 Coffee houses were like London's clubs in the days of Dr. Johnson　James Kirkup's *Tokyo* (Phoenix House, 1966), pages 68–9; 129–30. Kirkup writes of Shinjuku's Fugetsudo, an 'artistic' coffee shop 'displaying very deliberately *avant-garde* paintings and specializing in classical music of the drier type – Bach, Vivaldi, Buxtehude, Palestrina and Pergolesi, with occasional gushes of Tchaikovsky, Brahms, Mendelssohn and Grieg. When you enter the shop, write down your request for Chopin, Scarlatti or Debussy; you may have to wait nearly two hours to hear it played ... as Tokyo has no Soho or Bloomsbury or Greenwich Village, this place deserves one visit if you want to see a bit of pseudo-Left Bank atmosphere in Japan ... Again, as with restaurants, it is best just to wander round and drop into one coffee-shop after another. I prefer the rip-roaring modern jazz coffee-shops, particularly Dig, Village, Pony, Mokuba and a number that just call themselves Modern Jazz. Here, listening to Art Tatum or John Coltrane, one can strike up friendships with the jazz-mad Japanese and the more soberly appreciative Negro customers. Nearly all bars and coffee-shops are decorated with palms and tropical plants, goldfish or tropical birds ...' For postwar coffee culture, see also Jean Raspail's satire *Welcome, Honourable Visitors* (Jean Stewart, translator, Hamish Hamilton, 1960), pages 10–11.

12 **That man was rumored to throw out anyone who dared ask for milk or sugar with the holy liquid without warning him first**   Sekiguchi Ichiro, the owner of Café de l'Ambre, was born in 1913. He opened his coffee shop in 1948 using Indonesian beans that had been stored for shipment to Germany before World War Two. Merry White relates the story in the 'Masters of Their Universes: Performing Perfection' chapter of *Coffee Life in Japan.* Sekiguchi, writes White, 'has no compunctions about evicting customers who do not understand or who resist his authority. Sekiguchi serves [his coffee] without accompaniments; if you ask for sugar or milk after you receive the cup you may be denied them or even asked to leave . . . If you had wanted them, you should have asked while ordering, because the coffee is made for drinking a certain way: he would make it stronger or hotter, or with different beans, if sugar or milk were needed. One senses that these additives are actually a test: you shouldn't want them, and the coffee shouldn't need them . . .' (page 71).

Nihonbashi: The Zero Point

13 **Nihonbashi was the zero point**   Theodore C. Bestor, *Tsukiji: The Fish Market at the Center of the World* (University of California Press, 2004), page 98.

15 **like Zen *ensō***   See Audrey Yoshiko Seo's *Ensō: Zen Circles of Enlightenment* (Weatherhill, 2007) and Stephen Addiss' 'The Calligraphic Works of Fukushima Keidō,' in *Zen no Sho: The Calligraphy of Fukushima Keidō Rōshi* (Jason M. Wirth, editor, Clear Light Publishers, 2003). 'There is some debate on

whether *ensō* are paintings or calligraphy. On one hand, they are almost always created by a single calligraphic line, but on the other hand, they do not directly represent a word. Perhaps they form a category of their own' (Stephen Addiss, page 28). See also page 68: 'Its emptiness is the source of fullness: the *ensō* is a common expression of Zen mind, and Zen mind is not just the experience of the fullness of the self's own emptiness, but the emptiness of all things.'

16 **The jail was older than the Tokugawa shogunate and outlasted it too**   Edo's first jail stood nearby in Tokiwabashi; Tokugawa Iemitsu founded it around 1590–92, and then moved it to Kodenmachō at some point between 1596 and 1615. Hiramatsu Yoshirō, 'A History of Penal Institutions: Japan' (*Law in Japan*, volume 6 (1973), pages 1–2).

16 **Judgments were not subject to appeal and death sentences were carried out immediately**   Hiramatsu Yoshirō, 'A History of Penal Institutions: Japan', above, page 3.

16 **One inmate described the prison's atmosphere as 'reminiscent of the Warring States period'**   See Daniel Botsman's excellent but harrowing *Punishment and Power in the Making of Modern Japan* (Princeton, 2007), page 66.

16 **Edo also had two public execution grounds**   Daniel Botsman, *Punishment and Power*, pages 18–19; for the locations of the execution grounds, pages 20–4.

16 **'The creation of a horrifying spectacle was more important**   Daniel Botsman, 'Politics and Power in the Tokugawa Period', in *East Asian History*, #3 (June 1992), page 3. Also,

Punishment and Power, page 19, where Botsman notes: 'If we are to come to a better understanding of Tokugawa society, we must look beyond [its] brutality ... Tokugawa punishments were as much products of peace as of war, and while they could indeed be cruel, they did not take the form of arbitrary or unrestrained violence.'

Botsman also argues: 'There were no prisons in Tokugawa Japan,' but rather only prison-like institutions, because long-term imprisonment was rare, 'used as an official punishment only when there were extenuating circumstances that prevented the application of another penalty' ('Politics and Power' in *East Asian History*, above, page 9, and *Punishment and Power*, page 28).

17 ***kegare*** 'In the medieval period, crime itself was also seen as a form of pollution: criminals were driven out of their communities and their houses burned to the ground not just to punish them but also to purify and cleanse the place that had been sullied by their actions.' (Botsman, *Punishment and Power*, page 23.)

17 **The writer Hasegawa Shigure** See Hasegawa's autobiography: *Hasegawa Shigure sakuhinshū*, Fujiwara Shoten, 2009.

18 **The Golden Light Sutra** See Asuka Sango, *The Halo of Golden Light: Imperial Authority and Buddhist Ritual in Heian Japan* (University of Hawaii Press, 2015).

23 **Everyone always came back** Not quite everyone. The nineteenth-century physician Nakano Chōei bribed a laborer to set fire to one of the prison buildings so that he could

escape Kodenmachō. He eluded arrest for six years before being caught and killed.

23 In a late play about a samurai caught stealing from the shogun's vaults Botsman writes: 'Mokuami set the final scenes of the play [*Shisen ryō koban no ume no wa*, or *Four Thousand Gold Pieces, Like Plum Leaves*] inside the old jail-house, using descriptions from former guards to recreate for the public this previously hidden world' (*Punishment and Power*, page 246 note 17). For a description of the Far Road, see Botsman, *Punishment and Power*, page 66. For *Four Thousand Gold Pieces*, see Mokuami, *Kawatake Mokuami shū* (Tokyo Sōgen Shinsha, 1968).

See also James R. Brandon and Samuel L. Leiter in *Kabuki Plays on Stage: Restoration and Reform, 1872–1905* (University of Hawaii Press, 2003). 'Mokuami was deeply interested in, and very skilled at writing about, people caught up in the stressful life of the times . . . Individual freedom of choice was a new ethical concept learned from the West. Liberal and democratic social structures based on individualism were competing head-on with deeply entrenched feudal ideals that had not disappeared simply because the old political system had been abandoned . . .' (page 20).

Alan Cummings' doctoral thesis, *Kawatake Mokuami and Kabuki Playwriting, 1850–1893* (SOAS, 2010), has a very interesting passage on Mokuami's Edo and its 'romantic unreality': 'thieves speak in stylized verse instead of just picking your pocket' (page 74). Cummings adds: 'Mokuami preserved kabuki's essential escape from reality by creating his own stage version of an alternative Edo. This "other" Edo, while it certainly possessed many restrictive aspects of the real city, crucially allowed for flights of fantasy and wish fulfilment. It is against a recreated map of locations familiar to his audience that Mokuami's heroes are permitted, briefly, to dream of wealth, love and happiness. That these fantastic dreams are invariably shown to be crushed by the force of fate is a telling commentary on the popular bakumatsu [shogunate] mentality' (pages 57–8).

24 **a distorted mirror** Daniel Botsman has an interesting passage about the organization of the prison's inmates as representing in 'microcosm the overall structure of Tokugawa society.' He links the cityscape of Edo and the prison's interior ('Politics and Power', page 15).

24 **an ordinary prisoner who had arrived without money** For what tortures a penniless man might suffer on the Far Road, see Botsman: 'In the winter an inmate might be forced to stand for hours in a bucket of icy water ... or deprived of food and water, or suddenly force-fed with hot peppers or excrement from the latrines. Some inmates were simply beaten to death or smothered in their sleep.' (*Punishment and Power*, page 64.)

The samurai/warrior class were not, however, guaranteed more lenient treatment inside Kodenmachō. Botsman notes that they would instead be 'held to a higher standard of behavior than their social inferiors ... they were also less likely to receive pardons and more likely to be punished severely for relatively minor crimes ...' This punishment differential reflected the fact that 'warrior rule and the privileges that went with it were justified and legitimized in part through the claim that warriors were morally superior.' (*Punishment and Power*, pages 72 and 75.) There were 'special punishments (*junkei*) applied to people according to their social position. There were appropriate *junkei* for *bushi* [warriors], Buddhist priests, commoners and women; members of the [outcast] *hinin* class were subject to an entirely different system of punishment again' ('Politics and Power', page 6).

Asakusa: The Mythic Kantō Plain

31 **Sensō-ji demarked the border between this world and another world** Nam-lin Hur, *Prayer and Play in Late Tokugawa Japan: Asakusa Sensō-ji and Edo Society* (Harvard University Press, 2000), page 90. See also Royall Tyler, 'Buddhism in Noh', *Japanese Journal of Religious Studies* 14/ 1, 1987: 'The margin of water, where human beings suffer from the simultaneous pull of the heights and the depths' (page 27).

32 **It is rare to hear this Law** *The Lotus Sutra*, translated by Burton Watson (Soka Gakkai, 1993). 'We do not know where or when the Lotus Sutra was composed, or in what language', writes Watson in his Introduction. 'We have left the world of factual reality far behind. This is the first point to keep in mind in reading the Lotus Sutra. Its setting, its vast assembly of listeners, its dramatic occurrences in the end belong to a realm that totally transcends our ordinary concepts of time, space, and possibility. Again and again we are told of events that took place countless, indescribable numbers of kalpas or eons in the past, or of beings or worlds that are as numerous as the sands of millions and billions of Ganges rivers. Such "numbers" are in fact no more than pseudo-numbers or non-numbers, intended to impress on us the impossibility of measuring the immeasurable. They

are not meant to convey any statistical data but simply to boggle the mind and jar it loose from its conventional concepts of time and space. For in the realm of Emptiness, time and space as we conceive them are meaningless; anywhere is the same as everywhere, and now, then, never, forever are all one' (page xvi).

See also Royall Tyler, 'Buddhism in Noh', cited above, pages 23–4: 'There was a particularly intimate connection between the *Lotus Sutra* and the spirits of the dead as they hovered about the places where they were bound to earth. The sutra promised release to the lowliest and most lost of beings, and it affirmed at the same time the sanctity of the place where it was spoken . . .'

35 **The melancholy of the entire city flowed beneath that bridge**   Kawabata Yasunari, *The Scarlet Gang of Asakusa*, translated by Alisa Freedman (University of California Press, 2005), page 5.

35 **a village in a landscape empty but for grasses and a labyrinth of rivers**   See David Spafford, *A Sense of Place: The Political Landscape in Late Medieval Japan* (Harvard University Asia Center, 2013). The Kantō region's medieval history (mostly) lacks a clear plot and has neither obvious climax nor charismatic protagonists. The Kantō's political landscape was made up of *points*, not *areas* (pages 263 and 236).

During its medieval wars, the Kantō never had a coherent front line. 'No linear front could form because the lands of the various contenders were thoroughly intertwined . . . Nothing like Hadrian's Wall or the Great Wall of China could be built along the line delimiting a threshold between "us" and "them,"' (page 236). Every journey across the Kantō was a kind of crossing, 'through the lands of followers, allies, collaterals, neutral parties, and occasionally, enemies' (page 233).

For Spafford, the Kantō always 'referred to a space "beyond" rather than a place.' As immortalized in poetry, and in travel writings, it was 'untamed, unsettled, and timelessly peaceful. It was remote, programmatically so, for it was a distant land imagined as beyond the pale of civilization by those aristocrats in Kyoto who had collectively established the rules for writing about the world beyond the capital and its environs' (pages 18–19).

Much of the Kantō remained remote well into the seventeenth century: see the *Musashi Den'enbō*, a record of Tokugawa land surveys on the plain. Many villages were deemed too inaccessible to merit entries; others were so small that they were not recorded. (Kitajima Masamoto, editor, Kondō Shuppansha, 1977.)

For a discussion of modern Tokyo as a city with 'no clear boundaries, no defining walls,' see page 27 of *Tokyo: Form and Spirit* (Walker Art Center, catalogue, 1986).

35 **One medieval traveler, a nun from Kyoto** David Spafford, *A Sense of Place*, pages 39ff. Extracts from *The Diary of a Sarashina Lady*, see Ivan Morris' *As I Crossed A Bridge of Dreams: Recollections of a Woman in Eleventh Century Japan* (Penguin, 1989).

In the Middle Ages, the trope of the wayfarer hemmed in – even submerged – by the grasses, deprived of sight, became ubiquitous in travel literature about Musashino. The desolate landscape, featureless but for its grasses, empty of almost all human presence, was confined to a

curious placelessness, given purchase on the world
beyond the grasses by its poetic status ... (Spafford, *A
Sense of Place*, pages 39ff).

This isolated world survived into the Shōwa Era and beyond:
see Maki Fumihiko's beautiful essay 'My City: The Acquisition
of Mental Landscapes' in his *Nurturing Dreams: Collected
Essays on Architecture and the City* (MIT Press, 2008). 'Unlike
a village, Tokyo was an endless series of overlapping scenes,
and [as a child] I could even imagine a frontier starting just
beyond my vision. It was not so much a physical world as a
world of the imagination, a world that could expand at any
time in new directions. The twisting passageway through a display of figures created out of chrysanthemums, the dim interior
of a German circus tent, the mazelike spaces in a foreign ship
moored in Yamashita Wharf in Yokohama ...' (page 82).

36 **Beauty was first, in the year 628**　Nam-lin Hur's exquisite *Prayer and Play* includes plates depicting the
discovery of Benten's statue (pages 6–7). The object's dimensions are discussed (page 232 note 16), and the account for
how the statues were treated during fires: 'They were trans-
ferred to a boat standing by on the Sumida River. In every
case, the statues contained in the receptacles were placed
intact into a palanquin, and their secrecy was strictly main-
tained' (page 245 note 90).

36 **Tokyo Bay, which then didn't even have a name**　See
Roderick Ike Wilson's 'Placing Edomae: The Changing Environmental Relations of Tokyo's Early Modern Fisheries' for
context (*Resilience: A Journal of the Environmental Humanities*, vol. 3 (2016), pages 242–89).

37 **the thousandth traveler heard a reed flute**   *The Scarlet Gang of Asakusa*, cited above, page 82. Nam-lin Hur, *Prayer and Play*, pages 192–4: 'The people of Edo welcomed ghosts and evil spirits because they embodied the unpredictability of survival. The townspeople were fascinated with the topsy-turvy world of underground creatures and their volatile and violent energies. The fierce-faced deities and evil creatures meant disorder, hallucination, gloom, and indecency: things that slaked the townspeople's thirst for an upside-down society. These creatures gave anger, unhappiness, and frustration a form.'

38 **all the spirits (*kami*) have ascended to heaven; the Buddhas have left for the Western Paradise**   The anonymous author of *An Account of Things Seen and Heard*, published in 1816, quoted in Nam-lin Hur, *Prayer and Play*, page 203.

40 **what the Japanese call a *koffeemaniakku* ('coffee maniac') or coffee *otaku***   Definition taken from Hashimoto Miyuki, 'Visual Kei Otaku Identity – An Intercultural Analysis' (*Intercultural Communication Studies* XVI: 1 (2007), pages 88–9). For the term 'coffee maniac', see Merry White, *Coffee Life in Japan*, cited above: '*koffeemaniakku* – a fetishistic, obsessive, "maniac" eccentric, a dictatorial connoisseur' (page 72).

40 **Japan suddenly became a nation composed entirely of *otaku***   Quote from Jonathan Abel's translation of Azuma Hiroki's *Otaku: Japan's Database Animals* (University of Minnesota Press, 2009). From Abel's Notes, page 117. 'Japan in the 1980s was entirely a fiction. Yet this fiction, while it lasted, was comfortable to dwell in . . . This lightheartedness virtually dis-

appeared in the 1990s, which began with the collapse of the Bubble Economy, and was followed by the Kobe Earthquake, the Aum sarin gas incident, and the emergence of issues like "compensated dating" and the breakdown of classroom order. Yet it would appear that the world of otaku culture is an exception; there the 1980s illusion has remained alive and well' (page 19).

For origins of the word 'otaku' see Hashimoto Miyuki, 'Visual Kei Otaku Identity – An Intercultural Analysis', pages 87–99. Hashimoto tracks the evolution of otaku until it 'is used interchangeably with the word "nerds." ' By 1991, *Basic Knowledge* had amended the definition to be 'a new type of consumer . . . Otaku nowadays not only means just being a fan of cartoons and comics but generally character-ises people who have curious hobbies and indulge in intensive preoccupation with these objects of interest' (page 89). To differentiate between *otaku* and general juvenile culture, there must be, Hashimoto argues, *moe*. Role-playing-game players created this word; *moe* conveys the sexual implications of *otaku*. As a noun, 'it is used to char-acterize the love for a particular cartoon or comic character by emphasizing the idiosyncratic aspects of their appear-ance and behavior, such as glasses, school uniforms and a Lolita way of acting . . .'

41 **I knew someone who studied the effect of caffeine on monkeys** 'Behavioral Dependence on Caffeine and Phency-clidine in Rhesus Monkeys: Interactive Effects' (Carroll, M. E., Hagen, E. W., Asencio, M., and Brauer, L. H. in *Pharmacology, Biochemistry, & Behavior*, December 1988, 31 (4), pages 927–32).

Akasaka: The Invention of Edo

43 **Rat Mountain amazed no one**   Chris Drake translates the monk Gensei's poem; I owe him a great debt for his work.

For the original Japanese, see Toda Mosui's *A Sprig of Purple* (Suzuki Jun, editor, Shinpen Nihon Koten Bungaku Zenshū 82 (Shōgakkan, 2000), page 239).

In his notes on this cryptic poem, Chris Drake writes: **Rat Mountain,** or Bird-Rat Mountain, 'is in Gansu in Weiyuan Province in China. It was famous as a strange place, because rats and birds there lived together in the same holes or lairs. Here the image seems to be of generalized chaotic, pre-civilized existence, similar to the indiscriminate lairs on Rat Mountain.'

Bull king is a 'common epithet of Buddha, suggesting power and invincibility.' A **horned rabbit** is something that doesn't exist: a metaphor, in other words; allegory, fiction, parable.

The reference to a **Buddhist prince** is probably 'Shōtoku (574–622), who was known as Prince of the Stables. One legend claims that he was born in front of a stable. He became a passionate believer in Buddhism, and with his power he firmly established Buddhism in Japan despite opposition from Shinto groups. He himself is said to have written three commentaries on major Buddhist sutras.'

Goat, deer, and ox carts: 'One of three kinds of beautiful carts used as metaphors in Chapter 3 of the *Lotus Sutra*. There a man sees his children playing inside his burning house, which symbolizes existence in the world. His children are interested only in playing with toys, so, in order to lure the children outside to safety, that is, salvation, he promises them three kinds of carts. In the parable, the goat carts are a metaphor for the teachings and actions of the Buddha's original disciples, models who can lead suffering humans toward enlightenment. Gensei may be suggesting that such simple metaphors are no longer needed after Prince Shōtoku established and explained Buddhism in Japan.'

The rooster-man: 'A court official whose job was to call out to tell the court that dawn had come and to inform the court of the passing of the hours.'

Rājagṛha: 'A town in northern India that is a holy site for Buddhists. Here Buddha meditated and gave several important sermons, and after the Buddha's death or Parinirvana, the first Buddhist sutras were edited here.'

Gold Mountain: 'A mountain that appears in Chapter 30 of the *Mahā-prajñāpāramitā Sūtra*, where it is a symbol of learning and virtue. Thus the mountain grows higher and more sublime as people study and practice Buddhism.'

44 **the mathematical concept of chaos**   Yoshimura Hiroshi, *Ō-Edo toki no kane aruki* (Shūnjusha, 2002), page 97.

45 **The words make up a labyrinth, a secret code**   The Zodiac poem was written by a seventeenth-century monk called Gensei. For a useful introduction to his writing, and an explanation of his highly academic *kanbun* style (Chinese poems written by Japanese), see Burton Watson's *Grass Hill: Poems and Prose by the Monk Gensei* (Columbia University Press, 1983). 'Well-educated Japanese in the Tokugawa period ... learned to read and write in classical Chinese, in somewhat the same manner as American and European students during the same period learned Greek and Latin ... Their ability to write poetry in Chinese gave Japanese poets more possibilities for expression than did the thirty-one-syllable Japanese *waka* or *tanka*, and the seventeen-syllable haiku.'

(Thomas J. Rimer and Van C. Gessel, editors, *The Columbia Anthology of Modern Japanese Literature*, volumes 1–2, Columbia University Press, 2005, 2007.)

45 **he was perfectly placed to invent** Toda was the first writer to give Edo its own literary identity. Irreverent, witty, urbane, Toda Mosui is almost unknown in English translation. Jurgis Elisonas' wonderful chapter ('Notorious Places') in *Edo and Paris: Urban Life and State in the Early Modern Era*, James L. McClain, John M. Merriman and Ugawa Kaoru, editors (Cornell University Press, 1997) gives a greatest hits version of *A Sprig of Purple*, Toda's account of Edo in the late seventeenth century. Before Toda, Elisonas writes, Edo was 'written' as a 'sterile landscape.' But with Toda, 'whimsy, not orderly method, dictated the selection of what to discuss' (page 286).

For *A Sprig of Purple*, see Suzuki Jun, editor, *Kinsei zuisō shū*, Shinpen Nihon Koten Bungaku Zenshū 82 (Shōgakkan, 2000), pages 29–242. In classical literature, 'sprig of purple' is a 'metaphor for being "stained with passion." ' (Royall Tyler, *The Ise Stories*, University of Hawaii Press, 2010, page 15 note 1.)

45 **Not a bad name for a writer** Elisonas writes: *Iitsu* is 'the first word of a classical maxim meaning "discarded but not resentful" ' ('Notorious Places', page 285).

46 **Tokyo is a city of darkness, a city of light** 'Culturally, samurai society represented, in Kurimoto Shin'ichiro's words, a "sunshine city" (*hikari no toshi*), where hierarchy, subordination, status, privilege, and orthodox ideology were valued. As far as cultural politics was concerned, the "sunshine city" was supposed to subjugate commoner society.

Over time, however, commoner society gradually evolved in a "shadow city" (*yami no toshi*) with its own autonomy, where liberation, anti-order, cultural expression, individuality, and practical learning were passionately sought.' (Nam-lin Hur, *Prayer and Play*, page 175.) See also Marilyn Ivy, *Discourses of the Vanishing: Modernity, Phantasm, Japan* (University of Chicago Press, 1995), pages 206–7.

47 **Lucky Hole** See the photographer Araki Nobuyoshi's 1990 collection of this name (Tankobon Softcover) and Joan Sinclair's sublime *Pink Box: Inside Japan's Sex Clubs* (Abrams, 2006).

48 **The Japanese language has a modest number of words for the English word penis** This section is taken from Peter Constantine's *Japanese Slang: Uncensored* (Yen Books, 1994). The book should be read as a fantasia of mid-twentieth-century Japanese cinematic vocabulary, rather than as an academic lexicon.

49 **Even if their lives were bound by strict ancient rules** A direct quote from Peter Constantine's *Japanese Slang: Uncensored*, cited above; pages 154, 156 and 164.

49 **The themes change . . . but certain elements remain the same** All information here is condensed from Sarah Chaplin's *Japanese Love Hotels: A Cultural History* (Routledge, 2007). In the love-hotel business, she writes, 'Time is more keenly felt. Partly because all the arrivals and departures, the cleaning and replenishing are performed at accelerated speeds – this despite the perception of the love hotel as a respite from work.' Chaplin's study is more than a schematic map of the

average love hotel; she also considers the philosophical implications of 'the small inner world ... concealed in solid
concrete buildings with a hard-surfaced geometry [that] provides the conditions for moments of silence in which the
individual could recreate himself physically and spiritually'
(page 95). And: 'The emergence of selfhood requires the por-
nographic act' (page 200, note 40).

See *Japanese Love Hotels* page 181 for the love hotel's 'one-
way valve', and pages 185–7 for a hilarious diversion into
bedside reading at these establishments, which include dia-
grams of *kata*: the 'correct' erotic protocols. On page 95,
Chaplin analyzes how the space 'turns inward', and the
importance of threshold depths on page 76. A discussion of
how technology can extend desire (pages 92–4). See page 44
for the zones of unnamed space around love hotels and 24–5
for the love hotel's absence from conventional maps. 'The
lack of cartographic information in the public domain has
not only given rise to love hotel guidebooks, which literally
fill the gap for those wishing to find their location graphic-
ally represented, but more importantly, constructs a kind of
black market social imaginary, in which the only maps which
feature love hotels are mental maps in city dwellers' heads'
(page 25).

Chaplin quotes, however, the novelist Goto Aiko, who
complained:

> Sex was originally something to be done while bathed in
> sunlight in the middle of a field. The need to seek
> stimulation behind closed doors shows how weak people
> have become. Young people don't need stimulations like
> that! Young people should be doing it in the park: it's
> much more pleasant (page 61).

Chaplin's book was published in 2007, so doesn't cover trends like the Love Hotel iPhone app and blogs rating new establishments.

50 **Yoshiwara**   See Angelika Koch-Low's evocative essay in *Kronoscope* (17/1, 2017, pages 61–93): 'Timing the Pleasure Quarters in Early Modern Japan'. Koch-Low notes that in the 1807 book *Elegant Phrases from the Pleasure Quarter for Haikai Poets* (a guide 'to the connoisseur's language of prostitution for aspiring poets'), there was a complete section on words for 'hour'.

See also Joseph De Becker's *The Nightless City: Or, the History of the Yoshiwara Yūkwaku, by an English Student of Sociology* (Z. P. Maruya, 1899). De Becker writes of the old Yoshiwara: 'when one glances down the avenue at night, after the place is lighted up with thousands of brilliantly colored lanterns and flashing electric lamps, the whole quarter appears as if smothered in flowers . . .'

De Becker adds that the Yoshiwara's 'day' was from noon until 3 p.m., and its 'night' from 5 to 10 p.m.: 'Apparently finding that 10 o'clock PM was too early to close up the "shops," some genius hit on the pleasant fiction of causing the watchmen to strike their *hyōshigi* (wooden clappers) announcing the hour as 10 when in reality the temple bell was striking midnight: This originated the terms "real 10 o'clock" and "nominal 10 o'clock . . ."' (*The Nightless City*, pages 287–8).

De Becker further cites the seventeenth-century *Yoshiwara Ō-kagami* (*Mirror of the Yoshiwara*): closing hours were 'fixed at ten o'clock, but afterwards this was considered too early and no clapping of *hyōshigi* . . . was made at that hour. The great gate *Ō-mon* was shut at 10 o'clock but the *kuguri-do* (a small low door cut in a gate) was left so as to permit ingress and egress. When the hour of midnight struck (then called *kokonotsu-doki*) the *hyōshigi* were clapped together four times, and the place was finally closed up' (page 246).

Mejiro: A Failed Coup

55 The city plan of Edo was orientated Naito Akira, *Edo no toshi no kenchiku* ('The Architecture of the City of Edo', Mainichi Shinbunsha, 1972), pages 16–19. Quoted in 'Metaphors of the Metropolis: Architectural and Artistic Representations of the Identity of Edo', in *Japanese Capitals in Historical Perspective: Place, Power & Memory in Kyoto, Edo and Tokyo* (Nicolas Fiévé and Paul Waley, editors, RoutledgeCurzon, 2003), page 130.

57 By the steps before the old gate stood Fudō: He Who Shall Not Be Moved, most powerful of the Wisdom Kings Fudō's name literally means 'the immovable'. He is the 'central and paramount figure in the group of divinities known as the Godai Myōō, or Five Great Bright Kings, who in esoteric Buddhism stand as emanations or modes of activity of the Buddha. Where the Buddha exists static and immovable, withdrawn from activity, the five Myōō act as his agents and messengers . . . Fudō's right hand grasps a sword and his left a rope, and he stands not on a lotus or an animal mount as do many Buddhist deities, but on an immovable rock, which rises sometimes from curling waves. Always he is ringed with fire . . . This is the deity whom the great majority of ascetics look upon as their guardian, who appears to them in dreams, who directs their austerities, who endues them with vitality and confers upon them their powers.' (Carmen Blacker, *The Catalpa Bow*, Routledge, 1999, pages 175–6.) See also Mareile Flitsch's *Tokens of the Path: Japanese Devotional and Pilgrimage Images: The Wilfried Spinner Collection* (Arnoldsche Art Publishers, 2014). 'He has a muddy green-blue color, which is said to have been adopted while wading through the "swamp" of worldliness . . .' (page 152).

57 **See No Evil. Hear No Evil. Speak No Evil** Lafcadio Hearn wrote: 'Kōshin, Lord of Roads, is indeed yet with us; but he has changed his name and become a Shinto deity; he is now Saruda-hiko-no-mikoto; and his presence is revealed only by the statues of the Three Mystic Apes which are his servants – Mizaru, who sees no evil, covering his eyes with his hands, Kikazaru, who hears no evil, covering his ears with his hands, Iwazaru, who speaks no evil, covering his mouth with his hands.' (*Lafcadio Hearn, Japan's Great Interpreter: A New Anthology of His Writings: 1894–1904*, Louis Allen and Jean Wilson, editors, Japan Library, 1992, page 133.)

Figurines and charms featuring the Mystic Apes are still sold 'in the belief that they will maintain the buyer's health: if one does not see, hear, or speak about the weaknesses of others and evil in the world, one can maintain both peace of mind and physical health.' Writing in the late 1980s, Emiko Ohnuki-Tierney claimed 'a charred monkey's head, pounded into powder, is taken as medicine for illnesses of the brain, including mental illnesses, mental retardation, and head-aches, although this particular use was, no doubt, far more prevalent in the past.' (*The Monkey as Mirror: Symbolic Transformations in Japanese History and Ritual*, Princeton University Press, 1987, pages 50 and 69.)

57 **the rebel samurai Marubashi Chūya** For *Keian Taiheiki*, see Mokuami's collected works, *Kawatake Mokuami shū* (Tokyo Sōgen Shinsha, 1968). In this play, the Bell of Time is almost a character in its own right.

For furtive dissemination of the story under the Tokugawa shoguns, see Peter Kornicki, 'Manuscript, Not Print: Scribal Culture in the Edo Period' (*Journal of Japanese Studies*, 32:1 (2006)), pages 41–3: 'The threat to the *bakufu* [Tokugawa shogunate] had been real, and the reverberations lasted some years.' So long as the Tokugawa were in power, the story of Marubashi's attempted coup could circulate only in handwritten manuscripts later discovered throughout the Japanese peninsula. 'The successful transmission of this text shows that the story had an abiding appeal,' Kornicki writes. 'As soon as there was no longer anything to prevent publication, numerous printed editions appeared from the early Meiji era onward.'

58 **the citadel was clad in gleaming white tiles made of lead. It was 'delicately sculpturesque in appearance . . .** William H. Coaldrake's *Architecture and Authority in Japan* (Routledge, 1996), pages 134ff. Coaldrake discusses the three castle towers (*tenshu*) built during the seventeenth century, 'each representing a separate era in the creation and consolidation of authority . . . Each castle was an expression of a particular moment within a period of rule by control of the built as well as the political environment. Each castle, too, was a direct index to the political circumstances of its time . . . and was destroyed once those circumstances had changed . . .' (page 137).

For descriptions of Edo Castle, see Henry Smith II's articles, especially 'Tokyo and London: Comparative Conceptions of the City' in Albert M. Craig, editor, *Japan: A Comparative*

View (Princeton University Press, 1979). Smith's Columbia University webpage includes pdf links for all his publications, which is useful because print copies are rare. Henry Smith II's 'World Without Walls' and Naito Akira's *Edo, The City That Became Tokyo: An Illustrated History* (H. Mack Horton, translator, Kodansha International, 2003), especially pages 34–63, are excellent accounts of a place that is known primarily through inconsistent renderings on a six-panel screen painted about fifty years after the citadel burned in the Meireki fire of 1657. Also, Morton S. Schmorleitz's *Castles in Japan* (Tuttle, 1974).

Smith writes that Edo was built according to the highly *centered* design of ancient Chinese cities like Ch'ang-an: 'reaching out through axial roads and gates to the entire empire, and upward through a hierarchical series of enclosures to the imperial palace, the point of contact with Heaven. The entire city was an expression of the power and cosmology of the imperial order, perhaps the purest example of princely urbanity the world has ever known.'

Edo itself, however, was constructed '*not* as a national capital, but merely as the private castle town of a powerful feudal lord. It was not until Ieyasu's emergence as national hegemon after 1600 and the gradual institution of the *sankin kotai* system, by which provincial lords (daimyo) were required to spend alternate years in residence in Edo, that the city took on a truly national character. And even then, it was never the *miyako*: that ancient courtly concept remained with Kyoto, where the politically impotent emperor and imperial courtiers continued to reside . . .

'Militarily, the concern was not for the defence of the city as a whole, much less for that of the nation, but purely for the security of the shogun and his immediate retainers. There was no enclosing wall around the city, which blended impercept-ibly with the countryside, but merely around the shogunal castle, which sat in the centre . . .

'Edo shared with the Chinese city the character of "planned ephemerality" through construction in short-lived materials, and when the donjon was destroyed in the Meireki fire less than two decades later, it was never rebuilt. In time, the many trees in and around Edo Castle came to lend it a hidden and private aspect.' 'Tokyo and London: Comparative Concep-tions of the City', page 64.

58 **And a clock room, which set the official time for the entire city** Tsukuda Taisaburō, *Wadokei* (Tōhō shoin, 1960), pages 24–34, especially 33–4. Also Dylan McGee, 'Turrets of Time: Clocks and Early Configurations of Chronometric Time in Edo Fiction (1780–96)' (*Early Modern Japan: An Interdiscip-linary Journal*, volume 19 (2011), pages 44–57):

By the middle of the eighteenth century, Edo Castle had become a veritable bastion of punctuality. Major functions of the castle, such as the opening of the gates at six o'clock in the morning, the call to the *daimyō* to enter the castle at four o'clock in the morning, and the closing of the gates at six in the evening, were conducted in time with a large clock housed in the *tokei no ma*, (土圭の間), or the clock chamber. Accuracy was safeguarded through the marshalling of numerous auxiliary clocks throughout the castle and various back-up methods of keeping time, like candles and incense . . .

Within the castle, there developed a sophisticated – and indeed, labour-intensive – system of time notification whereby staff would sound drums at various points throughout the castle to notify inhabitants and *daimyō* living nearby of important times. All in all, the Tokugawa fascination with clocks may be characterized as a concerted effort to calibrate shogunal rule, with mechanical precision, to the rhythms of the cosmos. This enthusiastic adoption of technology was not without its drawbacks, however. In fact, the costs of procuring and maintaining the clocks, not to mention employing qualified staff to attend to these matters, placed a great strain on resources.

In 1701, fifty employees who attended to the clocks in the *tokei no ma* were dismissed, 'in an effort to reduce the castle's operating budget' ('Turrets of Time', pages 47–8).

58 The castle evolved in a whirlpool design 'Apart from the castle, Edo was laid out in a highly defensive manner, not from concern with external invaders, as in most cities, but rather with an eye to internal threats either from the resident *daimyō* or from commoner mobs. The principle was one of strict segregation of classes by residential area. The overall form of Edo was therefore not an ideal geometrical form with cosmic referents, but rather an irregular spiral leading clockwise outward from the castle in a pattern of descent down through the social ladder, passing through the residences of the great lords, into the area occupied by the *hatamoto* retainers of the shogun, finally through the central area of the *machi-chi* at Nihonbashi, and out the Tokaido which served as the main approach to the city . . .' (Henry Smith II, 'Tokyo and London', pages 65–6). See also Roman Cybriwsky, *Tokyo: The Shogun's City at the Twenty-First Century* (John Wiley, 1998), page 53.

59 Beyond the citadel, Edo itself was also laid out to confound invaders

This spiral, which seems to have been unique to Edo and was probably not an intellectually conceived design, was defined not by roads but by the wide moats and canals which served for defence and as the primary means of the transport of goods in the city. Defence planning was carried out within each of the residential areas as well. The commoner *machi-chi* was laid out . . . in a regular grid plan with barriers at every major intersection for close and efficient control. In the samurai *buke-chi* as well, barriers and checkpoints were frequent, with most streets intersecting in T's rather than in crosses so as to deny through access to any rebellious forces. This remains true of Tokyo today; one ambitious urban geographer has counted all of Tokyo's street intersections (total 155,767) and found that there are twice as many T-intersections as crossroads . . .

(See Henry Smith II in 'Tokyo and London', page 66 note 28.)

59 his life was preserved so he could be tortured and crucified

In *Punishment and Power in the Making of Modern Japan* (Princeton University Press, 2007), Botsman writes:

Punishments such as crucifixions and burning at the stake formed an extension of the system of signs, for although the executions themselves were not generally conducted in front of large crowds, the results, in the form of mutilated corpses strung up on crosses and stakes, were left on display for all to see. Next to these bodies-as-signs were conventional signposts that used the written word to make known the identity of the executed person, the offense committed, and the punishment that had been carried out . . .

One important corollary of this approach was that creating a horrifying spectacle (a memorable sign) was just as important as inflicting pain on the individual being executed – consequently, death was no limit to punishment. When a person who had been sentenced to crucifixion died before the punishment could be carried out, for example, the dead body was often pickled in salt and then crucified as if he or she was still alive . . . Death did not mark the end of the punishment, [which only ended with] a grotesque stump of humanity for the explicit purpose of display (pages 19–20).

59 **It was never rebuilt**   See Coaldrake, *Architecture and Authority*, page 137. 'The shogunate flirted briefly, once more, with the idea of rebuilding the tenshu in the reign of Ienobu (1709–1713). Once the projected cost had been ascertained, the idea progressed as far as the drawing up of detailed plans but the construction process was soon abandoned. The tenshu had become a political anachronism.'

60 *keigo*, **the formal Japanese used for extremely import-ant people**   My favorite account of *keigo* gone wrong appears in Donald Richie's *Japanese Portraits: Pictures of Different People* (Tuttle, 2006), and his description of a TV interview with one of his idols, the actress Yamada Isuzu, who played Lady Macbeth in Kurosawa's *Throne of Blood*.

62 **The Kanda River flowed past** See Youtube for versions of this song. 1970s nostalgia.

Nezu: Tokugawa Timepieces

65 **Those who watched never knew exactly how the clock's pieces worked** Timon Screech, 'Clock Metaphors in Edo Period Japan' (*Japan Quarterly*, 43.4 (Oct.–Dec. 1996), page 66).

The most common word for 'time' in modern Japanese (*jikan* 時間) first appeared in a late-nineteenth-century elementary school reader. The first character *jikan* has two elements: the left part signifies the sun, and the right part the temple. The character originally meant 'to change', and originally referred to the cycle of seasons. The concepts of minute and second were only introduced in the early nineteenth century, with the translations of Western books on astronomy. (Nishimoto Ikuko, 'The "Civilization" of Time', *Time & Society*, volume 6 #2–3 (July 1997), pages 237–59.)

A Japanese dictionary has claimed that the character 時 ji in *jikan* (which can also be pronounced '*toki*') derives 'perhaps from the very old Japanese verb toku, "to melt" or "to dissolve"'. (Ono Suzumi, *Nihongo o sakanoboru* (*Tracing the Origins of the Japanese Language*) (Iwanami Shisho, 1974), Chapter 2; quoted in Gunter Nitschke, *From Shinto to Ando: Studies in Architectural Anthropology in Japan* (John Wiley & Sons, 1993), page 53 note 9.)

For the hours, see Yulia Frumer's *Making Time: Astronomical Time Measurement in Tokugawa Japan* (University of Chicago Press, 2018). 'For most of the Tokugawa period 時 *(toki/ ji)*, 刻 (koku), 尅 *(toki, koku)*, and 辰 *(toki/ koku, shin)* were used interchangeably. A separate system was sometimes used for the nighttime hours, in which they were referred to as *kō* (更), and each *kō* was divided into five equal *ten* (点). Bell keepers would have a special conversion table that showed them at what hour (時) the beginning of each *kō* should be marked' (page 220 note 1).

The British diplomat Ernest Satow noted that in late-nineteenth-century Tokyo, when he first arrived, 'neither clocks nor punctuality were common. If you were invited for two o'clock, you most often went at one or three, or perhaps later. In fact, as the Japanese hour altered in length every fortnight, it was difficult to be certain about the time of day, except at sunrise, noon, sunset, and midnight . . .' (*A Diplomat in Japan*, Cambridge University Press, 2015), page 229.)

66 Then, in 1872, the Emperor Meiji abolished the old clock   See Donald Keene's *Emperor Meiji and His World, 1852–1912* (Columbia University Press, 2005), especially page 221: 'On December 10, the ceremony of changing the calendar was performed preparatory to adopting the solar in place of the lunar calendar. At ten that morning, after worshiping the Ise Shrine from afar, the emperor announced that the third day of the twelfth month would be January 1, 1873. The emperor reported this change to the spirits of his ancestors.'

The emperor then set out reasons for the change in an imperial rescript:

> First, the emperor mentioned the inconvenience of the
> lunar calendar, which required the insertion every two or
> three years of an intercalary month in order to match the
> solar year. The solar calendar was far more accurate,
> requiring only one extra day every four years; it would

not be off by a single day for 7,000 years. The emperor
decided to adopt the solar calendar because of its
superior accuracy.

But the emperor did not mention, Keene notes, what may
have been the chief reason for adopting the solar calendar. 'If
the lunar calendar were followed, it would become necessary
to pay salaries thirteen times every time a year had an interca-
lary month – obviously undesirable to any government.'

66 ***Nothing is the way it should be***   Direct quote from Stefan Tanaka's lyrical account of timekeeping after the Tokugawa
shogunate fell, when the solar calendar was introduced: *New
Times in Modern Japan* (Princeton University Press, 2004).
Tanaka quotes a newspaper article published just a few days
after the old timekeeping systems were abandoned in the early
Meiji era: 'Will one not lose reality when the moon is rising at
the end of the month?' And: 'Why did the government suddenly decide to abolish it? The whole thing is disagreeable.
The old system fitted in with the seasons, the weather, and the
movement of the tides. One could plan one's work or one's
clothing or virtually anything else by it. Since the revision . . .
nothing is the way it should be.' (*Ogawa Tameji, Kaika Mondō*
('Questions & Answers on Civilization & Enlightenment'),
quoted by Tanaka in *New Times*, pages 7–8.)

The new calendar, Tanaka concludes, fitted a political
rhetoric, 'that of legitimizing the new regime as compared to
the previous, Tokugawa rule. The message transmitted by
the solar calendar was that the lunar calendar, which had
guided people, was arbitrary, connected to ignorance and
backwardness, and an impediment to the achievement of
wisdom.' However, as Donald Keene notes in his biography

of the Emperor Meiji (cited below), although officially abolished, the lunar calendar was and still is used for religious ceremonies.

The new calendar was taken from the British naval almanac. See Jessica Kennett Cork's MA thesis, *The Lunisolar Calendar: A Sociology of Japanese Time* (University of Sheffield, 2010), pages 49ff. Cork cites Watanabe Toshio's *Nihon no Koyomi*: this first calendar had a preface that explained the differences between the old and the new methods of calculating time. But because of 'very complex terminology ("equatorial latitude" and "apparent radius of the sun")' the preface and calendar were 'utterly incomprehensible to the average user.'

Dylan McGee's 'Turrets of Time', cited above, provides a good survey of the literature, with fine illustrations. Cecilia Segawa Seigle's *A Courtesan's Day: Hour by Hour* (Hotei, 2004) sets out what time meant, and how it was measured, for those who lived in the Yoshiwara, Edo's brothel district. See also Nishimoto Ikuko's 'Teaching Punctuality: Inside and Outside the Primary School' (*Japan Review*, 14 (2002), pages 121–33).

For the *wadokei* themselves, see N. H. N. Mody's *Japanese Clocks* (Kegan Paul, Trench, Trubner, 1967) a photographic record of Mody's vast collection of timepieces, bought with the proceeds from his family's opium business. Also J. Drummond Robertson, *The Evolution of Clockwork: With a Special Section on the Clocks of Japan* (Cassell, 1931).

67 **There were riots over the changes**   See Jessica Kennett Cork's *The Lunisolar Calendar*, page 57: 'Rioters in Fukui, Tottori, Kyoto, and Fukuoka prefectures listed the reinstatement of the lunisolar calendar as one of their demands.' Cork is

quoting Okada Yoshirō's *Meiji Kaireki: 'toki' no bunmei kaika* (*Meiji Calendar Reform: The Cultural Enlightenment of 'Time'*) (Taishūkan Shoten, 1994), pages 244–5.

67 **an island of old clocks**   See Yulia Frumer's *Making Time* for the different characters once used to write the word 'clock', words associated with shadows and stars. 'The modern-day characters for this word are 時計, meaning "time/hour" and "gauge/measure." ' Before the twentieth century, however, 時計 was just one of the possible ways to write the word *tokei*. 'Other character combinations reveal associations with numerous non-mechanical means of gauging the passage of time. Examining Tokugawa-period sources, one sees combinations such as 土景 – "earth-shadow," – 斗計 "measuring the Big Dipper," and 土卦 "earth trigram"' (*Making Time*, page 40).

69 **On old Japanese clocks the hours were counted backwards**   See Kenneth Ullyett, *In Quest of Clocks* (Littlehampton Book Service, 1950), page 235.

69 **The clocks have no number greater than nine**   See Jessica Kennett Cork, cited above, page 38: 'The bells rang nine times each at midnight and noon, as nine is the epitome of the yang essence, then eight times during the following dual-hour, then seven, then on down to four, after which the cycle was repeated.' Cork cites Nagata Hisashi, *Nenjū gyōji o 'kagaku' suru: koyomi no naka bunka to chie* ('Making Annual Events "Scientific": Culture and Knowledge in Calendars') (Nihon Keizai Shinbunsha, 1989), page 179, and Akio Gotō, 'Jikokuhō' ('Time-Keeping Methods'), in *Koyomi o shiru jiten*, Okada Yoshirō et al., editors (Tōkyōdō Shuppan, 2006), page 174.

See also Yulia Frumer's *Making Time*: 'Wondering, "Why do we count the hours the way we do?" several early eighteenth-century [Tokugawa] scholars investigated classical Chinese texts, and concluded that the origins of this double sequence could be found in the ancient Classic of Changes (the Yi Jing). They came to believe that the system was supposed to represent correspondences between the twelve hours, the twelve months, and the annual cycle of birth and decay . . .' (pages 20–1 and 193).

71 ***we humans are slaves*** These extracts come from Guro's biographical sketch, courtesy of the Daimyo Dokei Museum in Yanaka. In Japanese.

72 **The Myriad Year Clock** See 'A Close Relationship between Japanese Art and Science with Roots in the Edo Period: Exploring the Man-nen Dokei, Western Timekeeping and the Japanese Flow of Time', exhibition catalogue, Toshiba International Foundation, 2014. This printing includes an excellent diagram of the clock's inner workings.

See also Yulia Frumer's *Making Time* for an analysis of the clock as representing 'the optimistic – and somewhat naïve – belief that there could and should be a universal device that would keep time correctly for eternity' (pages 169–74).

76 **pendulum and cogs and escapement wheels** See Yulia Frumer's *Making Time* for the enchanting technical vocabulary of clockmaking: the 'snowflake' gear (a six-toothed gear regulating the alarm's strikes), the 'sumo referee' gear (the clock's crown wheel), and the foliot, which was called the 'Seat of Heavens' (pages 41 and 223, notes 10–15).

Ueno: The Last Shogun

81 **The Flower Ornament Scripture** Translation of the *Avatamsaka Sutra* – page 66. Thomas Cleary, translator (Shambhala Press, 1993), page 1498.

84 **When the shogunate collapsed, samurai rallied first in Asakusa** See Conrad Totman's *The Collapse of the Tokugawa Bakufu, 1862–1868* (University of Hawii Press, 1980). 'During those days of disaster, Edo leaders proceeded unaware of the tumultuous events occurring to the west . . . The regime died in battle before its leaders at Edo even knew the question of life and death had at last been confronted . . . As the defeated army straggled into town, hospital facilities filled with wounded and sick survivors, and infantrymen and others fresh out of employment began to plunder and cause trouble' (pages 437ff.).

Katsu Kaishū planned to burn Edo, block by block, if his negotiations with the emperor's generals failed. (See Katsu's diaries, *KKZ* xi 358–9, Kodansha, 1982.) The best account of the *shōgitai* and their last stand comes in Yoshimura Akira's *Tengu sōran; shōgitai; bakufu gunkan kaiten shimatsu* (Iwanami Shoten, 2009), taken from the memoirs of the young monk who accompanied the abbot as he fled the burning temples.

My sources here are M. William Steele, 'Against the Restoration: Katsu Kaishū's Attempt to Reinstate the Tokugawa Family', *Monumenta Nipponica*, volume 36 #3 (Autumn 1981), pages 299–316. By the same author, 'Katsu Kaishū and the Limits of Bakumatsu Nationalism', in *Asian Cultural Studies* #10 (1978), pages 65–76. See also Mark Ravina's *The Last Samurai: The Life and Battles of Saigō*

Takamori (John Wiley and Sons, 2004), especially chapter five, 'To Tear Asunder the Clouds'. For a technical description of Edo Castle's surrender, see Haraguchi Kiyoshi, *Meiji Zenki Chihō Seiji-shi Kenkyū* (Hanawa shōbo, 1972). Also, Najita Tetsuo and J. Victor Koschmann, editors, *Conflict in Modern Japanese History: The Neglected Tradition* (Cornell University Press, 2005).

For Tokugawa Yoshinobu's departure from Edo, Shiba Ryōtarō's *The Last Shogun: The Life of Tokugawa Yoshinobu* (Juliet Winters Carpenter, translator, Kodansha, 1967) is a readable, though hardly rigorous, account. In *The Tokugawa Inheritance* (International House of Japan, 2009), Tokugawa Tsunenari describes how his branch of the Tokugawa family acclimated to politics in the twentieth century. The book is his attempt to rehabilitate the shogunal legacy. Takie Sugiyama Lebra's *Above the Clouds: Status Culture of the Modern Japanese Nobility* (University of California Press, 1993) is an anthropological survey of Japan's aristocrats and their vanishing culture.

After Tokugawa Yoshinobu left Edo, Henry Smith II estimated that the city's population (which he calculates to have been more than a million) dropped by half over the next seven years ('The Edo–Tokyo Transition' in Marius Jansen and Gilbert Rozman, editors, *Japan in Transition: From Tokugawa to Meiji*, Princeton University Press, 1986, page 347).

The policymakers of early Meiji even considered abandoning the city. According to the *Japan Times' Overland Mail*, on 5 September 1868: 'The mint and arsenal have both been transported to Osaka, the greater part of the palaces of the daimyo are dismantled, the hinges and heavy bronze ornaments torn off the doors, and in many cases the inner houses pulled down and their stone and timber sold to builders. A landslip has occurred at an important point in the second wall of the castle, where a breach now of some forty or fifty rods in width, the *debris* from which has fallen down and shallowed the moat. No attempt is being made to repair this . . .' (from M. William Steele, 'Edo in 1868: The View From Below' in *Monumenta Nipponica* 45:2, page 148).

See also J. H. Gubbins' *The Progress of Japan: 1853–1871* (Clarendon Press, 1911): 'In the twinkling of an eye, the flourishing city of Edo became like a desert . . . And so the prestige of the Tokugawa family, which had endured for three hundred years . . . fell to ruin in the space of one morning' (page 142).

86 **An English newspaper reported**   The *London and China Telegraph*, 7 September 1868.

86 **Edo was now Tokyo**   'A sense of the transition is also manifested in the way in which the city was named. In the period approximately between 1868 and 1889, the same Chinese characters which today are pronounced "Tokyo" were read "Tokei." The city was no longer Edo but not quite Tokyo yet' (Iwatake Mikako, 'From a Shogunal City to a Life City: Tokyo Between Two Fin-de-Siècles', in *Japanese Capitals in Historical Perspective: Place, Power and Memory in Kyoto, Edo and Tokyo*, Nicolas Fiévé and Paul Waley, editors, RoutledgeCurzon, 2003, page 253 note 3).

See also Henry Smith II, commenting on the proposed imperialist name 'Teito' as a 'pretentious sinicism . . . Visually, Tokyo never lived up to the grand ring of Teito' ('Tokyo and London: Comparative Conceptions of the City', in *Japan: A Comparative View*, Albert M. Craig, editor, Princeton University Press, 1979).

88 A single atom   *The Flower Ornament Scripture: Translation of the Avatamsaka Sutra*, cited above, pages 783 and 796.

90 Tsuno Daishi   'His power was legendary and he was venerated for his mastery of exorcism during his lifetime. The belief surrounding his ability to dispel evil gained cult status after his death. According to one myth, a plague once haunted the temple where the monk resided. He fought the affliction by changing into the shape of a powerful demon and requested that his demonic form be painted and kept for future generations in order to be able to dispel the plague should it haunt anyone again …' See Mareile Flitsch, editor, *Tokens of the Path: Japanese Devotional and Pilgrimage Images: The Wilfried Spinner Collection (1854–1918)* (Arnoldsche Art Publishers, 2014), pages 86–7.

90 One sounded a note of rest   On the three bells, see S. Katsumata, *Gleams from Japan* (Routledge, 2011), page 342. Katsumata (a pseudonym) is quoting from Yoshida Kenkō's thirteenth-century text, *Essays in Idleness*. (See Meredith McKinney's translation (Penguin Classics, 2013), pages 127–8 and page 182 notes 388–9.) 'A temple bell should be pitched to the *ōshiki*, a tone that resonates with a sense of impermanence or *mujō*.' McKinney notes that the *ōshiki* mode or scale is 'roughly equivalent to the C minor scale of Western music.'

See also Katsumata's note on how a bell's sound 'does not remain uniform throughout the four seasons: it is modified by atmospheric conditions and the density of the bell itself. To hear bells at their best … it is important to know the right time and place …' (page 335).

90 **rough** *ishigaki* **stone walls** See the Japanese Architecture and Art website JAANUS for a discussion of these dry stone walls, their properties and uses. Stones were often named according to their shapes ('chestnut') or the way they were cut ('tortoiseshell').

92 **Tsunayoshi's . . . 'Laws of Compassion'** In *The Dog Shogun: The Personality and Policies of Tokugawa Tsunayoshi*, Beatrice Bodart-Bailey argues, 'The issue at stake was not the protection of dogs. Like all other policies differentiating Tsunayoshi's government from those before and after him, the issue was the prerogatives of the samurai. Did the samurai have the right to set free unwanted dogs outside their walled compounds and let them hunt for food in areas of the city where commoners lived in cramped quarters, without the protection of such walls?' (University of Hawaii Press, 2006, page 153).

92 **Ueno should be one of the most attractive places in the city** From Paul Waley's classic *Tokyo Now & Then: An Explorer's Guide* (John Weatherhill, 1984), page 159.

Ishikawa Jun's short story, translated by William Tyler, appears in *Modern Japanese Literature* volume 2 (Columbia University Press, 2007; J. Thomas Rimer and Van C. Gessel, editors), pages 149–167.

For a comic description of the transformation of Ueno, see Thomas Raucat's *The Honorable Picnic* (Bodley Head, 1928): 'Tokio, Saturday, June 10, 1922, three o'clock in the afternoon. After the torrential downpour of the night, an ardent sun is blazing. In the public park of Ueno the Universal Peace Exposition hums its merriest. A multicolored crowd throngs about strange edifices which combine all styles of architecture and house the most diverse wares. But for the public, the chief attraction is to be found on the pond of Ueno. Last summer this was still a tranquil marsh covered with pale pink lotuses. On an island stood a little hushed temple. Today the pond is cut in two by a great concrete bridge. Jets of water spurt from the lake and at night the lanterns shine into its depths. All day long two noisy machines go spluttering back and forth across it while the crowd stares in amazement; these are the hydroplanes . . .'

96 **I met a man who recites medieval Buddhist sermons** See Matsuda Norio's Youtube pages for his performances, which include the passages 'There is a green willow tree' and 'The wind from Heaven . . .'

97 **Yamamoto's mother, who rang Ueno's Bell of Time** For women who rang bells, see *Gleams from Japan*, S. Katsumata, page 341: 'In 1921, a "Correct Time" propaganda was carried out in Japan under the sponsorship of the Education Department, and some eighty bell-ringers were rewarded for their long and faithful service. The recipients . . . included two women, one of whom was named Matsu Obata, aged 82. For fifty years she had struck the bell twenty-four times a day, and she had been admired for her accuracy in the execution of her duty, one requiring a great deal of watchfulness . . .'

98 **How can you tell when it's time to ring the bell?** J. J. Hoffmann, *Japanische Sprachlehre* (Leiden, 1877): 'The practice at Yedo was: first a single stroke given to the bell, then at an interval of about a minute a second blow, followed quickly by a third. There was then another long pause, and finally the

number of strokes corresponding with the hour was sounded, with an interval of about ten seconds between each stroke, except the last two, the final stroke following rapidly, to indicate the full number was completed.' Quoted in J. Robertson, *The Evolution of Clockwork*, page 200 note 1.

For an earlier outsider's account of one Bell of Time, see Yulia Frumer's *Making Time*, which cites a nineteenth-century Russian captain: 'First they strike the bell once, then after about a minute and a half they strike twice, one strike right after the other; those three strikes announce that the hours are about to be struck, as if they were saying: listen! Then, after another minute and a half, they start to strike the hours, strike after strike in intervals of some fifteen seconds, but the last two they strike quickly one after the other, as if to indicate: enough counting!' (page 33).

100 **An Austrian institute had just tested for radioactive particles** The Central Institute for Meteorology and Geodynamics in *New Scientist*, 24 March 2011.

100 **The foreign newspapers were full of horror stories** For a lyrical evocation of the post-Fukushima atmosphere of anxiety, see Andrew Fitzsimons' collection of haiku: *A Fire in the Head* (Isobar Press, 2014). Also Richard Lloyd Parry's 'Ghosts of the Tsunami' in *London Review of Books*, 6 February 2014.

For a visual evocation, see *In the Wake: Japanese Photographers Respond to 3/11*, Anne E. Havinga and Anne Nishimura Morse, curators, Museum of Fine Arts (Boston, 2015).

The Rokumeikan: The Meiji Restoration

103 **The Japanese have their eyes fixed on the future**   Erwin Bälz, *Awakening Japan: the Diary of a German Doctor*, Toku Baelz, editor; Eden and Cedar Paul, translators (Indiana University Press, 1974), page 17. Quoted in George Macklin Wilson, 'Time and History in Japan', *American Historical Review* 85 #3 (1980), page 570. Bälz may have misunderstood his interlocutor's meaning.

104 **'Do nothing to make the foreigners laugh at us.'**   Ellen P. Conant, *Challenging Past and Present: The Metamorphosis of Nineteenth-Century Japanese Art* (University of Hawaii Press, 2006), page 231.

105 **The deer call to one another**   This translation of Ode 183 is by the nineteenth-century Scottish missionary James Legge (*The Chinese Classics: with a Translation, Critical & Exegetical Notes, Prolegomena & Copious Indexes*, volume 4, Oxford University Press, 1893–5, page 246). For radically different versions of the same poem, see Arthur Waley ('Yu, yu, cry the deer/ nibbling the black southernwood . . .') and Ezra Pound (' "Salt/ lick!" Deer on waste sing . . .').

106 **Mishima's play *Rokumeikan***   In *My Friend Hitler and Other Plays* (Columbia University Press, 2002), Sato Hiroaki translates.

Perhaps the best description of the Rokumeikan building itself is Dallas Finn's. 'A lighthearted structure that bears a lot of weight,' the Rokumeikan became 'the scarlet woman of Meiji architecture: ambiguous and glamorous . . . The lost structure has become a legend.' (*Meiji Revisited: The Sites of Victorian Japan*, Weatherhill, 1995, pages 95–6.)

Pat Barr sets the building in its cultural context: *The Deer Cry Pavilion: A Story of Westerners in Japan 1868–1905* (Penguin, 1988). For the structure itself, see Ellen Conant's *Challenging Past and Present*. For the European reaction to Japan's Palladian villa on the Pacific, see Christopher Reed's translation, *The Pink Notebooks of Madame Chrysanthème and Other Documents of French Japonisme* (University of Hawaii Press, 2010). For the Japanese response to Pierre Loti (the author of *Madame Chrysanthème*), see Akutagawa Ryūnosuke's short story 'The Ball', and David Rosenfeld's 'Counter-Orientalism and Textual Play in Akutagawa's "The Ball",' *Japan Forum*, volume 12 #1 (2000), pages 53–63.

107 **the direct equation between Tokugawa rule and the order of the universe**   Quote from Naito Akira in William Coaldrake's essay, 'Metaphors of the Metropolis', in *Japanese Capitals in Historical Perspective: Place, Power and Memory in Kyoto, Edo and Tokyo* (Nicolas Fiévé and Paul Waley, editors, RoutledgeCurzon, 2003), pages 130–1. See also Coaldrake's *Architecture and Authority in Japan* Routledge, 1996), page 137: 'The castle was far more than the result of technological determinism: it stood on the boundary of the secular and the sacred, expressing the aspirations toward the eternal and the divine of those who were so bold as to reach towards the heavens with their earthly abodes.'

For changes the first Tokugawa shogun made to Edo and its landscape of mountains, hills, and rivers, see A. L. Sadler's classic *The Maker of Modern Japan: The Life of Shogun Tokugawa Ieyasu* (Tuttle, 1978), especially pages 163–75 (which describe Edo as the tiny village that Tokugawa Ieyasu was granted in 1590), and pages 224–32 (which give an overview of the changes Ieyasu made to the landscape). And Roman Cybriwsky's *Tokyo: The Shogun's City at the Twenty-First Century* (John Wiley, 1998), page 53.

109 **Boshin War** 'The surrender of Edo castle concluded the first phase of what Japanese historians call the Boshin War: *bo* (earth) and *shin* (dragon) were the Chinese zodiac signs for the year 1868', Mark Ravina, *The Last Samurai: The Life and Battles of Saigō Takamori* (John Wiley & Sons, 2004), page 157.

Tsukiji: The Japanese Empire

113 **Tsukiji regulars call the marketplace the *uoichiba*** Theodore C. Bestor, *Tsukiji: The Fish Market at the Center of the World* (University of California Press, 2004), page 21.

114 **Matsudaira's garden** Timon Screech's *The Shogun's Painted Culture: Fear and Creativity in the Japanese States, 1760–1829* (Reaktion Books, 2000), especially pages 24–5 and pages 210–16.

Peter Constantine's *Japanese Slang: Uncensored* (Yen Books, 1994) includes a wonderful section on the fish market's specialized argot, impenetrable to outsiders, which is still influenced by the Buddhist vocabulary of the almost eighty temples located in early eighteenth-century Tsukiji. See also Bestor, *Tsukiji*, pages 85–6: 'Market conversations are often enlivened with brief flurries of *beranme,* the extravagant shitamachi dialect in which even the most polite request can be issued (and received) as a bold challenge . . .'

Also, Bestor page 335 note 4: 'Wordplay is central to the slang. *Shari* means rice to a sushi chef, but originally it was a religious term for Buddha's white bones . . .' And when a live fish dies, the fishmonger might cry, '*Agatta!*': 'Its soul has risen!'

For the Bauhaus architecture of Tsukiji market, 'an almost perfect architectural mandala of a market's idealized physical functions: bulking and breaking', see Bestor, *Tsukiji*, above, page 70. Reading Bestor's book is almost – almost! – as good as visiting the old market itself.

115 **Hongan-ji** See Richard Jaffe, 'Buddhist Material Culture, "Indianism" and the Construction of the Pan-Asian Buddhism in Pre-War Japan' (*Material Religion* 23/3 (2006), pages 266–93; Cherie Wendelken, 'The Tectonics of Japanese Style: Architect and Carpenter in the Late Meiji Period', *Art Journal* 55 (3) (Autumn 1996); also Paride Stortini, 'East and West of the Tsukiji Honganji' (published on-line), for the realism of Tsukiji's elephants and lions, for the influence of Britain's Indo-Saracenic colonial style, and for 'travel' being the key to understanding Honganji: its Indian influence reflected the desire to achieve a meaning as close as possible to the original message of the historical Buddha. It was, Stortini writes, 'an inverted Orientalism' that reflected 'the search for a modern identity', one that stressed the role of Buddhism as a shared cultural element among contemporary Asian countries under the rule of imperial Japan.

For the elephant as an avatar of Japanese imperialism, see Ian Jared Miller's *The Nature of the Beasts: Empire and Exhibition at the Tokyo Imperial Zoo* (University of California Press, 2013). The elephants lived in Ueno Park, which during Meiji became 'a new kind of space designed to call forth a national public in the service of the state – [Ueno] was a stage for the enactment of a new relationship between the people and the government, Japan and the world' (page 37). Both the zoo and the museum were built 'with an eye to shaping the minds and behavior of the populace' (page 38).

Miller's chapter 'The Great Zoo Massacre' is essential reading. In it, he details the systematic slaughter of the zoo's most famous and valuable animals in the summer of 1943: the event was 'an early rip in the fraying fabric of wartime official culture, a culture that would, within two short years, call all imperial subjects to be ready to sacrifice themselves and their families in a Manichean struggle against the overwhelming power of the American military' (page 130).

Miller argues that Tokyo's governor general Ōdachi Shigeo used the zoo killings 'as a way to address one of the great taboos of official speech in Japan at the time: defeat. The public spectacle of men, women, and children processing into the zoo to mourn "animal martyrs" that had to be sacrificed because of the deteriorating war situation was the beginning of the governor general's campaign . . . to inure the people of Tokyo to the demands of a failing empire . . . It might also be seen as a small but important step toward the tragic mass suicides and hopeless unarmed charges that brought the war to a gory crescendo in 1945' (page 128). 'No longer would the cult of martyrs be limited to the soldiers on the frontlines.'

A Memorial Service for Martyred Animals 'transformed the dead victims, and especially the popular elephants, into fellow sufferers with the Japanese citizenry, willing to lay down their lives for the greater national good . . . preparing themselves to share in the traumatic national experience of defeat . . . The slaughtered elephants were enshrined in children's literature, and ultimately in national mythology, as representatives of the Japanese people, who were thus equally defined simply as victims of war, not as parties to it' (Harriet Ritvo, Preface, page xix).

116 **'hide'** For the culture around the singer hide (pronounced 'hee-day'), see Hashimoto Miyuki, 'Visual Kei Otaku Identity – An Intercultural Analysis' (*Intercultural Communication Studies* XVI: 1 (2007), pages 87–99).

117 **the metallurgical formulae for casting a temple bell were kept as a secret** S. Katsumata, *Gleams from Japan*, a collection of articles written under a pseudonym for the Japanese Tourist Bureau. First published in 1937, but reprinted by Routledge in 2011; pages 330–42.

'Katsumata' writes: 'The boom of a temple bell with a string of velvety tone[s] in its wake is perhaps the greatest of sedatives in a big city jarred with a bewildering confusion of noises proceeding from hooting automobiles, clanging streetcars, and loquacious and ubiquitous radios. The note is redolent of the romantic past and has the opposite of a Lethean influence on city dwellers: it enables them to forget the ugly present and live in the dreamy past. To the inhabitants of busy American cities, who are suffering from the madding [sic] din of civic life, I throw out the suggestion that the simplest and yet the most effective way of relief is the introduction into their midst of some Buddhist temple bells with their magically soothing note[s] ... this plan [would rescue] tens of thousands of Americans from intellectual bankruptcy' (pages 334–5).

118 **a vanished bridge** Tokyo remained a city of canals and rivers until the 1950s.

Roderick Ike Wilson, who specializes in the environmental history of nineteenth- and twentieth-century Japan, wrote me: 'I think it would be correct to say a nineteenth-century Edokko would hardly recognize the transformation of the riverbank and harbor after the Asia-Pacific War, let alone today.'

See Wilson's 'Placing Edomae: The Changing Environmental Relations of Tokyo's Early Modern Fisheries' in *Resilience: A Journal of the Environmental Humanities*, volume 3 (2016), pages 242–89.

'Edomae', Wilson writes of a district near Tsukiji, was 'one of many "seas", all clearly divided by capes, spits, and poles and together facing out onto the deep waters of the Naikai, "Inner Sea".

'Twice daily at low tide, the bay receded to create a landscape of shoals, shallow salty pools, and cooler freshwater streams . . . Across this surface of mud and sand, the constant flow of water carved out shoals which twice daily emerged as chimera-like islands. Some shoals appeared regularly enough to earn themselves names: "Appearing", "Front", "Offing".'

For the vertigo of wandering through the reclaimed land along the Sumida River, see Mishima Yukio's spiteful little story 'Seven Bridges'. In it, four geishas crisscross the Tsukiji district one night under a full moon, following a superstition: any wish would be granted to a believer who could cross seven bridges without speaking a single word. (Donald Keene, translator, *Death in Midsummer & Other Stories*, New Directions, 1966, pages 76–92.)

Yokokawa-Honjo: East of the River

123 **Of all Edo's beauties, the river is paramount** From Andrew Markus' translation of *An Account of the Prosperity of Edo* in *An Episodic festschrift for Howard Hibbett* (Highmoonoon Press, 2000).

For Yokokawa-Honjo, see Andrew Markus' *The Willow in Autumn: Ryūtei Tanehiko, 1783–1842* (Harvard Yenching-Institute, 1993), especially pages 8–11: Yokokawa-Honjo, the north–south Transverse Canal, became celebrated in the eighteenth century for its Bell of Time and its *kiri-mise*, 'low class brothels that charged on an hourly basis, and for its brazenly independent streetwalkers. These women – frequently superannuated castoffs from the Fukagawa pleasure quarter – had a reputation for desperate aggressiveness.' The preserve of petty samurai and minor functionaries, marshy Honjo 'enjoyed the dubious reputation of excelling in one thing only – a superabundance of mosquitoes.'

Markus cites a 1774 book called *The Carriage of Beautiful Ladies, Lavender Dappling,* and its depiction of Yokokawa-Honjo: 'No sooner does anyone pass by than he is pounced upon and seized; not even the mightiest thunderclap will make the women release their victims. It is a dreadful place. From here come the "hourly girls." '

Alan S. Woodhull's unpublished 1978 Stanford dissertation *Romantic Edo Fiction: A Study of the Ninjōbon and Complete Translation of Shunshoku Umegoyomi* is also a good source; Woodhull includes many details about the lost worlds of Fukagawa and Edogawa on the Sumida's eastern bank. He writes about the 'square net and torch illuminated fishing boats . . . a familiar spectacle along the Sumida in winter or early spring, as the whitebait moved upstream to spawn'; the vast plum tree orchards of Kameido; the river's ferries and water-taxis that spirited passengers to the brothels and back.

Woodhull looks more favorably on Markus' hourly girls and their teahouse district southeast of Edo Castle. 'Fukugawa, originally a port, was naturally filled with boathouses. Sometime in the late 1700s, it became something of a fad to go there for secret liaisons, small parties, etc. Gradually this practice grew to the point where the teahouse activity was the great part of the business. Again, since gondolas were the fastest means of transportation, these boathouses were very conveniently located' (page 357 note 47).

'Since Fukagawa was not a licensed Quarter, there were no courtesans as such, but only free-agent geisha. It was the fashion of these *haori-geisha* . . . that led the modish world' (page 363). Woodhull translates the nineteenth-century poet Tamenaga Shunsui: 'Fukagawa is/ port harbor of Romance./ Along the river banks are lined/ Storehouses filled with Love. / The gondolas which come and go/ Love-laden cross their paths,/ The shouts of boatmen to the docks/ "Ho, Master So-and-So's/ Arrived," ring out along beside/ the raucous, lively songs/ Which endless as this world drift forth, /from teahouse parlors ring' (page 228).

For Yokoami today, see Kit Nakamura's thoughtful 'Cool (Old) Japan Flourishes along Flowing Rivers of Edo', in the *Japan Times*, 27 June 2010. Nakamura describes the district's history as the shogunal – and later, imperial – lumberyard whose wood was essential for constructing the 'high city of gardens and villas'.

126 **the Sumida has been moved and merged** The Sumida remains strangely unexplored in English.

I have borrowed most facts from Roderick Ike Wilson's

excellent 'Changing River Regimes on the Kantō Plain, Japan, 1600–1900', in *A History of Water: Rivers and Society*, volume 2 (Terje Tvedt and Richard Coopey, editors, I. B. Tauris, 2010).

Helen Craig McCullough's commentary of *The Tales of Ise: Lyrical Episodes from Tenth Century Japan* (Stanford University Press, 1968) sums up the limits of understanding: 'It is still usual for different stretches of a Japanese river to have different names. Between 1621 and 1654, the government diverted the Tone River into its present channel, which carries the waters of five prefectures into the Pacific Ocean at Chōshi. There is disagreement about the exact location of the old channel ... The present Sumida River, which flows through the eastern part of the city of Tokyo into the bay, apparently was a tributary that joined the old Tone River further upstream, where it is still known as the Arakawa. It seems to have begun to follow its present course, and thus to have acquired its present name of Sumida, only after the Tone's diversion' (page 205, note 8).

Patricia Sippel researched the river's flood patterns and its channels during the Edo Period ('Japan's First Urban Water Disaster: The Great Kantō Flood of 1742', published on-line). This article is especially valuable for its historical maps of the river basins.

See also Gregory Smits' *Seismic Japan: The Long History and Continuing Legacy of the Ansei Edo Earthquake* (University of Hawaii Press, 2013). Smits notes that beneath the bottom of Tokyo Bay is 'a large valley or trough created by the flow of the Old Tokyo River roughly twenty thousand years ago. Sediments have gradually accumulated over this ancient valley.' The Tokugawa shogunate constructed artillery batteries (*o-daiba*) by piling up sacks of dirt on this poor soil base, in water 'about five meters deep'. When all five batteries inevitably collapsed, the public viewed the event 'as a direct strike by the cosmic forces on bakufu military capabilities . . .' (page 115).

127 **One nineteenth-century gazetteer claimed that the word is older** *Shinpen Musashi Fudoki-kō* (*A Description of the Musashi Region*) offers the earliest known etymology of the kanji used for *sumi* (隅). Thanks to Marky Star's *Japan This!* blog (31 May 2014) for the reference.

127 **Greenwich Village or Montmartre** Taken from Andrew Markus' 'Terakado Seiken's *Blossoms Along the Sumida*', in *Sino-Japanese Studies* 3 #2 (April 1991), pages 9–29. Markus describes Seiken's writing as 'an entire vision through fragments': 'the jumps, skips, and repetitions of the text suggest not an organized panorama but a true bird's-eye view, which darts from one salient feature to the next . . .'

127 **on the eastern embankment** See Markus' note in *Sino-Japanese Studies*, cited above: 'Although a broken series of levees and embankments some fifty miles long bordered the Sumida, "the embankment" usually refers more narrowly to [the segment] between Mimeguri Shrine on the south and Mokuboji temple in the north. The embankment, a good twelve feet above the surrounding lowlands, afforded a fine view of the river and "downtown" wharves of the central city . . . At the direction of the shogun Yoshimune, peach, cherry, and willow trees were planted along the Sumida embankment in 1725–26; Ienari expanded the project in 1790, and additional trees replaced dead stock in 1831. The trees – probably intended as a check to erosion – provided a continuous

canopy of buds and blossoms. "Until the end of the Third Month," notes the usually somber *Edo Meisho Zue* (*Pictorial Album of Famous Sites of Edo*), "branches brilliant with red, lavender, azure, and white blossoms mingle and intertwine. The effect is like brocade left out to air . . ." ' (page 19).

128 **The writer Nagai Kafū remembered** Quotes taken from 'The River Sumida', in Edward Seidensticker's *Kafū the Scribbler* (Stanford University Press, 1965). 'Lotuses blooming in rank profusion', page 184, and 'mossy shingled roofs', pages 215–16.

129 **Right-wing members of the Tokyo Metropolitan Assembly** The cultural geographer Cary Karacas wrote me: 'Despite Tsuchiya's best intentions . . . it is not used as Tsuchiya designed it: for people to actually be able to enter the site and view the *meibo* [books with memorial names written inside]. Another rather fascinating aspect of the memorial is the fact that, while modelled on his previous works, [Yokoami] unintentionally bears striking resemblance to certain wartime air raid shelters. One comment from a Tokyo air raid survivor, upon seeing the memorial: "It's as if they (those killed by fire-bombing) were once again forced into an air raid shelter . . ." [where so many died].'

See Karacas' extensive research on the Tokyo air raids, listed in the bibliography.

129 **His first art memorializes the salaryman** The 2001 volume *Tsuchiya Kimio: Remembrance* (Bijutsu Shuppan-sha) provides a good overview of the artist's work and philosophy. It includes several essays translated into English, and photographs of the war memorial's interior space. See Shioda

Junichi's essay in *Remembrance*: 'Ash is an extremely difficult material with which to work. As a material it has neither solidity nor hardness; consequently it lacks volume and possesses no unique shape . . . Ash transcends life; it is the symbol of the boundary with Nirvana. Ash is the condition of nothingness after worldly passions and the delusion of life have been burned away; one occasionally senses even purity. Ash is invested with a kind of supernatural power, being the first stage of rebirth, yet occurring at the completion of death. In this way, it possesses a dualist character' (page 13).

Shioda sees Tsuchiya as an artist of Japan's first 'lost decade': 'an age of absence, an age of shadows, from which substance has been lost. And even today, though the new century has begun, we are yet to escape this feeling: yet to reclaim the substance that we lost . . .' (page 12).

Marunouchi: New Origins

133 **Imperial rule over the eight corners of the earth**   In Japanese, '*Hakkō ichiu*': 'A saying attributed to the mythical Emperor Jimmu that by 1940 was pervasively invoked in support of Japan's expansionism', Kenneth J. Ruoff's *Imperial Japan at its Zenith: The Wartime Celebration of the Empire's 2600th Anniversary* (Cornell University Press, 2010), page 17. Also, Walter Edwards, 'Forging Traditions for a Holy War', *Journal of Japanese Studies* 29 #2 (2003), pages 289–324. Nanette Gottlieb translates the phrase as 'universal brotherhood' (*Kanji Politics: Language Policy and Japanese Script*, Kegan Paul International, 1995, page 98).

The past was invoked to affirm the present: the mythic Emperor Jimmu's accession marked 'the beginning of time, history, or narrative' (Fujitani Takashi, *Splendid Monarchy: Power and Pageantry in Modern Japan*, University of California Press, 1996).

134 **The city's most beautiful incarnation**   I discovered this Tokyo quite by chance, in the volume *Asakusa no misemono shūkyōsei erosu* (Wada Hirofumi, Ichiyanagi Hirotaka, et al., editors, Yumani Shoppō, 2005). The book's plates include theaters and staircases, bridges and buildings that did not last long enough to become landmarks. Not everyone was so enamored of that city, though; Kafū referred to it as 'a sham hallway, a grand façade with nothing behind it' (*Kafū the Scribbler: The Life and Writings of Nagai Kafū*, Edward Seidensticker, editor, Stanford University Press, 1965, page 108).

134 **the splendid achievement of completing the reconstruction of the Capital**   This rescript was reprinted in *The Reconstruction of Tokyo* (Tokyo Municipal Office, 1933).

135 **six thousand Koreans and the eight hundred Chinese**   The knowing eye here is Gennifer Weisenfeld's. See her *Imaging Disaster: Tokyo and the Visual Culture of Japan's Great Earthquake of 1923* (University of California Press, 2012), especially pages 171–3 and 306. 'The complicity of the quake's "innocent" victims and national saviors in the savage retribution visited upon Japan's resident colonial subjects and political dissidents has yet to be fully acknowledged . . .' Weisenfeld observes: 'There was a proliferation of rumors and gossip that accused "subversive" or "malcontent" resident Koreans of sedition, indicating that they had set off explosions and poisoned well water, and these rumors incited widespread

retributive violence, particularly among self-appointed vigilante squads organized by local neighborhoods through the region . . . Scholars have argued that Koreans were not just the victims of bigoted xenophobia in chaotic times but were specifically targeted as threatening colonial subjects who had been voicing desires for national independence from Japanese rule and evoking intense fear in the Japanese imagination. Despite the army's and police force's claims to be protecting this vulnerable population, the press later revealed these authorities to be organizers, instigators, and cohorts of the vigilantes in the persecution.'

Weisenfeld adds: 'Strict censorship laws prohibited representations of dead bodies and other potentially disturbing subjects, including the massacre of Koreans (although these measures could not stem the tide of contraband images available on the street that featured burned and bloated corpses in neighborhoods throughout the city). Visual culture both reveals and conceals in its visualizations. Although the photo-documentary images of the earthquake appeared to be displaying the bodies' stories so transparently, they in fact conflated the widely divergent histories of the mangled corpses into one generic narrative. Hidden beneath the surface of the earthquake presentations, visible only to the knowing eye, is an alternative history . . .' (pages 67–8). The media's visual authority 'perpetuated notions of resilience, unity, and innocence despite overwhelming evidence to the contrary' (page 69).

135 **'You thought it was perfectly normal** Kawabata follows this description with a deadpan segue into a description of the new city risen from the earthquake. 'But now, in the spring of 1930, there are big festivals celebrating the recon-

struction of Tokyo . . .' (*The Scarlet Gang of Asakusa*, translated by Alisa Freedman, University of California Press, 2005, pages 63–4).

135 The reckoning of time in Japan is tethered to the emperor's body 'The *nengō* system is said to have originated in imperial China around the second century AD. It had spread throughout the Chinese cultural world and started to be used in Japan between the mid seventh and the eighth century. The adoption of *nengō* in written records was a means by which the imperial family represented itself as the ruler of the country domestically as well as internationally in the wider East Asian world order . . . Before the Meiji era (1868–1912), the emperor adopted and changed *nengō* at critical moments during his reign. *Nengō*, which always consisted of two Chinese characters, were changed upon a new emperor's enthronement as it was seen to symbolically mark the start of the new era. *Nengō* were also changed after an earthquake, flood, famine, epidemic, fire, the appearance of a comet in the sky, or war. After natural as well as man-made catastrophes, a new era name was given and within it the first year started anew. This act was thought to nullify the polluted time and to bring in new time and order.

'In any social organization, time is one of the most fundamental organizing principles. Those who regulate time have power to rule, and for this reason, there have been fights over the power to control time. Many attempts were made by the shogun as well as other warriors to obtain the power to regulate time. For example, in the early part of the Tokugawa period, when the shoguns came to their post, the *nengō* was changed even though the shogun's accession to power should not have brought a change of *nengō*.' (Iwatake Mikako, 'From a Shogunal

City to a Life City: Tokyo Between Two Fin-de-Siècles', in *Japanese Capitals in Historical Perspective: Place, Power and Memory in Kyoto, Edo and Tokyo*, Nicolas Fiévé and Paul Waley, editors, RoutledgeCurzon, 2003, pages 235–6.)

'Following the Meiji Restoration in 1868, a new emperor and *nengō* system were created. The emperor served for life and was no longer to be threatened by political power games, and on his death, he was to be succeeded by his oldest son. A *nengō* was to start at the time of the new emperor's enthronement and remain unchanged until his death. The significance of this system is that time is fixed to the emperor's body . . .' (Iwatake Mikako, cited above, page 237).

M. William Steele notes that the introduction of the *nengō* 'Meiji' was controversial. 'A mocking rhyme popular in Edo at the time laughed at the new name: "Read from above it may mean 'bright rule,' but read from below, it means, 'ungoverned by anyone [*osamarumei*]." The pun is often interpreted to demonstrate residual pro-Tokugawa sentiment among the people of Edo. To be sure they resented being under imperial control, especially as it in effect meant under the control of boorish men from Satsuma and Chōshū. At the same time they had lost faith in the Tokugawa family. In saying, "We are not under the control of anyone," Edo commoners were expressing their contempt for any form of political authority.' (*Monumenta Nipponica*, vol. 45 #22 (1990), page 150.)

For an example of *nengō* changes in ancient Japan, see Delmer Brown and Ishida Ichirō, *The Future and the Past: A Translation and Study of the* Gukanshō: *An Interpretive History of Japan Written in 1219* (University of California Press, 1979), page 67: 'Following Ichijō's enthronement in 986 at the age of seven, a comet streaked across the sky in the last third of the sixth month of 989. The era name was changed to Eiso in the eighth month of that year. Then came the incomparable disaster known as the Eiso typhoon. And in the following year the era name was changed to Shōryaku . . .'

For a single instance when an era changed to reflect an *auspicious* event rather than a calamity, see Herbert E. Plutschow's *Matsuri: The Festivals of Japan* (Japan Library, 1996). 'Time was also renewed to reflect auspicious events. One of these was the discovery of a white heron in the imperial gardens in Kyoto . . .' (pages 34–5).

136 **When Emperor Hirohito died in 1989, 'tens of millions of calendars were discarded'** Gunter Nitschke, *From Shinto to Ando: Studies in Architectural Anthropology in Japan* (Academy Editions, 1993), pages 9–10. Quoted in Vinayak Bharne, *Zen Spaces and Neon Places* (ORO Editions, 2014), page 102. In the weeks before the Shōwa Emperor died, the media referred to the future day of his death in katakana, as X-day (Leo J. Loveday, *Language Contact in Japan: A Socio-linguistic History*, Clarendon Press, 1996, page 197).

136 **Shōwa was always Shōwa** After the Pacific War, the Occupation authorities decided to keep the *nengō* system, which 'continued unbroken, a calendrical declaration of fundamental continuity with the past' (John Dower, *Embracing Defeat: Japan in the Wake of World War II*, Norton, 2000, pages 279, 401 and 592 note two).

137 **emperor Jimmu** See Ben-Ami Shillony, *Enigma of the Emperors: Sacred Subservience in Japanese History* (Global Oriental, 2005): 'The belief that Japan is basically different from other countries because its royal house has never changed is almost as old as the dynasty itself . . . The

[eighth-century] chronicle *Nihon shoki* traces its beginnings to the foundation of the empire by the first "human" sovereign, Emperor Jimmu, on the first day of the first month of the year that corresponds to 660 BC. This date was first announced by Prince Shotoku in the early seventh century. Wishing to emphasize the antiquity of the imperial dynasty, he extrapolated backwards twenty sexagenary cycles from the year AD 601 . . . and arrived at the date of foundation (*kigen*). Although this date has no historical basis, and the actual foundation of the state probably occurred nearly one thousand years later, it was accepted for most of Japanese history, and was often quoted as proof of the immutability of Japan's political structure . . .' (pages 5–6).

Ironically, the concept of anniversaries is a Western one, so the foundation was not celebrated until the nineteenth century (Shillony, page 8). For the invention of *Kigen*, and its public reception, see Jessica Kennett Cork, *The Lunisolar Calendar: A Sociology of Japanese Time* (MA dissertation, University of Sheffield, 2010), pages 54–5, on Hayashi Wakaki's essay 'Kaireki no eikyō' ('The Effect of Calendar Reform' in *Shūko kaishi*). Cork also quotes Miyata Noboru: 'Important festivals such as the fire festival and O-bon were abolished and replaced with holidays like . . . Kigen-setsu, which no one had ever heard of' (Miyata Noboru in *Koyomi to saiji: Nihonjin no kisetsu kankaku*, Tokyo Shōgakkan, 1984, page 19).

137 The first emperor Jimmu's mother was the daughter of the sea god This passage is adapted and condensed from W. G. Aston's version of *The Nihongi* chronicles, first published in 1896. For Fujitani Misao's quote, see Kenneth J. Ruoff's *Imperial Japan at its Zenith: The Wartime Celebration of the Empire's 2600th Anniversary* (Cornell University Press, 2010), pages 21 and 49–50. For the Kigen celebrations as seen from the American perspective, see Joseph Grew's *Ten Years in Japan: A Contemporary Record Drawn from the Diaries and Private Papers of the US Ambassador to Japan 1932–1942* (Simon and Schuster, 1944). For the Japanese imperial army and its losses in China, see *Imperial Japan at its Zenith* (pages 17 and 215). Ruoff argues that Jimmu served as a figurehead for Japanese fascist ideology: while noting that even during wartime, Japan held parliamentary elections, he stresses the importance of 'the cult of the unbroken imperial line' in mobilizing the country. Though Emperor Hirohito did not 'give rousing speeches from balconies or behave in a manner that was similar to the charismatic styles of Hitler and Mussolini, and Japan at that time certainly did not produce another leader whose charisma remotely approached that of Germany's Fuhrer or Italy's Il Duce', Emperor Jimmu became 'a surrogate in this area' (page 19).

For more on Jimmu, see also Gustav Heldt's translation of *The Kojiki: An Account of Ancient Matters* (Columbia University Press, 2014). First written down in AD 712, this 'intensely political' text invented the past by tracing 'the genealogy of the ruling family back to the very beginnings of the world. It does so largely in mythical style, telling its tale through vignettes and poems.' *The Kojiki* narrative explains 'the greatest conundrums of existence: why the sun and moon; why death; how does life begin; what is our place in the order of things . . . The lack of creator is marked and there is no attempt to identify an absolute origin.' (Richard Bowring's *The Religious Traditions of Japan 500–1600*, Cambridge University Press, 2005, pages 46–50.)

For a sardonic account of imperial Japan's timekeeping, see Dazai Osamu's eerie short story 'December 8th', which was written during World War Two (*Modern Japanese Literature*, J. Thomas Rimer and Van Gessel, editors, Columbia University Press, 2005, volume 1, pages 660–67). Japanese historians were only free to critique the Jimmu myth after the end of World War Two. In February 1946, the president of Tokyo Imperial University 'called for critical analysis of imperial history, territory that largely had been off limits previously: "Until quite recently, we have held to the beliefs of our fore-fathers that the Japanese people had lived, from time immemorial, with immutable reverence toward the Imperial House as the founders of our nation, their unbroken line with an everlasting destiny. Today, however, may not be the year of twenty-six hundred and something as has been believed. How much of this is real historical fact? How much is myth and legend? Such questions must be solved by positive and comparative historical study . . ." ' (*Imperial Japan at its Zenith*, page 185).

138 **Kigen Anniversary nationalistic events were held** For the party itself, see Herbert Bix, *Hirohito and the Making of Modern Japan* (HarperCollins, 2000): 'One day before the start of the official commemorative events, on November 9, a government regulation established an "Office of Shinto Deities" within the Home Ministry to further the "spiritual mobilization" of the nation in preparation for total war . . . At the peak of the celebrations, on November 10 and 11, an estimated five million people attended banquets. Food prepared as military field rations, in remembrance of the troops on the front lines, was consumed by celebrants in the palace plaza' (page 384).

141 **One of the emperor's poems was set to music** Many thanks to Kaori Ungerer for help with this translation.

Chris Drake writes: 'The Shōwa emperor's poem was composed in 1933. Its words were slowly sung during a newly created Shinto dance performed all over the empire during the 1940 Kigen celebrations. A historical vortex of contested meanings makes translating and explicating this poem very difficult, since it is actually two poems, one antebellum and early war (when it was written) and one post-war (when it was popularized and performed).

'The poem is a *tanka:* five lines and thirty-one syllables. The emperor reversed normal prose word order (which would have positioned the verb at the very end); this reversal created a powerful tension within his *tanka*. It's as though the emperor, as a *kami* (deity) himself, were using the poem to (re)create the cosmos.

'The first line refers to the realm of the invisible *kami* and the realm of visible nature and humans. It's an immense, cosmic image that matches the hugeness of the 2600-year imperial line.

'The emperor is not praying to a single god of heaven and a single god of earth. He's praying to all the myriad gods: Shinto has innumerable (*yaoyorozu*) deities, with more always possible since new things are always appearing in the world.

'A translator must also note the (probably unconscious) conflation of the word "peace" with "pacification" implied in the original version: "May the empire be at peace with no problems or unfortunate unrest or violence by misguided rebellious ruffians anywhere." Any scholarly translation of the *tanka* needs to deal with its double meaning in a way that doesn't simply flatten out or dismiss history' (Chris Drake, in private correspondence).

141 a Shinto dance   See Terauchi Naoko's article in *Tōyō Ongaku Kenkyū* #81 (2016): 'Sounds of "War and Peace": New

Bugaku Pieces *Yūkyū* and *Shōwa raku* Created for the *Kigen nisen roppyakunen* in 1940': 'The dances were the embodiment of the nation-state of Japan as imagined by the Ministry of the Imperial Household. The presentation was in fact made a deliberate negotiation between contrasting concepts such as "the ancient and the contemporary," "Japan and the West," centralization within Japan and "expansion throughout Asia," and "purity and diversity." ... The dances pursued images of both a "strong Japan" by using "patriotic" old lyrics composed in the thirteenth century and a "pure, ancient Japan" by designing costumes based on warrior attire in the eighth century and older.' During the 1964 Olympic Games, *Yūkyū* was revived, in a style changed 'from a men's military dance to an elegant dance employing young women.'

David Hughes, who provided the reference to Terauchi's research, notes that in 1940 the composer (who was also the head of the palace court music ensemble) set the emperor's poem to the most appropriate music: 'the one most related to the emperor's [divinity] ... No evidence that such music or dance existed 2,600 years ago, but never mind' (by e-mail).

Kitasuna: The Firebombs of 1945

143 **Running/ On the road of fire**   Sō Sakon's poem 'Running' from *Mother Burning* (*Modern Japanese Literature*, J. Thomas Rimer and Van Gessel, editors, Columbia University Press, 2007, volume 2, pages 427–31) gives one of the most haunting accounts of the bombings' human cost. Leith Morton translates.

My English sources for the firebombings are Robert Guillain's *I Saw Tokyo Burning: An Eyewitness Narrative from*

Pearl Harbor to Hiroshima (William Byron, translator, Doubleday, 1981). Hoito Edoin's *The Night Tokyo Burned: The Incendiary Campaign Against Japan, March–August 1945* (St. Martin's Press, 1987). *Fire from the Sky: A Diary over Japan* (Ron Greer and Mike Wicks, 2013). In Japanese, oral histories and written testimonials at the Tokyo Air Raid Museum, including that of Nihei Haruyo. Also, the NHK 1978 documentary on the 9 March air raid; and Katsumoto Saotome's *Illustrated Tokyo Air Raid* (Kawade Shobo Shinsha, 2003). The research of Cary Karacas, cited above, is invaluable.

146 **the smell of death followed us**   Ron Greer and Mike Wicks, *Fire from the Sky*, cited above, page 115.

152 ***Yamato damashii!***   'Japanese spirit'. A phrase appropriated by nationalists in modern Japan. It appears first in *Genji Monogatari*, where it means only 'Japanese wit' as opposed to 'Chinese learning'. (Royall Tyler, translator, Penguin, 2002, page 381 note 9.)

153 **a young night watchman**   See especially Inoue's *Tokyo Air Raid*, a 'dream journal' found among his papers after his death (Iwanami Shoten, 1995).

157 ***When everything else has vanished***   Yoshimura Hiroshi, cited above, for Yokokawa-Honjo as 'the Drunkard's Palace', and on the importance of names – of any trace – when everything else has gone' (*Ō-Edo toki no kane aruki*, pages 41–2).

Shiba Kiridoshi: Tokyo Tower

163 **the largest of all the bells in the capital**   S. Katsumata, *Gleams from Japan* (Routledge, 2011), pages 342–3. *Gleams* is a compilation of articles written for Japan's Tourist Association during the 1930s: 'S. Katsumata' was a pseudonym. The current bell is not original to Zōjō-ji.

164 **Kawase Hasui**   Kendall H. Brown's *Kawase Hasui: The Complete Woodblock Prints* (Hotei, 2003). (The 'emotionally vapid, creatively stunted' quote was Brown's, page 23; also the description of the tram 'that never seems to come', page 592.) Lawrence Smith, *The Japanese Print Since 1900: Old Dreams and New Visions* (British Museum, 1983), includes a critique of Hasui as a limited artist of 'glib, picturesque but shallow tourist art'. For further sources, Helen Merritt, *Modern Japanese Woodblock Prints: The Early Years* (University of Hawaii Press, 1990). Also, 'Poet of Place: The Life and Art of Kawase Hasui', in Amy Reigle Newland's *Visions of Japan: Kawase Hasui's Masterpieces* (Hotei Publishing, 2008).

166 **The great Tōkaidō highway, which connected Kyoto and Edo, began and ended near Zōjō-ji**   See Nam-lin Hur, *Prayer and Play in Late Tokugawa Japan: Asakusa Sensō-ji and Edo Society* (Harvard University Press, 2000), page 103: Zōjō-ji helped create a ' "magical" cosmology for Edo. These symmetrical locations at the city's principal gateways constituted a liminal world within the shogunal capital, where religion and entertainment were fused and the social evils and defilement emanating from the inner city were dissolved . . .'

168 **Jizō who oversees life's transitions**   Taken from Hank Glassman's *The Face of Jizō: Image and Cult in Medieval Japanese Buddhism* (University of Hawaii Press, 2012), page 188.

169 **foreigners were reminded to 'leave your boots at the door'**   For bad behavior in the Shiba temples, see Rudyard Kipling: 'Distances are calculated by the hour in Tokyo. Forty minutes in a rickshaw, running at full speed, will take you a little way into the city; two hours from the Ueno Park brings you to the tomb of the famous Forty-Seven, passing on the way the very splendid temples of Shiba, which are all fully described in the guide-books. Lacquer, gold-inlaid bronze work, and crystals carved with the words "Om" and "Shri" ... In one of the temples was a room of lacquer panels overlaid with gold-leaf. An animal of the name of V. Gay had seen fit to scratch his entirely uninteresting name on the gold. Posterity will take note that V. Gay never cut his fingernails, and ought not to have been trusted with anything prettier than a hog-trough ...' (Hugh Cortazzi and George Webb, editors, *Kipling's Japan: Collected Writings,* Bloomsbury Academic, 2012, pages 180–1.)

171 **All figures of Buddha were removed from the main hall of the temple**   From James Edward Ketelaar's *Of Heretics and Martyrs in Meiji Japan: Buddhism and Its Persecution* (Princeton University Press, 1990), page 122. Ketelaar describes the enshrining of the Three Creator *kami* and the Imperial Ancestor Amaterasu in the Tokugawa family temple as 'a true ideological coup-de-grâce; in one stroke the Tokugawa bakufu was defaced and the Buddhism it had elevated to the status of a national religion was cast aside.'

For the early encounters of European and American

visitors with Japan, I also drew on Mary Crawford Fraser's eloquent memoir, *A Diplomat's Wife in Japan: Sketches at the Turn of the Century* (Hugh Cortazzi, editor, Weatherhill, 1982), and the second edition of Ernest Satow and A. G. S. Hawes's *A Handbook for Travellers in Central and Northern Japan* (John Murray, 1884).

171 **Arsonists burned down the main temple on New Year's Day, 1874** See John Reddie Black's *Young Japan: Yokohama & Yedo. A Narrative of the Settlement and the City from the Signing of the Treaties in 1858, to the Close of the Year 1879. With a Glance at the Progress of Japan During a Period of Twenty-One Years* (Oxford University Press, 1968), volume 2, page 411. 'The new year had hardly been ushered in, when in Tokio the fierce alarum bells rung out their startling peals, not the less appalling because they are so frequently heard. The great temple of Zojoji, Shiba, had been set on fire by incendiaries, and in the space of about an hour it was totally consumed . . . The wooden frame campanile in which the great bell was hung, was destroyed, and the fine toned bell fell, and has never been re-hung to this day. It was one of the four celebrated bells of Japan, only one of which remains suspended – each of the other three having been damaged by fire . . .'

173 **The M-69s become miniature flamethrowers** Quoted in A. J. Baime, *The Accidental President: Harry S. Truman and the Four Months That Changed the World* (Houghton Mifflin Harcourt, 2017), page 215.

176 **'When one weeps, the other tastes salt'** A Japanese friend, on reading Arthur's translation, said, 'The problem is,

he tried to translate everything. You have to leave some things unsaid. What about, (愛する人の涙しょっぱい)?'

Daylight Savings Time: The Occupation

176 'The Sorting That Evens Things Out' In *Chuang-tzu: Textual Notes to a Partial Translation* (A. C. Graham, SOAS, 1982). Quoted in *Sources of Chinese Tradition*, volume 1 (William Theodore de Bary and Irene Bloom, editors, Columbia University Press, 1999), pages 99–101. 'This chapter [deals with] matters of knowledge and language, life and death, dream and reality ..' That like the sun 'simultaneously at noon and declining, a thing is simultaneously alive and dead', was a paradox of the fourth-century BCE philosopher Hui Shi.

180 the seven-year Allied Occupation of Japan This paragraph is condensed from Cary Karacas' excellent chapters 'Blackened Cities: Blackened Maps' and 'The Occupied City' in *Cartographic Japan: A History in Maps* (Kären Wigen, Fumiko Sugimoto and Cary Karacas, editors, University of Chicago Press, 2016). Also, Lucy Herndon Crockett's *Popcorn on the Ginza: An Informal Portrait of Postwar Japan* (William Sloane Associates, 1949).

180 Language, too, reflected the new order See Nanette Gottlieb: 'Matsuzaka Tadanori ... silenced criticism of proposed reforms by pointing out the window at the ruins of Tokyo and asserting that the devastation had come about because the people of Japan had not had the words to criticize the military – what they saw was hard won evidence of the need to democratize the language.'

Gottlieb adds that in those unsettled days of the immediate postwar period, the general mood was one of 'revulsion for the xenophobia and the reactionary conservatism and ultra-nationalism of the war period; there was a yearning for things that were modern and western and rational' ('Language and Politics: The Reversal of Postwar Script Reform Policy in Japan', *Journal of Asian Studies*, volume 53 #4, November 1994, page 1178).

Firebombs wiped out newspaper and typeface factories; in 1945, new typeset matrices were needed, so as an economy measure the print media supported an overhaul of the country's language system. Before World War Two, newspapers used a font 'of some 7500 kanji, actually almost double that number if we count pieces of type which combined kanji with furigana.' (John DeFrancis, *Visible Speech: The Diverse Oneness of Writing Systems*, University of Hawaii Press, 1989, page 142.)

For statutes and the Constitution written in colloquial Japanese, see Kyoko Inoue, *MacArthur's Japanese Constitution: A Linguistic and Cultural Study of Its Making* (University of Chicago Press, 1991), page 29 and page 31 note 35.

181 *palanquin, inkstone,* and *desire*   Examples taken from Christopher Seeley, *A History of Writing in Japan* (University of Hawaii Press, 2000), page 152. For foreign loan words banned during the 1930s, see Nanette Gottlieb, *Kanji Politics: Language Policy and Japanese Script* (Kegan Paul International, 1995), pages 87–8. The list included baseball, radio announcer, shower, slipper, spanner, bolt, and handle. 'The aim was not just to prevent the use of foreign words belonging to the language of the enemy, but also to prevent foreign ideas from entering along with them.'

181 **Quiz. Body-building. Leisure. OK.** Examples taken from Leo Loveday, *Language Contact in Japan: A Socio-linguistic History* (Oxford University Press, 1996), page 76. Loveday includes an amusing list of words left off the Ministry of Education's new list of kanji for general use, issued in 1946: '*Dog* appeared, but *cat* did not; *pine*, but not *cedar*' (page 141). 'In place of profusion, complexity and tradition, now reigned restrictions, simplicity and convenience' (page 147).

181 **'the marvelous new pidgin terminology of the moment'** John Dower, *Embracing Defeat: Japan in the Wake of World War Two* (Norton, 2000), page 105.

Tokugawa Tsunenari, in conversation with me, had a matter-of-fact explanation of why Daylight Savings Time was so resented during the Occupation: 'When the office opens at nine, everyone gets in for nine. Then at 5 p.m., you're officially off, but usually people stay much longer, until eighteen or nineteen or so, just to clean up all the work. But if the start time is an hour earlier, then sixteen o'clock is off time, but – the sun is still up! So Daylight Savings Time means you're working an hour extra. It's a question of overtime. I used to work until 10 or 11 p.m. in the office . . . I had so many things to do. For that kind of salaryman, starting at eight would mean you were working an hour free of charge.'

Ichigaya: Postwar Prosperity

185 **The Jetavana Temple** In his note on this famous passage, Tyler writes: 'The Japanese reader must always have heard in the opening lines the familiar boom of a bronze temple bell, but scripturally these bells were silver and glass. At

the Jetavana Vihāra (Japanese: Gion Shōja, built for the Buddha by a wealthy patron) they hung at the four corners of the temple infirmary and were rung when a disciple died. At the Buddha's passing, the twin-trunked sal trees that stood around where he lay, including their yellow flowers, turned pure white' (*The Tale of the Heike*, Viking, 2012, page 3).

187 **I'd seen fortune-tellers before** According to the anthropologist Carmen Blacker, the word for divination in Japanese is '*ura* or *uranai*, a term which appears to indicate primarily "that which is behind, and hence invisible" '(*Divination and Oracles*, Michael Loewe and Carmen Blacker, editors, (Shambhala, 1981, page 64).

Blacker wrote several interesting articles and books on Japan's pre-modern belief systems, focusing on shamans, oracles and divination. Some rituals – fortune-telling by means of turtle divination, or the interpretation of dreams – became extinct during the medieval era. Others lasted into the mid-1960s and beyond. Blacker found vestiges of these traditions in professional healers who possessed *gantsū*, or 'second sight': 'No sooner was her patient seated before her than the image of a fox, or a resentful ancestor, would appear before her seeing eyes . . .' Cures included reciting *The Heart Sutra*, or performing certain ceremonies. Other ascetics Blacker interviewed claimed to be able to see 'whether a tree or a stone were holy or not' (*The Collected Writings of Carmen Blacker*, Edition Synapse, 2000, page 61).

In *The Catalpa Bow* (Routledge, 1999), Blacker writes: 'Our familiar human world is no more than a narrow segment of the cosmos which now confronts us. Beyond it lies a further realm, altogether "other", peopled by beings non-human, endowed with powers non-human, whose whole order of existence is ambivalent, mysterious and strange. Between these two worlds there is no ordinary continuity. Each is contained, like a walled garden, by its own order of being, and separated by a barrier which represents a rupture of level, a break in the ontological plane. This barrier the ordinary man or woman is powerless to cross. They cannot at will make the passage to this other perilous plane, nor can they see, hear or in any way influence the beings who dwell there.

'Ordinary men and women are powerless to deal with these perilous and ambivalent forces. Certain special human beings, however, may acquire a power which enables them to transcend the barrier between the two worlds. This power bears no relation to the physical strength or mental agility with which we are ordinarily endowed . . . It is a special power to effect a rupture of plane, to reach over the bridge and influence the beings on the other side . . .' (pages 20–1).

189 the writer Mishima Yukio took a four-star general hostage here My sources for Mishima are John Nathan's *Mishima: A Biography* (Da Capo Press, 2000) and Henry Scott Stokes' *The Life and Death of Yukio Mishima* (Cooper Square Press, 2000). For Mishima's own stylized portraits of himself, *Confessions of a Mask,* Meredith Weatherby, translator (Peter Owen, 1960) and *Forbidden Colours* (Alfred H. Marks, translator, Penguin, 2008). The 1985 BBC documentary *The Strange Case of Yukio Mishima* is also useful, and Paul Schrader's 1985 movie *Mishima.*

190 James Kirkup *Tokyo* (Phoenix House, 1966), pages 155–8.

190 A military court Nakazato Nariaki, *Neonationalist Mythology in Postwar Japan: Pal's Dissenting Judgment at the*

Tokyo War Crimes Tribunal (Lexington Books, 2016), Part 1: 'Pal and the Tokyo Trial', especially pages 9–13.

Also Yuma Totani's *The Tokyo War Crimes Trial: The Pursuit of Justice in the Wake of World War II* (Harvard University Press, 2008). 'The physical immediacy of the court [in Tokyo] was essential for the trial to achieve its educational function, that is, to give history lessons to the Japanese public . . .' (page 10).

For Nuremberg Trials of Nazi war criminals as a model for the Tokyo Tribunal, see Totani, pages 8–10 and page 265 note 7: 'A Japanese contractor later recalled a photographic image of the Nuremberg court, which was presented to him as the model he should follow.'

The Tokyo Tribunal and its legacy remain controversial. Critics have cited the Tribunal's dispensation of justice that amounted to 'political expediency for the victor nations', because of its failure to address the Imperial Army's germ-warfare units, its use of poison gas against Chinese combatants, and the victor nations exempting themselves from prosecution for war crimes. The first generation of trial analysts regarded the Tribunal as a success while its critics characterized it as 'a pseudo-legal event' (Totani, page 246). Recent historians like Awaya Kentarō, with access to new archival records, however, argue that the Tribunal was 'neither a revenge trial nor a just trial, but one that fell somewhere in between' (Totani, pages 247–8).

192 **In 1968 and 1969, university students took over their campuses, sometimes taking their professors hostage** The era was known for its photo essays. Watanabe Hitomi's *Todai Zenkyotō* (Shinchosha, 2007) is a good one; if nostalgic. It includes an essay by the leader of the student

revolts. Also, Yoshimoto Takaaki's *The End of Fiction* for the counterculture's most articulate criticism of Japan's post-war establishment. For the Shinjuku protest in a foreign policy context, see Thomas R. H. Havens' *Fire Across the Sea: The Vietnam War and Japan, 1965–75* (Princeton University Press, 1987), pages 126–7.

Nick Kapur has argued that the Japanese authorities used the 1964 Olympics as an opportunity to shut down Tokyo's open spaces. 'If you look at pictures of big train stations in the 1950s – in Shinjuku and Shibuya – you can see really broad open spaces where street cars were pulling in and out. [But in the 1960s] these train stations were chopped up and subdivided, and other plazas were cut by highways. [The authorities] cut down public space and gave people less room to have large street protests. In front of the National Diet, they put a huge median in front of the big road [between passersby and the House of Councilors and the House of Representatives] and police booths every ten meters. Even today, they keep people away.' (*Japan at the Crossroads: Conflict and Compromise after Anpo*, Harvard University Press, 2018. Quotes taken from podcast on newbooksnetwork.com/ 21 September, 2018.)

192 **Mishima's contemporary and sometime adversary Terayama Shūji** For Terayama Shuji's beliefs on revolution and art, see the chapter 'Cultural Outlaw in a Time of Chaos' in Carol Fisher Sorgenfrei's *Unspeakable Acts: The Avant-garde Theatre of Terayama Shūji and Postwar Japan* (University of Hawaii Press, 2005), pages 31ff.

Prime Minister Nakasone Yasuhiro's memoir, *The Making of the New Japan: Reclaiming the Political Mainstream* (Lesley Connors, translator, Curzon Press, 1999, pages 164–7), includes a tribute to General Masuda Kanetoshi, the four-star general whom Mishima held hostage, and who was forced to watch Mishima commit suicide. After the fall of Saipan, Masuda walked in as a colleague was disemboweling himself. 'It is hard not to feel a sort of karma in the fate of the inspector general who . . . once again observed a second tragedy.' After the incident, Masuda retired, blaming himself. '"I had met with Mishima on three occasions but had not thought him to be brooding to such an extent. I think that if I could have talked to him quietly, on a one-to-one basis, things might have worked out very differently. When public opinion will allow it, in the future, I intend to meet with the bereaved families and ask them to let me visit the spirits of the dead."'

'By chance,' Nakasone wrote, 'I had received some wild duck meat from the Emperor and I gave it to him. Masuda accepted it reverently and took it for a last dinner with his subordinates.'

For Nakasone, Mishima's death was 'neither an aesthetic event nor an artistic martyrdom, but a philosophical protest, a death in anger at the nature of the age.'

It is possible to visit the old Barracks. Gashes that Mishima's sword left in the doorframe are still visible, and General Masuda's office has been left as it was.

The War Crimes Tribunal chambers are intact, too.

193 **The writer and film critic Donald Richie remembered his last meeting with Mishima** From Donald Richie's *Japanese Portraits* (Tuttle, 2006), page 31.

195 **anyone could have his own pocket watch** See Yulia Frumer, *Making Time*, for how the possession of a European *jishingi* (a term used to refer to both marine chronometers and pocket watches) 'was enough to cast the glow of sophisti-

cation on the owner, even if he or she did not understand how to read time off the foreign dial.' Frumer further quotes indignant Japanese intellectuals who complained about how such owners played with their timepieces 'for fun', without appreciating their *jishingi* as expressing 'heaven's movement' (pages 175 and 194).

See also Shibusawa Keizō, *Japanese Life and Culture in the Meiji Era* (Obunsha, 1958). 'The pocket watch was first introduced as a gift from Commodore Perry to the shogun. An article on Yokohama, written in 1862, mentions that Westerners were always consulting little round silver timepieces, which sold for around five *ryō* apiece . . .' (page 41).

195 **notes of temple bells, lyrical but imprecise**   In *Making Time* (cited above), Yulia Frumer argues for a more nuanced understanding of the traditional view that Western timekeeping methods introduced during Meiji were 'more accurate' reflections 'of astronomical reality' than the Japanese timekeeping methods they replaced.

195 **Time fascinated Mishima**   These quotes come from Mishima's *Sea of Fertility* tetralogy. 'The world was like a leather bag', and 'a whirlpool', from *Spring Snow* (Michael Gallagher, translator, Vintage, 1999), pages 18 and 163. 'A sundial that can stop time passing', *Spring Snow*, page 219. 'A palace's great hall', from *The Temple of Dawn* (E. Dale Saunders and Cecilia Segawa Seigle, translators, Vintage, 2001: 'Honda felt as if he were standing in the center of time, as if in some enormous hall in which all partitions had been removed . . .' (page 48). 'A vast river': '. . . a flood of past and future might have occurred subconsciously in the mind of Princess Moonlight, and the isolated phenomena of this world, like islands dotting

the vast stretch of water clearly reflecting the moon after the rains, might be the more difficult of the two to believe. The embankments had been broken down and all divisions had disappeared. The past had begun to speak freely . . .' *The Temple of Dawn*, page 118. 'The most enchanting hourglass in the world', *Spring Snow*, page 248.

197 **Mishima writes about a young extremist who is planning a coup in the 1930s** *Runaway Horses* (Michael Gallagher, translator, Vintage, 2000), page 261.

Shinjuku

199 **Shinjuku sits at the intersection of perception and reality** Taken from the beautiful manga *Shinjuku*, a collaboration between Christopher Morrison and the artist Amano Yoshitaka (Dark Horse, 2010).

201 **the publisher Kaizōsha invited Einstein to lecture in Japan** Tsutomu Kaneko has argued that the country's interest in relativity reflected 'the general intellectual class which supported the wide-spread Taishō democracy movement [and saw relativity] not as an isolated physics theory, but as an idea opening up new horizons.' 'Einstein's Impact on Japanese Intellectuals: The Socio-Cultural Aspects of the "Homological Phenomena",' in *The Comparative Reception of Relativity* (Thomas F. Glick, editor, Reidel, 1987), pages 351–79, and Tsutomu Kaneko, 'Einstein's View of Japanese Culture' in *Historia Scientiarum* #27, 1984, pages 51–76.

The theory of relativity further appealed to the Japanese because, 'contrary to its name, the theory ultimately depicts an absolute world, an idea-like world. Individual events that occupy actual space and follow time are shadows of this idea-like world. Even so, unless *things* exist, this absolute world (space-time) will also cease to exist.' Also, relativity 'dissents radically from man's commonsense feeling that he is the center of the universe. Previously it had been thought that by using watches, it would be an extremely simple matter to determine that it was the same time . . . According to relativity, however, if twins were to hold two perfectly-synchronized watches and one travels in space while the other remains on earth, immediately the pace of the watch hands and the speed at which the twins age, would come to differ . . . Thus, relativity set a theoretical limit on man's five senses.'

Not everyone in Japan was so enamored of Einstein, however. The great philosopher Nishida Kitarō said that Einstein 'himself may not know the philosophical implications of his own thought', and observed that crowds 'flocked around him as if to see an exhibit of an exotic animal rather than to listen to him' (*Letters*, 26 August 1922 and 17 December, 1922, in Yusa Michiko, *Zen & Philosophy: An Intellectual Biography of Nishida Kitarō*, University of Hawaii Press, 2002, page 187). And one writer complained to a newspaper: 'These days even science is nothing more than a kind of superstition that makes one lose one's "balance of mind".' Another observed that the scientist's press tour reflected 'handing over a cheap article at a night stall.'

201 **There were fierce arguments in the government Cabinet Council over whether the Japanese public would understand Einstein's lectures on relativity** *Japan Weekly Chronicle*, quoted in Tsutomu, 'Einstein's Impact on Japanese Intellectuals', page 376 note 18.

202 And confusion over how to pronounce the word for 'relativity' (*sōtai-sei*) meant that it was mixed up with a word for 'sex' (*aitai-sei*) The character 相 used in the word 'relativity' has many pronunciations, among which are both '*sō*' and '*ai*'. In the early 1920s, writes Tsutomu, 'there was a flood of articles on sex, and spectacular love affairs which had no regard for class or age were creating a sensation, so it is understandable that the theory of relativity (*sōtai-sei*) was immediately mistaken for sex between lovers (*aitai-sei*).'

202 At Tokyo University, Katori Hidetoshi builds clocks Professor Katori first achieved international prominence in 2001 after engineering the so-called 'magic wavelength trap' within optical lattice clocks: this trap allowed accuracy and stability to be possible within a single system. The optical lattice clock thus became a sensor for which 'stability' – that is, 'precision over time' – is key: Katori's magic wavelength revolutionized the field of quantum optics.

Helen Margolis, Principal Research Scientist at Britain's National Physical Laboratory, describes Katori's contribution this way: Katori 'made it possible to use, really use, the number of atoms that you can trap, with light, *but without perturbing the atoms*' (interview, August 2015), something technically impossible before.

Shinjuku: Tokyo Tomorrow

205 Shinjuku is a monster, a chimera Quotes from the photographer Moriyama Daido, who has been shooting the district since the 1960s. 'In Shinjuku, "Blade Runner" in Real Life', *New York Times*, 1 August 2016.

205 **Honma Kunio** In 1914, Honma Kunio published *Impressions of Tokyo*. Quoted in Alisa Freedman, *Tokyo in Transit: Japanese Culture on the Rails and Road* (Stanford University Press, 2011), pages 127 and 284.

205 **Shadows are paler here** Contrast Ryūtanji Yū, below, and his comment that Shinjuku is a place where the 'colors of daily life are deeper than those of pleasure.'

206 **Hayashi Fumiko** This passage appears in the May 1931 issue of 'Examining the City' (*Tokai o shinsakusuru*), a collection of fifteen one- to two-page sketches by modernist writers; also taken from Freedman, *Tokyo in Transit*. For the writer Ryūtanji Yū, Shinjuku was the single neighborhood that best exemplified the 'vortex of modern life' in Tokyo; a place where the 'colors of daily life are deeper than those of pleasure' (page 168). Ryūtanji's description of Shinjuku Station and the commuters streaming out of it: 'like the inundation of the high tide on the night of a full moon.' Writing about Ryūtanji, Alisa Freedman observes: 'He presents the motion of passengers and passersby through various areas of the station, which cannot be seen by the human eye all at once, but is occurring in reality all at the same time.'

With its motion and crowds, Tokyo has not changed between Ryūtanji's early 1930s and the twenty-first century.

207 **Raymond Lucas** 'Getting Lost in Tokyo' in *Footprint*, 1 July 2014, vol. 2 #1, pages 91–104. Lucas' graphics are wonderful. A true schematic diagram of *aporia*.

208 **'Yes, we have the original!'** Japan's temple bells often carried great political significance. The first Tokugawa shogun Ieyasu used the casting of a Kyoto bell as an excuse to

eliminate his last political rival, when the bell (which that lord's faction had commissioned) was found to contain an ambiguous inscription. The bell itself 'was fourteen feet high and seventy-two tons in weight . . . As usual, it had an inscription written in elaborate Chinese text . . . Great was the surprise and agitation of everyone when the Governor of Kyoto interposed with a demand for the postponing of all the celebrations on the grounds that the inscription on the bell was an insult to the dignity of the Shogun and his family.

'The objections formally made to the inscription on the bell were that: Ieyasu ought to have been written immediately after the name of the era . . . Also [the phrase] "In the East it greets the pale moon, and in the West bids farewell to the set-ting sun" was interpreted as alluding to the lord of the east [Ieyasu] as the lesser luminary' (A. L. Sadler, *The Maker of Modern Japan: The Life of Shogun Tokugawa Ieyasu*, cited above, pages 273–4).

For the destruction of temple bells, see S. Katsumata, *Gleams from Japan* (Routledge, 2011): 'About the time of the arrival of the Perry fleet', the emperor issued an edict that 'his-toric bells and bells used for telling the hour should be spared' from being melted down into war materiel. The author notes that this edict came too late in certain domains, where the bells had already been melted down and recast as cannon and 'other weapons' (page 344).

Hibiya: The Imperial Hotel

211 **At every turn, it is possible to leave the major spaces for minor ones** Cary James, *Frank Lloyd Wright's Imperial Hotel* (Tokoudo Shoten, 1972), page 16.

212 **a colossal evening glow**   Mishima Yukio, *The Temple of Dawn* (E. Dale Saunders and Cecilia Segawa Seigle, translators, Vintage, 2001), page 12.

213 **'the fusion of extreme electronics with extreme sentimentality is typically Tokyo'**   Waldemar Januszczak, 'Countdown Conundrum', in the *Sunday Times Culture* Magazine, 9 November 2009. See also Tom Lubbock, 'To Infinity and Beyond', in the *Independent*, 24 June 1997, and Rosanna de Lisle, 'To the Light Fantastic', in the *Independent*, 14 June 1997.

214 *Time is not what we think it is*   Miyajima Tatsuo quotes taken from his Youtube interview on the 'Ashes to Ashes' installations.

For information on Miyajima Tatsuo and his work, see his website, and catalogues: *Time Train* (Kerber Art, 2009); *Big Time* (Hayward Gallery, 1997); *MEGA DEATH: shout! shout! count!* (Tokyo Opera City Art Foundation, 2000), *Opposite Level/ Counter Circle*, (Richard Gray Gallery, 2001), *Art in You* (Esquire Magazine Japan, 2008), and Cristina Garbagna's *Tatsuo Miyajima* (Electa, 2004). The website of the Lisson Gallery, which represents Miyajima, is also a good resource.

215 **'They were in the business of bathhouses'**   See Joseph De Becker, *The Nightless City* (Z. P. Maruya, 1899), page 13 note: 'These "*bath-houses*" were in reality houses of assignation and unlicensed brothels. Carrying on their business under this innocent title they engaged women called "*kami-arai-onna*," or (for want of a better word) "shampooers," but these females were really "*jigoku*" ("Hell women") and were

selected for their beauty in order to attract persons to *"take baths."* The *"bath-house"* women were not only as beautiful and accomplished as the regular courtesans, but they were cheaper and would accommodate guests either day or night, whereas the regular girls were only permitted to exercise their calling in the day-time. These unlicensed prostitutes were so numerous that they seriously interfered with the business of the real *Yoshiwara*, and it was to the interest of regular brothel-keepers that they should be suppressed . . .'

Also, James L. Huffman's *Down and Out in Late Meiji Japan* (University of Hawaii Press, 2018), 'Earning a Living: Movers and Servers', especially page 93.

215 **samurai doctors for the shoguns**   Quotes taken from Marius B. Jansen, *The Making of Modern Japan* (Belknap Press, 2002), page 213. See also *The Introduction of Modern Science and Technology to Turkey and Japan* (Kuriyama Shigehisa and Feza Günergun, editors, International Research Centre for Japanese Studies, 1998).

217 **a set of surprisingly glum motivations**   Waldemar Januszczak, 'Countdown Conundrum', cited above.

219 **no architect would admit to designing**   See Paul Waley for the Imperial Hotel's demise: 'an act of cultural barbarism . . . Frank Lloyd Wright's hotel was idiosyncratic, and it was unique', *Tokyo Now & Then: An Explorer's Guide* (John Weatherhill, 1984), page 32.

220 **In Asia, it's a circle'**   See the writings of aristocrat and philosopher-poet Kuki Shūzō for the contrast between 'Western' and 'Asian' concepts about time. Kuki crystallized his

ideas in two lectures ('Considerations on Time' and 'The Expression of the Infinite in Japanese Art') delivered in 1928 to a gathering of French literati (Stephen Light translates both in his *Shūzō Kuki and Jean-Paul Sartre: Influence and Counter-Influence in the Early History of Existential Phenomenology*, Southern Illinois University Press, 1987).

See also Kuki's 'Metaphysics of Literature': 'The past is not simply something that has already gone. The future is not simply something that has not yet come. The past comes again in the future; the future has already come into the past. If we follow the past far enough, we return to the future; if we follow the future far enough, we return to the past. Time forms a circle; it is recurrent. If we locate time in the present, we can say that this present possesses as present an infinite past and an infinite future and, moreover, that it is identical with a limitless present. The present is the eternal present with an infinite depth; in short, *time is nothing but the infinite present, the eternal now*' (quoted in Michael Marra's *Kuki Shūzō: A Philosopher's Poetry & Poetics*, University of Hawaii Press, 2004, page 34 and note 91).

221 'The flow of time has completely changed . . .' See Rob Gilhooly's dispatch from Ishinomaki, one year after the 2011 earthquake: 'Time Has Stopped for Parents of Dead and Missing Children: Closure Next to Impossible at School Where 70 Pupils Were Washed Away' (*Japan Times*, Sunday, 11 March 2012). Gilhooly quotes Ono Dairyu, a Buddhist priest who worked with bereaved families: 'Everyone says that the flow of time has completely changed; that the clocks have stopped . . .'

223 **Edo was imagined as a place that could not be entered, or might not be left** Katō Takashi, 'Governing Tokyo', in *Edo and Paris: Urban Life and the State in the Early Modern Era* (James L. McClain, John M. Merriman and Ugawa Kaoru, editors, Cornell University Press, 1997), Chapter 2, page 43.

Bibliography

Addiss, Stephen. 'The Calligraphic Works of Fukushima Keidō', in *Zen no Sho: The Calligraphy of Fukushima Keidō Rōshi*. Jason M. Wirth, editor. Clear Light Publishers. 2003, pp. 15–29.

Araki Nobuyoshi. *Lucky Hole*. Tankobon Softcover. 1990.

Aston, W. G., translator. *Nihongi: Chronicles of Japan from the Earliest Times to AD 697*. Kegan Paul. 1896.

Azuma Hiroki. *Otaku: Japan's Database Animals*. Jonathan E. Abel and Shion Kono, translators. University of Minnesota Press. 2009.

Baime, A. J. *The Accidental President: Harry S. Truman and the Four Months That Changed the World*. Houghton Mifflin Harcourt. 2017.

Bälz, Erwin. *Awakening Japan: the Diary of a German Doctor*. Toku Baelz, editor; Eden and Cedar Paul, translators. Indiana University Press. 1974.

Barnes, Gina. 'The New Big Picture', *Japan Review*, 15:3–50 (2003).

Barr, Pat. *The Deer Cry Pavilion: A Story of Westerners in Japan 1868–1905*. Penguin. 1988.

De Becker, Joseph Ernest. *The Nightless City: Or, the History of the Yoshiwara Yūkwaku, by an English Student of Sociology*. Z. P. Maruya. 1899.

Bellah, Robert. 'Japan's Cultural Identity: Some Reflections on the Work of Watsuji Tetsuro', *Journal of Asian Studies*, volume 24 #4 (August 1965).

Bestor, Theodore C. *Tsukiji: The Fish Market at the Center of the World*. University of California Press. 2004.

Bharne, Vinayak. *Zen Spaces and Neon Places*. ORO Editions. 2014.

Bix, Herbert. *Hirohito and the Making of Modern Japan*. HarperCollins. 2000.

Black, John Reddie. *Young Japan: Yokohama & Yedo. A Narrative of the Settlement and the City from the Signing of the Treaties in 1858, to the Close of the Year 1879. With a Glance at the Progress of Japan During a Period of Twenty-One Years.* Oxford University Press. 1968. (Facsimile reprint of the first edition, Baker & Pratt, 1883.)

Blacker, Carmen. *The Collected Writings of Carmen Blacker.* Edition Synapse. 2000.

—. *The Catalpa Bow.* Routledge. 1999.

Bodart-Bailey, Beatrice. *The Dog Shogun: The Personality and Policies of Tokugawa Tsunayoshi.* University of Hawaii Press. 2006.

Botsman, Daniel. 'Politics and Power in the Tokugawa Period', *East Asian History*, #3 (June 1992), pp. 1–32.

—. *Punishment and Power in the Making of Modern Japan.* Princeton University Press. 2007.

Bower, Blair T. and Katsuki Takao, editors. *Who Speaks for Tokyo Bay?* CRC Press. 1993.

Bowring, Richard. *The Religious Traditions of Japan 500–1600.* Cambridge University Press. 2005.

Brandon, James R. and Leiter, Samuel L. *Kabuki Plays on Stage*, volume 4: *Restoration and Reform, 1872–1905.* University of Hawaii Press. 2003.

Brecher, W. Puck. 'Down and Out in Negishi: Reclusion and Struggle in an Edo Suburb', *Journal of Japanese Studies* 35:1 (2009), pp. 1–35.

Brown, Delmer M. and Ishida Ichirō. *The Future and the Past: A Translation and Study of the* Gukanshō: *An Interpretive History of Japan Written in 1219.* University of California Press. 1979.

Brown, Kendall H. *Kawase Hasui: The Complete Woodblock Prints.* Hotei. 2003.

Chaplin, Sarah. *Japanese Love Hotels: A Cultural History.* Routledge. 2007.

Cleary, Thomas. *The Flower Ornament Scripture: A Translation of the Avatamsaka Sutra.* Shambhala Press. 1993.

Coaldrake, William H. *Architecture and Authority in Japan.* Routledge. 1996.

—. 'Metaphors of the Metropolis' in *Japanese Capitals in Historical Perspective: Place, Power and Memory in Kyoto, Edo and Tokyo*. Nicolas Fiévé and Paul Waley, editors. RoutledgeCurzon. 2003.

Conant, Ellen P. *Challenging Past and Present: The Metamorphosis of Nineteenth-Century Japanese Art*. University of Hawaii Press. 2006.

Constantine, Peter. *Japanese Slang: Uncensored*. Yen Books. 1994.

Cork, Jessica Kennett. *The Lunisolar Calendar: A Sociology of Japanese Time*. MA dissertation, University of Sheffield. 2010.

Crockett, Lucy Herndon. *Popcorn on the Ginza: An Informal Portrait of Postwar Japan*. William Sloane Associates. 1949.

Cummings, Alan. *Kawatake Mokuami and Kabuki Playwriting, 1850–1893*. Doctoral dissertation, School of Oriental and African Studies. 2010.

Cybriwsky, Roman. *Tokyo: The Shogun's City at the Twenty-First Century*. John Wiley. 1998.

Daibo Katsuji. *Coffee Manual*. Eguchi Ken and Kei Benger, translators. Nahoko Press. 2015.

DeFrancis, John. *Visible Speech: The Diverse Oneness of Writing Systems*. University of Hawaii Press. 1989.

Deleuze, Gilles and Guattari, Félix. *Kafka: Toward a Minor Literature*. Dana Polan, translator. University of Minnesota Press. 1986.

de Lisle, Rosanna. 'To the Light Fantastic', *Independent*, 14 June 1997.

Derschmidt, Eckhart. 'The Disappearance of the *Jazz-Kissa*: Some Considerations about Jazz Cafes and Jazz Listeners', in *The Culture of Japan as Seen Through its Leisure*. Sepp Linhart and Sabine Frühstück, editors. State University of New York Press. 1998.

Dower, John. *Embracing Defeat: Japan in the Wake of World War II*. Norton. 2000.

Edwards, Walter. 'Forging Traditions for a Holy War', *Journal of Japanese Studies* 29 #2 (2003), pp. 289–324.

Elisonas, Jurgis. 'Notorious Places' in *Edo and Paris: Urban Life and the State in the Early Modern Era*. James L. McClain, John

M. Merriman and Ugawa Kaoru, editors. Cornell University Press. 1997.

Field, Norma. *In the Realm of a Dying Emperor.* Pantheon. 1991.

Fiévé, Nicolas and Waley, Paul, editors. 'Metaphors of the Metropolis: Architectural and Artistic Representations of the Identity of Edo', in *Japanese Capitals in Historical Perspective: Place, Power & Memory in Kyoto, Edo and Tokyo.* RoutledgeCurzon. 2003.

Finn, Dallas. *Meiji Revisited: The Sites of Victorian Japan.* Weatherhill. 1995.

Fitzsimons, Andrew. *A Fire in the Head.* Isobar Press. 2014.

Flitsch, Mareile, editor. *Tokens of the Path: Japanese Devotional and Pilgrimage Images: The Wilfried Spinner Collection (1854–1918).* Arnoldsche Art Publishers. 2014.

Fraser, Mary Crawford. *A Diplomat's Wife in Japan: Sketches at the Turn of the Century.* Hugh Cortazzi, editor. Weatherhill. 1982.

Freedman, Alisa. *Tokyo in Transit: Japanese Culture on the Rails and Road.* Stanford University Press. 2011.

Frellesvig, Bjarke. *A History of the Japanese Language.* Cambridge University Press. 2011.

Friedman, Mildred, editor. *Tokyo, Form and Spirit.* Walker Art Center exhibition catalogue. Abrams Press. 1986.

Frumer, Yulia. 'Translating Time: Habits of Western-Style Timekeeping in Late Edo Japan', *Technology and Culture*, volume 55, #4 (October 2014).

—. *Making Time: Astronomical Time Measurement in Tokugawa Japan.* University of Chicago Press. 2018.

Fujitani Takashi. *Splendid Monarchy: Power and Pageantry in Modern Japan.* University of California Press. 1996.

Garbagna, Cristina. *Tatsuo Miyajima.* Electa. 2004.

Garcia, Hector. *A Geek in Japan* blog. 'Yuyake Koyake'. 9 May 2007. http://www.ageekinjapan.com/夕焼け小焼け-yuyake-koyake/

Gilhooly, Rob. 'Time Has Stopped for Parents of Dead and Missing Children', *Japan Times*, 11 March 2012.

Glassman, Hank. *The Face of Jizō: Image and Cult in Medieval Japanese Buddhism.* University of Hawaii Press. 2012.

Gottlieb, Nanette. 'Language and Politics: The Reversal of Postwar
Script Reform Policy in Japan', *Journal of Asian Studies*, volume
53 #4 (November 1994), pp. 1175–98.

—. *Kanji Politics: Language Policy and Japanese Script*. Kegan Paul
International. 1995.

—. *Language and Society in Japan*. Cambridge University Press.
2005.

Graham, A. C. *Chuang-tzǔ: Textual Notes to a Partial Translation*.
SOAS. 1982.

Greer, Ron and Wicks, Mike. *Fire from the Sky: A Diary over
Japan*. 2013.

Gubbins, J. H. *The Progress of Japan: 1853–1871*. Clarendon Press.
1911.

Guillain, Robert. *I Saw Tokyo Burning: An Eyewitness Narrative
from Pearl Harbor to Hiroshima*. William Byron, translator.
Doubleday. 1981.

Haraguchi Kiyoshi. *Meiji Zenki Chihō Seiji-shi Kenkyū*. Hanawa
shobō. 1972.

Harich-Schneider, Eta. *A History of Japanese Music*. Oxford
University Press. 1973.

Hasegawa Shigure. *Hasegawa Shigure sakuhinshū*. Fujiwara
Shoten. 2009.

Hashimoto Koji. https://www.youtube.com/
watch?v=hQRQgljIWtw&feature=youtu.be

Hashimoto Miyuki. 'Visual Kei Otaku Identity – An Intercultural
Analysis', *Intercultural Communication Studies* XVI: 1 (2007),
pp. 87–99.

Havens, Thomas R. H. *Fire Across the Sea: The Vietnam War and
Japan, 1965–1975*. Princeton University Press. 1987.

Havinga, Anne E. and Morse, Anne Nishimura, curators. *In the
Wake: Japanese Photographers Respond to 3/11*. Museum of Fine
Arts, Boston. 2015.

Hayashi Hiroki, Kasahara Keiji, Kimura Hisanori. 'Pre-Neogene
Basement Rocks in the Kanto Plain, Central Japan', *Journal of
the Geological Society of Japan*, volume 112, #1 (January 2006),
pp. 2–13.

Hearn, Lafcadio. *Lafcadio Hearn, Japan's Great Interpreter: A New*

Anthology of His Writings: 1894–1904. Louis Allen and Jean Wilson, editors. Japan Library. 1992.

Heldt, Gustav, translator. *The Kojiki: An Account of Ancient Matters.* Columbia University Press. 2014.

Hiramatsu Yoshirō. 'A History of Penal Institutions: Japan', *Law in Japan*, volume 6 (1973), pp. 1–48.

Hoito Edoin. *The Night Tokyo Burned: The Incendiary Campaign Against Japan, March–August 1945.* St. Martin's Press. 1987.

Hoffmann, J. J. *Japanische Sprachlehre*, volumes 1–3. Leiden. 1877.

Huffman, James L. *Down and Out in Late Meiji Japan.* University of Hawaii Press. 2018.

Hur Nam-lin. *Prayer and Play in Late Tokugawa Japan: Asakusa Sensō-ji and Edo Society.* Harvard University Press. 2000.

Inoue Hisashi, *Tales from a Mountain Cave: Stories from Japan's Northeast.* Angus Turvill, translator. Thames River Press. 2013.

Inoue Kyoko. *MacArthur's Japanese Constitution: A Linguistic and Cultural Study of Its Making.* University of Chicago Press. 1991.

Inoue Yuichi. *Tokyo Air Raid.* Iwanami Shoten. 1995.

Ivy, Marilyn. *Discourses of the Vanishing: Modernity, Phantasm, Japan.* University of Chicago Press. 1995.

Iwatake Mikako. 'From a Shogunal City to a Life City: Tokyo Between Two Fin-de-Siècles', in *Japanese Capitals in Historical Perspective: Place, Power and Memory in Kyoto, Edo and Tokyo.* Nicolas Fiévé and Paul Waley, editors. RoutledgeCurzon. 2003.

Iwata-Weickgenannt, Kristina. 'Precarity Beyond 3/11, or "Living Fukushima" – Power, Politics, and Space in Wagō Ryōichi's Poetry of Disaster', in *Visions of Precarity in Japanese Popular Culture and Literature.* Iwata-Weckgenannt and Roman Rosenbaum, editors. Routledge. 2014.

Jaffe, Richard M. 'Buddhist Material Culture, "Indianism," and the Construction of Pan-Asian Buddhism in Pre-War Japan', in *The Journal of Objects, Art and Belief*, volume 2 #3 (2006), pp. 266–92.

James, Cary. *Frank Lloyd Wright's Imperial Hotel.* Tokoudo Shoten. 1972.

Jansen, Marius. *The Making of Modern Japan.* Belknap Press. 2000.

Januszczak, Waldemar. 'Countdown Conundrum', *Sunday Times Culture* Magazine, 9 November 2009.

Kamiguchi Sakujiri. 'Autobiographical Sketch'. Courtesy of the Daimyo Dokei Museum.

Kapur, Nick. *Japan at the Crossroads: Conflict and Compromise after Anpo*. Harvard University Press. 2018. Podcast on newbooksnetwork.com/ 21 September, 2018.

Karacas, Cary. 'Place, Public Memory, and the Tokyo Air Raids', *Geographical Review* 100 (4), (October 2010), pp. 521–37.

—. 'The Fire-Bombing of Tokyo: Views from the Ground', *Asia-Pacific Journal* 9 (3), (January 2011).

—. 'A Cartographic Fade to Black: Mapping the Destruction of Urban Japan', *Journal of Historical Geography* 38 (2), (July 2012), pp. 306–28.

—. 'The Optics of Ruination: Towards an Archaeological Approach to the Photography of the Japan Air Raids', *Journal of Urban History*, 40 (5), (September 2014), pp. 959–84.

—. 'Blackened Cities: Blackened Maps' and 'The Occupied City' in *Cartographic Japan: A History in Maps*. Kären Wigen, Fumiko Sugimoto and Cary Karacas, editors. University of Chicago Press. 2016.

Katō Takashi. 'Governing Tokyo', in *Edo and Paris: Urban Life and the State in the Early Modern Era*. James L. McClain, John M. Merriman and Ugawa Kaoru, editors. Cornell University Press. 1997.

Katsu Kaishū. *Zenshū*. Kodansha. 1982.

Katsumata S. *Gleams from Japan*. Routledge. 2011.

Katsumoto Saotome. *Illustrated Tokyo Air Raid*. Kawade Shobo Shinsha. 2003.

Kawabata Yasunari. *The Scarlet Gang of Asakusa*. Alisa Freedman, translator. University of California Press. 2005.

Kawatake Mokuami. *Kawatake Mokuami shū*. Tokyo Sōgen Shinsha. 1968.

Keene, Donald. *Emperor of Japan: Meiji and His World, 1852–1912*. Columbia University Press. 2002.

Ketelaar, James Edward. *Of Heretics and Martyrs in Meiji Japan: Buddhism and Its Persecution*. Princeton University Press. 1990.

Kipling, Rudyard. *Kipling's Japan: Collected Writings*. Hugh Cortazzi and George Webb, editors. Bloomsbury Academic. 2012.

Kirkup, James. *Tokyo*. Phoenix House. 1966.

Kitajima Masamoto, editor. *Musashi den'enbo*. Kondō Shuppansha. 1977.

Koch-Low, Angelika. 'Timing the Pleasure Quarters in Early Modern Japan', *Kronoscope*, 17/1 (2017), pp. 61–93.

Kornicki, Peter. 'Manuscript, Not Print: Scribal Culture in the Edo Period', *Journal of Japanese Studies*, 32:1 (2006).

Kuriyama Shigehisa and Günergun, Feza, editors. *The Introduction of Modern Science and Technology to Turkey and Japan*. International Research Centre for Japanese Studies. 1998.

LaFleur, William R. *The Karma of Words: Buddhism and the Literary Arts in Medieval Japan*. University of California Press. 1983.

Lebra, Takie Sugiyama. *Above the Clouds: Status Culture of the Modern Japanese Nobility*. University of California Press. 1993.

Legge, James. *The Chinese Classics: with a Translation, Critical & Exegetical Notes, Prolegomena & Copious Indexes*, volumes 1–5. Oxford University Press. 1893–5.

Light, Stephen. *Shūzō Kuki and Jean-Paul Sartre: Influence and Counter-Influence in the Early History of Existential Phenomenology*. Southern Illinois University Press. 1987.

Lloyd-Parry, Richard. 'Ghosts of the Tsunami', *London Review of Books*, 6 February 2014.

Loewe, Michael and Blacker, Carmen, editors. *Divination and Oracles*. Shambhala. 1981.

Loveday, Leo J. *Language Contact in Japan: A Socio-linguistic History*. Clarendon Press. 1996.

Lubbock, Tom. 'To Infinity and Beyond', *Independent*, 24 June 1997.

Lucas, Raymond. 'Getting Lost in Tokyo', *Footprint*, 1 July 2014, volume 2 #1, pp. 91–104.

McCullough, Helen Craig. *The Tales of Ise: Lyrical Episodes from Tenth Century Japan*. Stanford University Press. 1968.

McGee, Dylan. 'Turrets of Time: Clocks and Early Configurations of Chronometric Time in Edo Fiction (1780–96)', *Early Modern Japan: An Interdisciplinary Journal*, volume 19 (2011), pp. 44–57.

Maeda Ai. *Text and the City: Essays on Japanese Modernity*. Duke University Press. 2004.

Maki Fumihiko. *Nurturing Dreams: Collected Essays on Architecture and the City*. MIT Press. 2008.

Markus, Andrew. 'Tang Poetry on Ruins'. Unpublished paper. 1978.

—. 'Terakado Seiken's *Blossoms Along the Sumida*', *Sino-Japanese Studies* 3 #2 (April 1991), pp. 9–29.

—. *The Willow in Autumn: Ryūtei Tanehiko, 1783–1842*. Harvard University Press. 1992.

—. 'Time in Premodern Japan'. Unpublished paper. 1994.

—. *An Account of the Prosperity of Edo* in *An Episodic festschrift for Howard Hibbett*. Highmoonoon Press. 2000.

Marra, Michael F. *Modern Japanese Aesthetics: A Reader*. University of Hawaii Press. 1999.

—, translator and editor. *Kuki Shūzō: A Philosopher's Poetry and Poetics*. University of Hawaii Press. 2004.

Mayeda, Graham. *Time, Space and Ethics in the Philosophy of Watsuji Tetsurō, Kuki Shūzō, and Martin Heidegger*. Routledge. 2006.

Merritt, Helen. *Modern Japanese Woodblock Prints: The Early Years*. University of Hawaii Press. 1990.

Miller, Ian Jared. *The Nature of the Beasts: Empire and Exhibition at the Tokyo Imperial Zoo*. University of California Press. 2013.

Morris, Ivan, translator. *As I Crossed A Bridge of Dreams: Recollections of a Woman in Eleventh Century Japan*. Oxford University Press. 1971.

Mishima Yukio. *Death in Midsummer & Other Stories*. Donald Keene, translator. New Directions. 1966.

—. *Spring Snow*. Michael Gallagher, translator. Vintage. 2000.

—. *Runaway Horses*. Michael Gallagher, translator. Vintage. 2000.

—. *The Temple of Dawn*. E. Dale Saunders and Cecilia Segawa Seigle, translators. Vintage. 2001.

—. *The Decay of the Angel*. Edward Seidensticker, translator. Vintage. 2001.

—. *My Friend Hitler and Other Plays*. Sato Hiroaki, translator. Columbia University Press. 2002.

—. *Confessions of a Mask*. Meredith Weatherby, translator. Peter Owen. 1960.

—. *Forbidden Colours*. Alfred H. Marks, translator. Penguin. 2008.

Mitamura Yasuko. *Let's Learn Katakana*. Kodansha. 1985.

Miyajima Tatsuo. *Big Time*. Hayward Gallery. 1997.

—. *MEGA DEATH: shout! shout! shout!*. Tokyo Opera City Art Foundation. 2000.

—. *Opposite Level/ Counter Circle*. Richard Gray Gallery. 2001.

—. *Art in You*. Esquire Magazine Japan. 2008.

—. *Time Train*. Kerber Art. 2009.

Miyata Noboru. *Shūmatsukan no minzokugaku*. Tokyo Kōbundō. 1987.

Mody, N. H. N. *Japanese Clocks*. Kegan Paul, Trench, Trubner. 1967.

Moriyama Daido. 'In Shinjuku, "Blade Runner" in Real Life', *New York Times*, 1 August 2016.

Morrison, Christopher and Amano, Yoshitaka. *Shinjuku*. Dark Horse. 2010.

Naito Akira. *Edo no toshi no kenchiku* ('The Architecture of the City of Edo'). Mainichi Shinbunsha. 1972.

—. *Edo, The City That Became Tokyo: An Illustrated History*. H. Mack Horton, translator. Kodansha International. 2003.

Najita Tetsuo and Koschmann, J. Victor, editors. *Conflict in Modern Japanese History: The Neglected Tradition*. Cornell University Press. 2005.

Nakamura Kit. 'Cool (Old) Japan Flourishes along Flowing Rivers of Edo', *Japan Times*, 27 June 2010.

Nakasone Yasuhiro. *The Making of the New Japan: Reclaiming the Political Mainstream*. Lesley Connors, translator. Curzon Press. 1999.

Nakazato Nariaki. *Neonationalist Mythology in Postwar Japan: Pal's Dissenting Judgment at the Tokyo War Crimes Tribunal*. Lexington Books. 2016.

Nathan, John. *Mishima: A Biography*. Da Capo Press. 2000.

Nishimoto Ikuko. 'The "Civilization" of Time', *Time & Society*, volume 6 #2–3 (July 1997), pp. 237–59.

—. 'Teaching Punctuality: Inside and Outside the Primary School,' *Japan Review*, 14 (2002), pp. 121–33.

Nitschke, Gunter. *From Shinto to Ando: Studies in Architectural Anthropology in Japan*. Academy Editions. 1993.

Nouët, Noël. *The Shogun's City: A History of Tokyo*. Paul Norbury. 1990 reprint of the 1934 edition: *Tokyo Vue par un Étranger: Cinquante Croquis*. John and Michèle Mills, translators.

Ohnuki-Tierney, Emiko. *The Monkey as Mirror: Symbolic Transformations in Japanese History and Ritual*. Princeton University Press. 1987.

Okada Yoshirō. *Meiji Kaireki: 'toki' no bunmei kaika* (*Meiji Calendar Reform: The Cultural Enlightenment of 'Time'*). Taishūkan Shoten. 1994.

Ono Suzumi. *Nihongo o sakanoboru* (*Tracing the Origins of the Japanese Language*). Iwanami Shisho. 1974.

Plutschow, Herbert E. *Matsuri: The Festivals of Japan*. Psychology Press. 1996.

Raspail, Jean. *Welcome, Honourable Visitors*. Jean Stewart, translator. Hamish Hamilton. 1960.

Raucat, Thomas. *The Honourable Picnic*. Bodley Head. 1928.

Ravina, Mark. *The Last Samurai: The Life and Battles of Saigō Takamori*. John Wiley & Sons. 2004.

Reed, Christopher, translator. *The Chrysanthème Papers: The Pink Notebook of Madame Chrysanthème and Other Documents of French Japonisme*. University of Hawaii Press. 2010.

Reigle, Amy Newland. *Visions of Japan: Kawase Hasui's Masterpieces*. Hotei Publishing. 2008.

Remmelink, Willem Gerrit Jan, editor. *The Patriarch of Dutch Learning. Shizuki Tadao: Papers of the Symposium Held in Commemoration of the 200th Anniversary of His Death*. *Journal of the Japan-Netherlands Institute*, volume 9 (2008).

Richie, Donald. *Japanese Portraits: Pictures of Different People*. Tuttle. 2006.

Rimer, J. Thomas and Gessel, Van C., editors. *The Columbia Anthology of Modern Japanese Literature*, volumes 1–2. Columbia University Press. 2005, 2007.

Robertson, J. Drummond. *The Evolution of Clockwork: With a Special Section on the Clocks of Japan*. Cassell. 1931.

Rosenfeld, David. 'Counter-Orientalism and Textual Play in Akutagawa's "The Ball" ', *Japan Forum*, volume 12 #1 (2000), pp. 53–63.

Ruoff, Kenneth J. *Imperial Japan at its Zenith: The Wartime Celebration of the Empire's 2,600th Anniversary*. Cornell University Press. 2010.

Ryan, Judith, ' "Lines of Flight": History and Territory in *The Rings of Saturn*', in *W. G. Sebald: Schreiben ex patria/Expatriate Writing*. Gerhard Fischer, editor. Rodopi. 2009.

Sadler, A. L. *The Maker of Modern Japan: The Life of Shogun Tokugawa Ieyasu*. Tuttle. 1978.

Sango Asuka. *The Halo of Golden Light: Imperial Authority and Buddhist Ritual in Heian Japan*. University of Hawaii Press. 2015.

Satow, Ernest Mason. *A Diplomat in Japan: The Inner History of the Critical Years in the Evolution of Japan When the Ports Were Opened and the Monarchy Restored*. Cambridge University Press. 2015.

—, and Hawes, A. G. S. *A Handbook for Travellers in Central and Northern Japan: Being a Guide to Tōkiō, Kiōto, Ōzaka, Hakodate, Nagasaki, and Other Cities; the Most Interesting Parts of the Main Island; Ascents of the Principal Mountains; Descriptions of Temples; and Historical Notes and Legends*. John Murray. 1884.

Schmorleitz, Morton S. *Castles in Japan*. Tuttle. 1974.

Screech, Timon. 'Clock Metaphors in Edo Period Japan', *Japan Quarterly*, 43.4 (Oct.–Dec. 1996), pp. 66–75.

—. *The Shogun's Painted Culture: Fear and Creativity in the Japanese States, 1760–1829*. Reaktion Books. 2000.

Seeley, Christopher. *A History of Writing in Japan*. University of Hawaii Press. 2000.

Seidensticker, Edward. *Kafū the Scribbler: The Life and Writings of Nagai Kafū, 1879–1959*. Stanford University Press. 1965.

—. *Low City, High City: Tokyo from Edo to the Earthquake: How the Shogun's Ancient Capital Became a Great Modern City, 1867–1923*. Allen Lane. 1983.

Seigle, Cecilia Segawa. *A Courtesan's Day: Hour by Hour*. Hotei. 2004.

Seo, Audrey Yoshiko. *Ensō: Zen Circles of Enlightenment*. Weatherhill. 2007.

Shiba Ryōtarō. *The Last Shogun: The Life of Tokugawa Yoshinobu*. Juliet Winters Carpenter, translator. Kodansha. 1967.

Shibusawa Keizō. *Japanese Life and Culture in the Meiji Era*. Obunsha. 1958.

Shikibu Murasaki. *The Tale of Genji*. Royall Tyler, translator. Penguin. 2003.

Shillony, Ben-Ami. *Enigma of the Emperors: Sacred Subservience in Japanese History*. Global Oriental. 2005.

Siebold, Philipp Franz von. *Nippon*, volumes i–iv. Leyden. 1852.

Sinclair, Joan. *Pink Box: Inside Japan's Sex Clubs*. Abrams. 2006.

Sippel, Patricia. 'Japan's First Urban Water Disaster: The Great Kantō Flood of 1742', https://toyoeiwa.repo.nii.ac.jp/index.php?action=pages_view_main&active_action=repository_action_common_download&item_id=483&item_no=1&attribute_id=22&file_no=1&page_id=13&block_id=17.

Smith, Henry II. 'Tokyo and London: Comparative Conceptions of the City', in *Japan: A Comparative View*. Albert M. Craig, editor, Princeton University Press. 1979.

—. 'The Edo–Tokyo Transition', in *Japan in Transition, From Tokugawa to Meiji*. Marius B. Jansen and Gilbert Rozman, editors, Princeton University Press. 1986.

—. 'World Without Walls', in *Japan and the World: Essays on Japanese History and Politics in Honour of Ishida Takeshi*. Gail Lee Bernstein and Haruhiro Fukui, editors, Macmillan. 1988.

Smith, Lawrence. *The Japanese Print Since 1900: Old Dreams and New Visions*. British Museum. 1983.

Smits, Gregory. *Seismic Japan: The Long History and Continuing Legacy of the Ansei Edo Earthquake*. University of Hawaii Press. 2013.

Sorgenfrei, Carol Fisher. *Unspeakable Acts: The Avant-garde Theatre of Terayama Shūji and Postwar Japan*. University of Hawaii Press. 2005.

Spafford, David. *A Sense of Place: The Political Landscape in Late Medieval Japan.* Harvard University Asia Center. 2013.

Star, Marky. *Japan This!* blog (31 May 2014). https://japanthis.com/2014/05/25/rivers-of-edo-tokyo/

Steele, M. William. 'Katsu Kaishū and the Limits of Bakumatsu Nationalism', in *Asian Cultural Studies* #10 (1978), pp. 65–76.

—. 'Against the Restoration: Katsu Kaishū's Attempt to Reinstate the Tokugawa Family', in *Monumenta Nipponica*, volume 36 #3 (Autumn 1981), pp. 299–316.

—. 'Edo in 1868: The View From Below', in *Monumenta Nipponica*, 45:2 (1990), pp. 127–55.

Steineck, Raji. 'Time in Old Japan: In Search of a Paradigm', in *KronoScope*, 17 #1 (2017), pp. 16–36.

Stokes, Henry Scott. *The Life and Death of Yukio Mishima.* Cooper Square Press. 2000.

Suzuki Jun, editor; Toda Mosui, *Murasaki no hitomoto* ('A Sprig of Purple') in *Kinsei zuisō shū*, Shinpen Nihon Koten Bungaku Zenshū 82, pp. 29–242 (Shōgakkan, 2000).

Tanaka, Stefan. *New Times in Modern Japan.* Princeton University Press. 2004.

Terauchi Naoko. 'Sounds of "War and Peace": New *Bugaku* Pieces *Yūkyū* and *Shōwa raku* Created for the *Kigen nisen roppyakunen* in 1940', in *Tōyō Ongaku Kenkyū* #81 (2016).

Tokugawa Tsunenari. *The Tokugawa Inheritance.* Iehiro Tokugawa, translator. International House of Japan. 2009.

Toshiba International Foundation. 'A Close Relationship between Japanese Art and Science with Roots in the Edo Period: Exploring the Man-nen Dokei, Western Timekeeping and the Japanese Flow of Time', exhibition catalogue. 2014.

Totani Yuma. *The Tokyo War Crimes Trial: The Pursuit of Justice in the Wake of World War II.* Harvard University Press. 2008.

Totman, Conrad. *The Collapse of the Tokugawa Bakufu, 1862–1868.* University of Hawaii Press. 1980.

Treat, John Whittier. *Writing Ground Zero: Japanese Literature and the Atomic Bomb.* University of Chicago Press. 1995.

Tsuchiya Kimio. *Tsuchiya Kimio: Remembrance.* Bijutsu Shuppan-sha. 2001.

Tsukuda Taisaburō. *Wadokei.* Tōhō shoin. 1960.

Tsutomu Kaneko. 'Einstein's Impact on Japanese Intellectuals: The Socio-Cultural Aspects of the "Homological Phenomena"', in *The Comparative Reception of Relativity.* Thomas F. Glick, editor. D. Reidel. 1987, pp. 351–79.

—. 'Einstein's View of Japanese Culture', *Historia Scientiarum* #27 (1984), pp. 51–76.

Tyler, Royall. 'Buddhism in Noh'. *Japanese Journal of Religious Studies* 14/ 1 (1987).

—, translator. *The Tale of the Heike.* Viking. 2012.

— and Joshua S. Mostow. *The Ise Stories.* University of Hawaii Press. 2010.

Ullyett, Kenneth. *In Quest of Clocks.* Rockcliff. 1950.

Wada, Hirofumi and Ichiyanagi Hirotaka, et. al., editors. *Asakusa no misemono shūkyōsei erosu.* Yumani Shoppō. 2005.

Waley, Paul. *Tokyo Now & Then: An Explorer's Guide.* John Weatherhill. 1984.

Watanabe Hitomi. *Todai Zenkyotō.* Shinchosha. 2007.

Watson, Burton, translator. *Grass Hill: Poems and Prose by the Japanese Monk Gensei.* Columbia University Press. 1983.

—. *The Lotus Sutra.* Soka Gakkai. 1993.

Watsuji Tetsurō. *Pilgrimages to the Ancient Temples in Nara.* Hiroshi Nara, translator. Merwin Asia. 2012.

Weisenfeld, Gennifer. *Imaging Disaster: Tokyo and the Visual Culture of Japan's Great Earthquake of 1923.* University of California Press. 2012.

Wendelken, Cherie. 'The Tectonics of Japanese Style: Architect and Carpenter in the Late Meiji Period', *Art Journal* 55 (3) (Autumn 1996).

White, Merry. *Coffee Life in Japan.* University of California Press. 2012.

Wilson, George Macklin. 'Time and History in Japan', in *American Historical Review* 85, #3 (1980).

Wilson, Robert Ike. 'Changing River Regimes on the Kantō Plain, Japan, 1600–1900', in *A History of Water: Rivers and Society,* volume 2. Terje Tvedt and Richard Coopey, editors. I. B. Tauris. 2010.

Wirth, Jason M., editor. *Zen no Sho: The Calligraphy of Fukushima Keidō Rōshi.* Clear Light Publishers. 2003.

Woodhull, Alan S. *Romantic Edo Fiction: A Study of the Ninjōbon and Complete Translation of Shunshoku Umegoyomi.* Stanford University, doctoral dissertation. 1978.

Yoneyama, Lisa. *Hiroshima Traces: Time, Space, and the Dialectics of Memory.* University of California Press. 1999.

Yoshida Kenkō. *Essays in Idleness.* Meredith McKinney, translator. Penguin Classics. 2013.

Yoshida Tadashi. 'From Mind Travel to Plurality of Worlds', in *The Patriarch of Dutch Learning. Shizuki Tadao: Papers of the Symposium Held in Commemoration of the 200th Anniversary of His Death.* Remmelink, Willem Gerrit Jan, editor. *Journal of the Japan-Netherlands Institute,* volume 9 (2008).

Yoshimura Akira. *Tengu sōran; shōgitai; bakufu gunkan kaiten shimatsu.* Iwanami Shoten. 2009.

Yoshimura Hiroshi. *Ō-Edo toki no kane aruki.* Shūnjusha. 2002.

Yusa Michiko. *Zen & Philosophy: An Intellectual Biography of Nishida Kitarō.* University of Hawaii Press. 2002.

Acknowledgments

Daibo Katsuji and Keiko: where would I have been, without you both, and without your kindness? You made Tokyo what it became for me: 理想郷.

I owe much to Hamish Macaskill, for first bringing me to see the Snake Lady, and for all that followed. Gratitude to Christopher MacLehose for this book's first word; to Ravi Mirchandani for its last, and for turning sand into crystal.

My thanks also to my copy-editor at Macmillan, Nicholas Blake; Nick carded out many errors and returned to Daibo's coffee house its vanished top floor. In the US, I am grateful to Melanie Jackson and her diamond knife. And to Anna deVries and Josh Zajdman at Macmillan and to Nicole Dewey at Shreve Williams.

Special thanks to Kaori Ungerer, whose intelligence and sensitivity have brought lights to this book, and given it depths, that it would not have had otherwise.

What merit this book has is light reflected from those Tokyo-ites who granted me interviews: Lord Tokugawa Tsunenari, who answered in granular detail my questions about time-keeping and society not only under the Tokugawa shogunate but also in the modern era. Nakayama Hiroshi at Dai-Anra-ku-ji, and his family, for their warmth and great generosity. Tsuchiya Kimio, who arranged for me to enter the Air Raid Memorial monument and shared his thoughts on art, litera-ture and history. Nihei Haruyo, who spoke about the firebombs to an American stranger. The monk Tsuyoshi, formerly of

Konjō-in, for his correspondence on Marubashi Chūya. Arthur Binard, for dashing off translations and discussing the language of time. Yamamoto Makoto, for offering me tea in his home, and letting me ring the Kanei-ji bell. Kobayashi Enkan and Takahashi Kazuyuki, for guiding me through Kanei-ji's history and its hidden spaces. Naruse Takurō, who showed me around his Nagoya workshop. Miyajima Tatsuo, who explained his LEDs and the philosophy behind them. Katori Hidetoshi, who gave complex answers to simple questions, and simple answers to complex questions. Professor Katori's universe is a beautiful one: the universe of numbers.

I have tapped the books of many scholars, and am grateful to them for answering my questions: in particular Nam-lin Hur, whose book *Prayer and Play at Sensō-ji* should be read by everyone – professionals and tourists alike – with an interest in the culture that surrounds Japanese temples. Ken Ruoff, whose *Imperial Japan at its Zenith* is an elegant and incisive account of a brief but critical moment in Japan's long history. Roderick Ike Wilson, whose work on Japanese waterways is indispensable: his writing is the best source in English on an extremely complex, and poorly understood, subject. I am extremely grateful to Gina Barnes, for talking me through the technical literature on Japan's geology and archaeology. To David Hughes, for interpreting the Kigen *kagura* dances; to Robert Garfias, who explained post-war Imperial court music. To Jurgis Elisonas, for directing me to Suzuki Jun's new *Murasaki no hitomoto* and saving me from struggling with the 1915 edition. To Cary Karacas, for explaining the ideological background of the Yokoami memorials. To Alan Cummings, for clarifying the title of Mokuami's late play *Four Thousand Gold Pieces, Like Plum Leaves*; for saving me from several embarrassing errors; and especially for sharing his doctoral thesis.

Liz Bridge and Helen Margolis at the UK National Physical Laboratory, for putting Katori Hidetoshi's research into context. To Chris Drake, for translating the Gensei poem inscribed on the Zodiac bell; for his rigorous notes on that difficult text; and for thoughtful commentary on the Shōwa emperor's *tanka*, which was performed for the Kigen ceremonies.

All mistakes and misinterpretations are, of course, my own.

This book exists in this form because of a chance meeting in 2009 with Professor Hashimoto Koji, his lovely wife Hashimoto Haruko, and their oldest daughter. I will always be grateful to Professor Hashimoto for his nonchalance in explaining difficult ideas to a non-physicist. I'm also grateful you were wearing that CERN T-shirt, sensei. What are the odds?

To my first teacher of Japanese, Nakajima Reiko, thank you: for answering every question, for reading the dictionary with me (the many, many entries on time and timekeeping), and for going on research trips. I am also grateful to my teachers at the Naganuma School, especially Morimura Fuyuko, who always put up with my mistakes, both the trivial and the terrible. I saw my first Bell of Time on one of Morimura sensei's trips. This book would not have the form it has, without her class.

I am grateful to Eguchi Ken, philosopher king of translators and once and future footballer, who went with me to Nagoya and to Dr. Katori's Todai labs. Also to Yoshida Kozue, who translated on visits to Kanei-ji and at meetings with Tsuchiya Kimio. Many thanks to Shizuko Richardson and Yamada Toko, who taught me Japanese when I moved back to Oxford, and for sourcing materials.

Thank you to Jens Wilkinson, who arranged visits to Dr. Katori's laboratories. To Kusakari Hidenori of World Wildlife Fund Japan, for arranging my interview with Lord Tokugawa Tsunenari. To Waga Setsu at the Mandarin Oriental, for her interest in this book, and for arranging interviews; also to Iida Takashi at the Tokyo American Club, for his great efforts on my behalf. Many thanks to Kubota Maho of SCAI the Bathhouse, for arranging the interview with Miyajima Tatsuo.

In Tokyo, I owe much to Caroline Trausch. Caroline died in 2017 but will forever be *la dame aux lumières*. I am also indebted to Yamaguchi Nahoko, Aaron Hames and Henry Tricks; to Betsy Wiedenmayer Rogers for introducing me to String Theory manga. I am very grateful to Monica Anstey, for sharing her heart, her mind, and her fax machine. To Mumi Trabucco, always willing to visit the ends of the earth for photographs and adventures. To Kyoko Hunter, for facilitating my interviews with Tsuchiya Kimio. To Geeta Mehta, whose lectures on Tokyo architecture opened up the city's culture beyond its skyscrapers and temples. To Komatsu Taka, for sharing his strength. And to Matsubara Yoshi, for discussing Kanto loam with me, and for his family's friendship with mine, which is an honor.

In Hong Kong, for their great generosity, thanks to the Mole Sisters, Leslie and Caroline. In Nagoya, to Hamanaka Masashi, for discussing String Theory.

In England, special thanks to Lionel Mason for introductions, patient explanations of extra dimensions in space (but not time), for friendship, and for believing in this book when it was still in its infancy; to Alison Etheridge for the same. And to Chang Heuishilja, for her painstaking translations of Japanese tracts on geology. At the Nissan Institute in Oxford, the librarians: Izumi Tytler, Yuki Kissick, Hitomi Hall and Rie Williams. Also to Fusa McLynn for several corrections to my manuscript. In Oxford, I am grateful to Robert Chard, Bjarke Frellesvig and Jenny Guest for welcoming me into classical language classes; and to Brian Powell for sharing his erudition and for editing a late version of the manuscript.

Special thanks to Simon Collings, who, with a few light touches, greatly improved early drafts. And to James Baer, who influenced the book's structure, and whose sensitive editing saved me from several mistakes.

I am grateful for friendship and encouragement from Simon Altmann, Charlotte Apostolides, Ewen Bowie, Giles Goodland, Simon Hornblower, Ito Mitsuko, Maria Stamatopoulou and Nadine Willems. I am also indebted to Vivian Lee, Elizabeth Factor and Diviya Madhvani. And to Lucien Senna and Marlene Hauser, the Muses.

Profound thanks to my teacher and friend Madoka Chase Onizuka, 心: for what I owe, I have no words.

And to my parents, William and Carole Sherman, who have always believed that ideas were as important as people; who insist on kindness to strangers; and the necessity of learning foreign languages. For love and support, to Matilda Buchanan, and the McKuins: Joel, Bob, Mary and Andrew. And to Babak Pahlavan.

Thank you, Neva Sibucao. Your work underpins mine.

Thank you, Alex and Laura, for sharing the world of this book. You are both more beautiful than any word could ever be. I wish for you both your own adventures.

This book is dedicated to Ian, first reader and believer.